CALLINGS AND CONSEQUENCES

MCGILL-QUEEN'S STUDIES IN THE HISTORY OF RELIGION

Volumes in this series have been supported by the Jackman Foundation of Toronto.

SERIES ONE G.A. RAWLYK, EDITOR

1 Small Differences
Irish Catholics and Irish Protestants, 1815–1922
An International Perspective
Donald Harman Akenson

2 Two Worlds
The Protestant Culture of Nineteenth-Century Ontario
William Westfall

3 An Evangelical Mind
Nathanael Burwash and the Methodist Tradition in Canada, 1839–1918
Marguerite Van Die

4 The Dévotes
Women and Church in Seventeenth-Century France
Elizabeth Rapley

5 The Evangelical Century
College and Creed in English Canada from the Great Revival to the Great Depression
Michael Gauvreau

6 The German Peasants' War and Anabaptist Community of Goods
James M. Stayer

7 A World Mission
Canadian Protestantism and the Quest for a New International Order, 1918–1939
Robert Wright

8 Serving the Present Age
Revivalism, Progressivism, and the Methodist Tradition in Canada
Phyllis D. Airhart

9 A Sensitive Independence
Canadian Methodist Women Missionaries in Canada and the Orient, 1881–1925
Rosemary R. Gagan

10 God's Peoples
Covenant and Land in South Africa, Israel, and Ulster
Donald Harman Akenson

11 Creed and Culture
The Place of English-Speaking Catholics in Canadian Society, 1750–1930
Edited by Terrence Murphy and Gerald Stortz

12 Piety and Nationalism
Lay Voluntary Associations and the Creation of an Irish-Catholic Community in Toronto, 1850–1895
Brian P. Clarke

13 Amazing Grace
Studies in Evangelicalism in Australia, Britain, Canada, and the United States
Edited by George Rawlyk and Mark A. Noll

14 Children of Peace
W. John McIntyre

15 A Solitary Pillar
Montreal's Anglican Church and the Quiet Revolution
Joan Marshall

16 Padres in No Man's Land
Canadian Chaplains and the Great War
Duff Crerar

17 Christian Ethics and Political Economy in North America
A Critical Analysis
P. Travis Kroeker

18 Pilgrims in Lotus Land
Conservative Protestantism in British Columbia, 1917–1981
Robert K. Burkinshaw

19 Through Sunshine and Shadow
The Woman's Christian Temperance Union, Evangelicalism, and Reform in Ontario, 1874–1930
Sharon Cook

20 Church, College, and Clergy
A History of Theological Education at Knox College, Toronto, 1844–1994
Brian J. Fraser

21 The Lord's Dominion
The History of Canadian Methodism
Neil Semple

22 A Full-Orbed Christianity
The Protestant Churches and Social Welfare in Canada, 1900–1940
Nancy Christie and Michael Gauvreau

23 Evangelism and Apostasy
The Evolution and Impact of Evangelicals in Modern Mexico
Kurt Bowen

24 The Chignecto Covenanters
A Regional History of Reformed Presbyterianism in New Brunswick and Nova Scotia, 1827–1905
Eldon Hay

25 Methodists and Women's Education in Ontario, 1836–1925
Johanne Selles

26 Puritanism and Historical Controversy
William Lamont

SERIES TWO IN MEMORY OF GEORGE RAWLYK

DONALD HARMAN AKENSON, EDITOR

1 Marguerite Bourgeoys and Montreal, 1640–1665
Patricia Simpson

2 Aspects of the Canadian Evangelical Experience
Edited by G.A. Rawlyk

3 Infinity, Faith, and Time
Christian Humanism and Renaissance Literature
John Spencer Hill

4 The Contribution of Presbyterianism to the Maritime Provinces of Canada
Edited by Charles H.H. Scobie and G.A. Rawlyk

5 Labour, Love, and Prayer
Female Piety in Ulster Religious Literature, 1850–1914
Andrea Ebel Brozyna

6 The Waning of the Green
Catholics, the Irish, and Identity in Toronto, 1887–1922
Mark G. McGowan

7 Religion and Nationality in Western Ukraine
The Greek Catholic Church and the Ruthenian National Movement in Galicia, 1867–1900
John-Paul Himka

8 Good Citizens
British Missionaries and Imperial States, 1870–1918
James G. Greenlee and Charles M. Johnston

9 The Theology of the Oral Torah
Revealing the Justice of God
Jacob Neusner

10 Gentle Eminence
A Life of Cardinal Flahiff
P. Wallace Platt

11 Culture, Religion, and Demographic Behaviour
Catholics and Lutherans in Alsace, 1750–1870
Kevin McQuillan

12 Between Damnation and Starvation
Priests and Merchants in Newfoundland Politics, 1745–1855
John P. Greene

13 Martin Luther, German Saviour
German Evangelical Theological Factions and the Interpretation of Luther, 1917–1933
James M. Stayer

14 Modernity and the Dilemma of North American Anglican Identities, 1880–1950
William H. Katerberg

15 The Methodist Church on the Prairies, 1896–1914
George Emery

16 Christian Attitudes towards the State of Israel
Paul Charles Merkley

17 A Social History of the Cloister
Daily Life in the Teaching Monasteries of the Old Regime
Elizabeth Rapley

18 Households of Faith
Family, Gender, and Community in Canada, 1760–1969
Edited by Nancy Christie

19 Blood Ground
Colonialism, Missions, and the Contest for Christianity in the Cape Colony and Britain, 1799–1853
Elizabeth Elbourne

20 A History of Canadian Catholics
Gallicanism, Romanism, and Canadianism
Terence J. Fay

21 The View from Rome
Archbishop Stagni's 1915 Reports on the Ontario Bilingual Schools Question
Edited and translated by John Zucchi

22 The Founding Moment
Church, Society, and the Construction of Trinity College
William Westfall

23 The Holocaust, Israel, and Canadian Protestant Churches
Haim Genizi

24 Governing Charities
Church and State in Toronto's Catholic Archdiocese, 1850–1950
Paula Maurutto

25 Anglicans and the Atlantic World
High Churchmen, Evangelicals, and the Quebec Connection
Richard W. Vaudry

26 Evangelicals and the Continental Divide
The Conservative Protestant Subculture in Canada and the United States
Sam Reimer

27 Christians in a Secular World
The Canadian Experience
Kurt Bowen

28 Anatomy of a Seance
A History of Spirit Communication in Central Canada
Stan McMullin

29 With Skilful Hand
The Story of King David
David T. Barnard

30 Faithful Intellect
Samuel S. Nelles and Victoria University
Neil Semple

31 W. Stanford Reid
An Evangelical Calvinist in the Academy
Donald MacLeod

32 A Long Eclipse
The Liberal Protestant Establishment and the Canadian University, 1920–1970
Catherine Gidney

33 Forkhill Protestants and Forkhill Catholics, 1787–1858
Kyla Madden

34 For Canada's Sake
Public Religion, Centennial Celebrations, and the Re-making of Canada in the 1960s
Gary R. Miedema

35 Revival in the City
The Impact of American Evangelists in Canada, 1884–1914
Eric R. Crouse

36 The Lord for the Body
Religion, Medicine, and Protestant Faith Healing in Canada, 1880–1930
James Opp

37 Six Hundred Years of Reform
Bishops and the French Church, 1190–1789
J. Michael Hayden and Malcolm R. Greenshields

38 The Missionary Oblate Sisters
Vision and Mission
Rosa Bruno-Jofré

39 Religion, Family, and Community in Victorian Canada
The Colbys of Carrollcroft
Marguerite Van Die

40 Michael Power
The Struggle to Build the Catholic Church on the Canadian Frontier
Mark G. McGowan

41 The Catholic Origins of Quebec's Quiet Revolution, 1931–1970
Michael Gauvreau

42 Marguerite Bourgeoys and the Congregation of Notre Dame, 1665–1700
Patricia Simpson

43 To Heal a Fractured World
The Ethics of Responsibility
Jonathan Sacks

44 Revivalists
Marketing the Gospel in English Canada, 1884–1957
Kevin Kee

45 The Churches and Social Order in Nineteenth- and Twentieth-Century Canada
Edited by Michael Gauvreau and Ollivier Hubert

46 Political Ecumenism
Catholics, Jews, and Protestants in De Gaulle's Free France, 1940–1945
Geoffrey Adams

47 From Quaker to Upper Canadian
Faith and Community among Yonge Street Friends, 1801–1850
Robynne Rogers Healey

48 The Congrégation de Notre-Dame, Superiors, and the Paradox of Power, 1693–1796
Colleen Gray

49 Canadian Pentecostalism
Transition and Transformation
Edited by Michael Wilkinson

50 A War with a Silver Lining
Canadian Protestant Churches and the South African War, 1899–1902
Gordon L. Heath

51 In the Aftermath of Catastrophe
Founding Judaism, 70 to 640
Jacob Neusner

52 Imagining Holiness
Classic Hasidic Tales in Modern Times
Justin Jaron Lewis

53 Shouting, Embracing, and Dancing with Ecstasy
The Growth of Methodism in Newfoundland, 1774–1874
Calvin Hollett

54 Into Deep Waters
Evangelical Spirituality and Maritime Calvinist Baptist Ministers, 1790–1855
Daniel C. Goodwin

55 Vanguard of the New Age
The Toronto Theosophical Society, 1891–1945
Gillian McCann

56 A Commerce of Taste
Church Architecture in Canada, 1867–1914
Barry Magrill

57 The Big Picture
The Antigonish Movement of Eastern Nova Scotia
Santo Dodaro and Leonard Pluta

58 My Heart's Best Wishes for You
A Biography of Archbishop John Walsh
John P. Comiskey

59 The Covenanters in Canada
Reformed Presbyterianism from 1820 to 2012
Eldon Hay

60 The Guardianship of Best Interests
Institutional Care for the Children of the Poor in Halifax, 1850–1960
Renée N. Lafferty

61 In Defence of the Faith
Joaquim Marques de Araújo, a Comissário in the Age of Inquisitional Decline
James E. Wadsworth

62 Contesting the Moral High Ground
Popular Moralists in Mid-Twentieth-Century Britain
Paul T. Phillips

63 The Catholicisms of Coutances
Varieties of Religion in Early Modern France, 1350–1789
J. Michael Hayden

64 After Evangelicalism
The Sixties and the United Church of Canada
Kevin N. Flatt

65 The Return of Ancestral Gods
Modern Ukrainian Paganism as an Alternative Vision for a Nation
Mariya Lesiv

66 Transatlantic Methodists
British Wesleyanism and the Formation of an Evangelical Culture in Nineteenth Century Ontario and Quebec
Todd Webb

67 A Church with the Soul of a Nation
Making and Remaking the United Church of Canada
Phyllis D. Airhart

68 Fighting over God
A Legal and Political History of Religious Freedom in Canada
Janet Epp Buckingham

69 From India to Israel
Identity, Immigration, and the Struggle for Religious Equality
Joseph Hodes

70 Becoming Holy in Early Canada
Timothy Pearson

71 The Cistercian Arts
From the 12th to the 21st Century
Edited by Terryl N. Kinder and Roberto Cassanelli

72 The Canny Scot
Archbishop James Morrison of Antigonish
Peter Ludlow

73 Religion and Greater Ireland
Christianity and Irish Global Networks, 1750–1950
Edited by Colin Barr and Hilary M. Carey

74 The Invisible Irish
Finding Protestants in the Nineteenth-Century Migrations to America
Rankin Sherling

75 Beating against the Wind
Popular Opposition to Bishop Feild and Tractarianism in Newfoundland and Labrador, 1844–1876
Calvin Hollett

76 The Body or the Soul?
Religion and Culture in a Quebec Parish, 1736–1901
Frank A. Abbott

77 Saving Germany
North American Protestants and Christian Mission to West Germany, 1945–1974
James C. Enns

78 The Imperial Irish
Canada's Irish Catholics Fight the Great War, 1914–1918
Mark G. McGowan

79 Into Silence and Servitude
How American Girls Became Nuns, 1945–1965
Brian Titley

80 Boundless Dominion
Providence, Politics, and the Early Canadian Presbyterian Worldview
Denis McKim

81 Faithful Encounters
Authorities and American Missionaries in the Ottoman Empire
Emrah Şahin

82 Beyond the Noise of Solemn Assemblies
The Protestant Ethic and the Quest for Social Justice in Canada
Richard Allen

83 Not Quite Us
Anti-Catholic Thought in English Canada since 1900
Kevin P. Anderson

84 Scandal in the Parish
Priests and Parishioners Behaving Badly in Eighteenth-Century France
Karen E. Carter

85 Ordinary Saints
Women, Work, and Faith in Newfoundland
Bonnie Morgan

86 Patriot and Priest
Jean-Baptiste Volfius and the Constitutional Church in the Côte-d'Or
Annette Chapman-Adisho

87 A.B. Simpson and the Making of Modern Evangelicalism
Daryn Henry

88 The Uncomfortable Pew
Christianity and the New Left in Toronto
Bruce Douville

89 Berruyer's Bible
Public Opinion and the Politics of Enlightenment Catholicism in France
Daniel J. Watkins

90 Communities of the Soul
A Short History of Religion in Puerto Rico
José E. Igartua

91 Callings and Consequences
The Making of Catholic Vocational Culture in Early Modern France
Christopher J. Lane

Callings and Consequences

The Making of Catholic Vocational Culture in Early Modern France

CHRISTOPHER J. LANE

McGill-Queen's University Press
Montreal & Kingston • London • Chicago

ISBN 978-0-2280-0854-5 (cloth)
ISBN 978-0-2280-0855-2 (paper)
ISBN 978-0-2280-0975-7 (ePDF)
ISBN 978-0-2280-0976-4 (ePUB)

Legal deposit fourth quarter 2021
Bibliothèque nationale du Québec

Printed in Canada on acid-free paper that is 100% ancient forest free (100% post-consumer recycled), processed chlorine free

---

Library and Archives Canada Cataloguing in Publication

Title: Callings and consequences : the making of Catholic vocational culture in early modern France / Christopher J. Lane.
Names: Lane, Christopher J., author.
Series: McGill-Queen's studies in ethnic history. Series two ; 91.
Description: Series statement: McGill-Queen's studies in ethnic history. Series two ; 91 | Includes bibliographical references and index.
Identifiers: Canadiana (print) 20210286601 | Canadiana (ebook) 20210286695 | ISBN 9780228008552 (paperback) | ISBN 9780228008545 (cloth) | ISBN 9780228009757 (ePDF) | ISBN 9780228009764 (ePUB)
Subjects: LCSH: Catholic Church—Clergy—Appointment, call, and election. | LCSH: Vocation, Ecclesiastical—History of doctrines. | LCSH: Vocation—Catholic Church—History of doctrines. | LCSH: Reformation—France. | LCSH: France Church history.
Classification: LCC BX2380 .L36 2021 | DDC 253/.20944—dc23

This book was typeset in 10.5/13 Sabon.

For Dixie

Contents

Acknowledgments

With apologies for omissions, due to forgetfulness or necessary brevity, I offer some words of thanks to some of the individuals and institutions who made this book possible.

Funding has come from a variety of sources. A 2010–11 research year in Paris was supported chiefly by a Bourse Jeanne Marandon from the Société des Professeurs Français et Francophones d'Amérique. Also important were large and small grants over the course of my graduate studies from various sources at the University of Notre Dame and Saint Louis University, including both Graduate Schools, the Institute for Scholarship in the Liberal Arts, the Nanovic Institute, and the Center for Medieval and Renaissance Studies. Funded summer programs at the University of Geneva's Institut d'histoire de la Réformation, at the Newberry Library, and at Calvin University's Meeter Center for Calvin Studies provided crucial opportunities for research and scholarly development. Generous book publication subventions were provided by McGill University, Queen's University, and Christendom College.

I heartily thank the staff at various libraries and archives, including the Bibliothèque nationale de France, the Archives nationales, the Bibliothèque Sainte-Geneviève, the Bibliothèque de la Société de l'Histoire du Protestantisme Français, the Newberry, the Huntington, the Hekman Library at Calvin University, the Hesburgh Library at Notre Dame, and the St John the Evangelist Library at Christendom College.

Many thanks to all at McGill-Queen's University Press, especially senior editor Kyla Madden. Her initial interest in the manuscript, her continual encouragement, and her attentive hard work helped spur on my writing efforts and have been essential in bringing the book to light. The manuscript was significantly strengthened by many suggestions from the two anonymous reviewers and from Kathryn Simpson at Minerva Writing Services. My appreciation goes to the editors of the *Journal of Ecclesiastical History* and the two anonymous reviewers of "Vocational Freedom, Parental Authority and Pastoral Persuasion in Seventeenth-Century France" (2018). Chapter 5 of this book is based partially on that article. I also thank the editors of *Lived Religion and Everyday Life in Early Modern Hagiographic Material* (Palgrave Macmillan, 2019) and the delightful group of scholars who participated in a workshop in Rome on that topic. Some material from my chapter ("Gentle Holiness in the Vocational Culture of Seventeenth-Century French Visitandine Nuns") in that volume appears at points in this book. Any text drawn from those two works is included here by permission of Cambridge University Press and Palgrave Macmillan, respectively.

Mentors, colleagues, and friends from various institutions – especially faculty members at ND, SLU, and Christendom – have also made this book possible. My first efforts in the study of early modern history and of vocation as an object of scholarly inquiry were facilitated by Christopher O. Blum, Andrew Sulavik, Mack Holt, Charles H. Parker, James Hitchcock, and the late Philip Gavitt. David d'Avray, in a brief email exchange, first set me on my specific research path by alerting me to the concept of vocation as it appeared in seventeenth-century French sermons on marriage. Teaching, critique, and encouragement from my doctoral adviser Brad S. Gregory and the rest of my dissertation committee – Thomas Kselman, Margaret Meserve, and John Van Engen – were fundamental to my scholarly formation and to the shape of this book. Jotham Parsons and the late Anne Jacobson Schutte gave insightful commentary on pieces of my research at meetings of the Society for French Historical Studies and the Sixteenth Century Society and Conference, respectively.

Perseverance in this work would have been impossible without the supportive scholarly communities of my fellow graduate students at SLU and at ND, and, more recently, of my colleagues and students at Christendom College. So many could be mentioned, but I will content myself to highlight Joseph Brutto, Michael Kelly, John W. McCormack, Richard Oosterhof, Ben Reinhard, Adam Schwartz, Christopher Shannon, Steve Snyder, and Greg Townsend.

In the course of over two decades of friendship, the late Brendan J. McGuire offered advice, encouragement, debate, camaraderie, and more than a couple of good words to others on my behalf. My scholarly journey is indebted to him in ways I hope one day fully to grasp. Student assistants Lily Mann and Milanna Fritz read and offered invaluable suggestions on substantial parts of the manuscript, and several cohorts of students sharpened my thinking by being game for a course puzzlingly entitled "The History of Vocation."

Most of all, I thank Dixie Dillon Lane – graduate colleague, friend, wife, and faculty colleague – whose joyful encouragement and supportive hard work at every moment of this book project have been essential to its completion. Her keen scholarly mind has been a constant help and inspiration. A final thanks also to Mary, David, Henry, and Nora, who bring untold joy.

CALLINGS AND CONSEQUENCES

Introduction

> If we search into the cause of the disorders which we see in each state of life – ecclesiastical, religious, and lay – in which so many acquit themselves of their duties so poorly, we shall find that a great part of the evil comes from this source: namely, that their entry has been evil; and we shall find that a majority of people enter into a condition of life lightly, without examining whether they are fit for it, or whether they are called there by God.[1]

These words, published in 1655 by the priest Charles Gobinet (1614–1690), theologian at the Sorbonne and rector of the Collège du Plessis-Sorbonne, exemplify the efforts of many seventeenth-century French Catholic reformers to highlight the problem of bad vocational discernment. To help build a new vocational culture, Gobinet devoted roughly one quarter of his seven hundred–page *Instruction for Youth in Christian Piety* – which remained in print into the nineteenth century, in dozens of editions and in several languages – to the art of coming to know God's call and then choosing marriage, religious life, or the priesthood in response to that call.[2] Alongside many bishops, preachers, writers of spiritual treatises, spiritual directors, and educators of his era, he taught that "all the good of a man, both for this life and for eternal salvation" depended upon choosing rightly in this matter.[3] Given the images of nuns and priests typically conjured up when the words "Catholic" and "vocation" are spoken in one breath, we may be surprised to learn how frequently these seventeenth-century reformers insisted that life in the world demanded a calling no less than life in the cloister. The renowned Jesuit preacher Louis Bourdaloue (1632–1704), for example, asked the following in a late seventeenth-century sermon: "Are the states of the world any less under the sovereign domain of God, and of his Providence, than are those of the Church? Is not the grace of vocation necessary for the state of marriage, just as much as for that of religion? Do not the conditions of the world have as much relation with salvation as the other conditions?"[4] The main thrust of this sermon was that parents were not to impose their own will on their children in the choice of a state of life, but rather were to facilitate their children's freely discerning and accepting God's call. That this need be said in the patriarchal context of Old Regime France is unsurprising, and it speaks to but one of the many challenges that reformers faced in building a new vocational culture.

The words of Gobinet and Bourdaloue suggest important questions about Catholicism and vocation in the early modern era. Why did some clergy and other reformers begin to pay close attention to vocation? In particular, what led them to become anxious about Catholics' poor choices of a state of life? Why did reformers place the choice of marriage or even that of a secular profession within the same framework as a choice to enter the priesthood or a religious house? If each Catholic's temporal happiness and eternal salvation depended on these choices, by what means could young people come to know God's will? To what extent was free individual choice even possible, given the patriarchal context of Old Regime France? Finally, how did this strand of vocational reform affect the long-term development of Catholic modernity?

This book seeks to address such questions by analyzing the origins, characteristics, and enduring effects of Catholic efforts to form young men and women in the discernment of God's call and the choice of a state of life. In a manifestation of the "rigorist turn" in seventeenth-century French Catholicism, reformers developed an inherited repertoire of medieval and sixteenth-century vocational culture into more coherent, systematic forms that were meant to remake the Church and the kingdom. Four characteristics marked this transformed approach: urgency, inclusiveness, method, and liberty. Good vocational discernment was believed to be urgent, because the consequences of missing or rejecting God's call were grave: for the individual, unhappiness in this life and likely damnation in the next; for society, the disorder caused by people being unfit for the duties of their respective states of life. This reforming effort was inclusive of the laity, both in the sense that discernment of a calling was required for entrance into marriage and in the sense that, ideally, every Catholic was to discern God's call prior to choosing any state of life. In their attempt to universalize vocational discernment, reformers packaged it into systematic methods, which, even though they were designed to ease the way to a good choice, tended to make choosing rightly look very difficult. The last of these four characteristics, liberty from coercion – especially by parents – in the choice of a state of life, had been a major concern of the church hierarchy for many centuries. In the seventeenth century, rigorist principles raised the stakes on the question of vocational liberty precisely at a time when patriarchal authority was growing in France. Hence, reformers sought to persuade parents that they could be involved in their children's choices of state without violating God's authority to distribute vocations as he saw fit. Finally, this book argues that the vocational reforms of seventeenth-century France were not passing phenomena but gave rise to enduring beliefs and practices in the repertoire of global Catholic modernity, even to the present.

VOCATION AND MODERNITY

The study of this reform effort helps not only to deepen our understanding of the Catholic Reformation – both within and beyond France – but also to reframe our understanding of vocation and its connection to modernity. In both religious and secular contexts today, concepts of calling are cultural tools that often shape life choices and the stories people tell themselves and others about their path in life. But vocation is often defined vaguely and deployed equivocally. How is calling distinguished from work? Can any professional status be considered a calling, and under what conditions? Is a sense of vocation necessary for satisfaction in life, and does it demand some higher purpose? In other words, is vocation "the place where your deep gladness and the world's deep hunger meet"?[5] Can Western vocational concepts, so rooted in Christianity, be coherently secularized? Can one be called by anything other than a divine caller?[6] And has the whole concept become quixotic in the face of "liquid modernity," wherein our daily life and work are "cut out from the grand design of humankind's shared mission and no less grandiose design of a life-long vocation"?[7] Or can one still "rebel from liquid modernity" and embrace a "Counterculture of Commitment"?[8] Behind such varied visions of vocation are many historical threads, and precisely analyzing past vocational cultures in context helps us to untangle the web of vocational modernities. If we are to understand more fully "what we talk about when we talk about vocation," we need to study "what *they* talked about when *they* talked about vocation."

Among contributions to modern vocational beliefs and practices, the French Catholic vocational reforms analyzed in this book have been comparatively neglected in both scholarly analysis and popular awareness. Max Weber's *The Protestant Ethic and the Spirit of Capitalism* helped establish a consensus that early modern Protestant approaches to vocation still influence contemporary culture.[9] The concept of vocation was but one piece of evidence for the Weber thesis, with which the present study is not concerned. More relevant to our purposes is recognizing that Weber's focus on vocation in Protestantism still draws our own focus away from vocation in Catholicism. Typical historical narratives of vocation in early modernity emphasize how Protestants extended the concept to lay callings in the world. Yet when the term vocation is used today in relation to early modern Catholic history, the subject matter is nearly always clerics and members of religious orders. Little attention has been paid to the inclusiveness of early modern Catholic vocational reform. Consequently, Catholic reformers' efforts to build a universalized culture of vocational discernment have been seldom mentioned as forces of modernization.

This neglect of early modern Catholic vocational reform contributes to a perception that only in the twentieth century did Catholics take up the concept of lay vocation. An American priest and seminary professor, for example, wrote in 1942 as one fighting an uphill battle against ordinary Catholics' "impression that vocation is something reserved for priests or nuns, and that it has nothing to do with a man or woman in the world."[10] In 1953, the Dominican theologian Yves Congar wrote that only in recent decades had there been a "rediscovery … that lay people are fully 'of the Church.'"[11] As new approaches to lay vocation emerged before, during, and after the Second Vatican Council, the inclusiveness of early modern vocational reform was obscured.[12] And yet, although many questions, principles, and debates were new, the twentieth-century conversation rested partly on seventeenth-century foundations, for those earlier Catholic reformers had already treated laymen and women as called by God to their state.

Even if the inclusive, comprehensive aspirations of early modern Catholic vocational reform have received little attention, many studies have expanded our understanding of other aspects of early modern Catholic vocational choice. Scholars have tended to analyze the states of life separately, partly because of natural divisions among collections of archival records and even among prescriptive texts. A source collection might yield evidence only about marital court cases, or only about members of a single religious congregation or house, or only about clerics of one particular diocese. Yet certain patterns have emerged across the states of life, and we can see how young people's choices were embedded in France's web of social, cultural, and legal contexts. Tensions between individual choice and parental authority have been repeatedly scrutinized, and it has become clear that familial inheritance strategies – in which young men and women were not always pawns but often willing participants – helped to determine marriage matches and choices of the priesthood or of religion.[13] In a less discordant vein, it has been demonstrated that families often had close connections with particular religious houses for reasons of spiritual affinity. A single monastery, for example, might include a multi-generational set of sisters, aunts, nieces, and cousins.[14] While such studies illuminate the social context of vocation, they typically leave out the pastoral context in which the very concept of vocation was being transformed. Even when scholars have directly commented on lay vocation, they have not often seen it as part of a larger phenomenon of lay-inclusive vocational reform. Hence, François de Sales has been treated as an exceptional figure for treating marriage as a vocation, even though the vocational view of marriage was integral to many subsequent reformers' agendas.[15] Some important and wide-ranging studies have briefly discussed seventeenth-century French reformers' claims that a vocation was needed for marriage.[16] Yet even these follow the pattern of analyzing only one state of life at a time, rather than exploring the reformers' push for vocational discernment as the one process that might lead to any state – married, religious, or clerical.

Given this scholarly habit of isolating the states of life, therefore, direct analysis of inclusive vocational reform in early modern Catholic France is only just beginning.[17] We can reassess what we have come to know about early modern life choices, by looking at those choices in light of the comprehensive vocational reform that was promoted at the time. If we know, for example, that a young woman was taught by her spiritual director that both entering a monastery and entering a marriage required discernment of a call from God, then we can better understand her ultimate decision to join the Carmelites or to wed a notary. Whereas scholars have deftly put vocational choices into social, familial, and legal contexts, my research suggests that we have insufficiently engaged the persuasive efforts of reformers in the contested context of pastoral care and spiritual practices.

Analyzing this specific seventeenth-century French vocational phenomenon illuminates distinctively Catholic experiences of and contributions to modernity. In the second half of the twentieth century, historians established a consensus that the rise of modernity was a complex, cross-confessional process. Long-term Catholic reform was an integral part of the Reformation Era rather than a mere reaction to the success of Protestantism, and developments in all Christian confessions were fundamental to modernizing the institutions and cultures of the West.[18] But it has been notoriously difficult for scholars to agree on exactly what constitutes modernity, and some have embraced the concept of "multiple modernities" coexisting among different groups within global civilization.[19] This attention to group identity points us to some of the thorniest questions about modern times: to what extent and in what contexts has there been a rise of individual autonomy and subjective identity, and how have individuals related to communities? Two sociologists have summarized this tension: "On the one hand, modernity liberates individuals from the constraining bonds of tradition, generating a multiplicity of options that give rise to choice and pluralism. At the same time, modernity imposes certain forms of discipline, uniformity, rationalization, and social control that counter individual liberation."[20] Although it is generally agreed that early modern Christianity contributed to and was affected by this tension between individual autonomy and social identity, accounts vary considerably in their details.[21]

Some scholars have sought to integrate early modern Catholic beliefs and practices more coherently into their accounts of the "modern self," a concept intertwined with these debates on the nature of modernity.[22] One historian has recently emphasized that Catholics, rather than seeking "liberation from social and metaphysical restrictions," pursued "practices of belief" or "practices of self-formation" (especially spiritual direction, spiritual exercises, general confessions, and examinations of conscience) as "means of getting closer to God, enhancing the awareness of one's lack of autonomy, and fine-tuning one's desires to follow a prescribed set of behaviors, practices, and beliefs that connected the person to larger frames of reference."[23] To alter one classic formulation, individual autonomy was thus oriented toward belonging to a "body of people" who lived by a "body of beliefs."[24] Contradictions between the self and the community – especially between the self and the community's norms – were not so apparent for early modern Catholic practitioner-believers. Fundamentally, these Catholics' goals were not anti-modern, but rather were "part and parcel of the reconfiguration of modern selfhoods."[25]

This nuanced perspective helps us see how individual-communal dynamics were at the heart of seventeenth-century Catholic vocational culture. Reformers pushed for the liberty of young people's vocational choices, while also seeking to make those choices conform entirely to a higher divine will. Reformers exhorted young men and women to seek counsel humbly from authorities such as spiritual directors and parents, but not to abdicate their individual responsibility to make a choice. And ultimately, the goals of the discernment process were both individual and communal. Young men and women who chose a state of life were placing themselves in spiritually and socially ordered hierarchies, in relation to a diocese and bishop, a religious house and superior, or a household and spouse. For the community, these structures would function rightly only if the right people were in the right places, in accord with God's providential plan. For the individual, conforming within these structures would facilitate greater happiness in this life and personal salvation in the next. The history of Catholic vocational reform therefore makes us rethink whether modernity necessitates discord between individual and communal identity.

SOURCES AND KEY ANALYTICAL TERMS

This book's core evidence comes from French-language prescriptive texts, printed from the middle of the seventeenth century through the beginning of the eighteenth century, related to vocational discernment and the choice of a state of life. Most of the authors were clerics, and the genres include sermons (printed for devotional reading and as models for priests' live preaching), pious spiritual handbooks, catechisms, and guides for priestly care of the faithful. Seeking to reveal how reformers employed and solidified new commonplaces about right vocational discernment and choice, I inevitably have had to choose among many possible authors and texts as demonstrative examples. One of my goals has been to show the diversity of these clerical authors. Because Ignatius of Loyola was an important influence on subsequent vocational reformers, Jesuits have an important place here. But it is crucial to recognize that many secular clerics and non-Jesuit regular clerics promoted identical or similar principles and tropes. Authors of my sources varied in their attitudes toward Jansenism and other forms of rigorism, even though, as I will argue, almost all of them manifested what I call "vocational rigorism." Because my analysis centres around the use and establishment of a shared spiritual and pastoral repertoire, biographical information on authors is often minimal, being more expansive when it serves the argument. The note to the first mention of an author often includes further biographical details.

Some justification is needed for my frequent use of the terms "reformers" and "rigorists" to describe these authors (not to mention related words such as "reform," "rigorism," "rigoristic," etc.). The very meaning of the term "reform" has been debated by historians of early modern Christianity in large part because it was a matter of contention during the early modern era itself – not only between confessions but even within Catholicism.[26] Personal reform and institutional reform were mutually reinforcing manifestations of early modern Catholic reform. Catholic leaders indeed often explicitly intended this symbiosis between personal holiness and the remaking of institutions.[27] In seventeenth-century France, vocational reformers came to see the choice of a state of life as the lynchpin of all Catholic reform, which included a desire for a "remade society" which would "embody unequivocally the demands of the gospel in a stable and … rational order."[28] God had a providential plan for the Church and for Christendom, a plan in which each individual had a proper role, a place to which each was called. When people took up their assigned places, they could lead holy lives and thereby make the institutions of church and world to run properly. But when people were in the wrong places, they lacked the fitness and divine aid needed to fulfill their duties, and so their sins and failings undermined the common good. The needs of others would be unmet, and Christian society would be still more deeply mired in sin and scandal. No institutional reforms could gain traction unless the individuals whom God intended were manning those institutions as priests, religious, and married laity. Vocational reform in seventeenth-century France can thus ultimately be described as a theologically driven attempt to "infiltrate the social imaginary, first of élites perhaps, and then of the whole society." A "social imaginary" is not simply an intellectual theory but a life tool, consisting in the ways in which people "imagine their social existence, how they fit together with others, how things go on between them and their fellows, the expectations which are normally met, and the deeper normative notions and images which underlie these expectations."[29] But in order to transform society and establish a Catholic social imaginary rooted in vocation, reformers needed to target their prescriptive texts at the next generation. They spoke primarily to uncommitted young men and women and to the parents who could support or thwart youthful choices. Rightly formed young Catholics, it could be hoped, might seek out and accept their God-given callings and thus help to remake society.

But a hopeful outlook was not a chief mark of vocational reformers, for they were participants in a "rigorist turn" in French Catholicism that began roughly in the middle of the seventeenth century. Rigorism in seventeenth-century France was not coextensive with the Jansenist movement, and applying the label "rigorist" to any given figure or text is not always simple. Broadly defined, rigorism was the tendency to have a narrow view of the path to eternal salvation, and French Catholic discourse tended in a more rigorist direction as early as the 1630s. Due to the term's varied applications, it is often best to ask whether an author or work is rigorist on a *particular* question of theology or pastoral care, such as the abundance of grace, moral advice given in confession, or withholding absolution from habitual sinners.[30] This latter approach enables us to speak specifically of "vocational rigorism," the idea that choosing a state of life wrongly – that is, choosing a state other than that to which one was called by God – would entail both great suffering in this life and likely damnation in the next. Vocational rigorism cut across theological and institutional divides in mid to late seventeenth-century French Catholicism, and this phenomenon helps us see that rigorism was not always embodied in a particular set of doctrines or even persons. Rather, it was a mood or tendency that pervaded much of later seventeenth-century Catholic reform.

Neither rigorism nor vocational reform were exclusively French possessions, but France was a central locus for the development of both. Partly because it was delayed by the Wars of Religion, France's

Catholic Reformation was especially able to absorb phenomena that first developed elsewhere (especially Spain and Italy) and give them new ground in which to flourish. And during the mid-century rigorist turn, French and francophone ecclesiastics intensified and systematized many of these phenomena, including vocational culture. Thus, during its "great century," also known as the "century of saints," France became once again, as it had been throughout much of the Middle Ages, the most important nursery of Catholic religious culture. Although the "imitation of things French by other parts of Europe," from the late seventeenth century onward, was selective and varied according to local circumstances, in the end, "France had built a religious culture that increasingly appealed to the Catholic elites of Europe" and "was credited with diffusing a more refined, elevated kind of religion, not merely among the elites, but beyond them to the mass of the population."[31] Future studies focusing on early modern vocational reform beyond France could help us find convergences and distinctions across languages and regions.[32] But it is evident, as I will suggest in this book's conclusion, that seventeenth-century francophone vocational reform has exerted a particularly strong long-term influence on global Catholic culture.

Aside from prescriptive exhortations on right vocational discernment and choice, this study makes more limited use of religious biographical narratives from books, funeral orations, and obituary notices. Biographies were both descriptive and prescriptive, and they reveal the establishment of commonplaces, consciously or unconsciously integrated with the complexities of narrated human experiences. Read with caution, these biographical texts – concerning individuals in the clerical state, in the religious state, and in the married state – illuminate some of the concrete challenges that reformers faced in seeking to make human experience conform to idealized principles and processes.

THE BIBLICAL AND MEDIEVAL FOUNDATIONS OF CATHOLIC VOCATIONAL CULTURE

We cannot ultimately understand the work of early modern reformers without addressing the terms and principles that they inherited and reinterpreted. It is not self-evident why Christians came to conceive of certain aspects of life in terms of "vocation" or why it might make sense to believe that individuals had some choice in the matter.

Building that foundation was a centuries-long process, and various kinds of vocational reform had already been integral to every major period of Catholic reform. After the New Testament authors established the religious import of the language of being "called," the third- and fourth-century explosion of monasticism expanded that concept's meaning. The Carolingian Renaissance of the eighth and ninth centuries was rooted in the monasteries, sought better formation of the secular clergy, and reconfigured laws of marriage. The high Middle Ages gave rise to a plethora of monastic reforms and new religious orders, renewed attention to the formation of clergy (especially with the rise of the universities), and a reconceptualization of the theology and law of marriage.

And so, the basic concepts that fed into early modern vocational culture were defined during the Middle Ages, but not necessarily as parts of one whole. The development of early modern vocational culture thus exemplifies that of many medieval Catholic "practices of belief," in that pieces of it evolved separately for distinct purposes and were subject in the early modern period to processes of "adopting and adapting, choosing and rejecting, and above all reinterpreting."[33] This section of the introduction will outline the medieval traditions that came to be reinterpreted as part of a changing early modern vocational culture. To understand what the central terms and concepts meant to our early modern protagonists, we must look especially to the Latin and French forms of these terms. Although Greek New Testament usage influenced early modern theology and pastoral care, it did not fundamentally alter the vocation-related terms that Catholics had long developed in light of the Latin Vulgate.

The term "vocation" itself is of immediate biblical origin. Forms of the verb "to call" (Latin *vocare*; French *appeler*) and the noun "calling" or "vocation" (Latin *vocatio*; French *vocation* or *appel*) occur frequently in the bible, though not typically in reference to a call to a state of life. In Hebrew, Greek, Latin, and French, as in modern English, "call" words are often used simply for an invitation to meet ("called them to the sacrifice" in 1 Sam. 16:5) or for stating a name ("the street called Straight" in Acts 1:9).[34] A related and more theologically significant usage occurs repeatedly in the New Testament, where "calling" is an element in the salvation of all Christians ("those whom he called he also justified" in Rom. 8:30; "called to be saints" in 1 Cor. 1:2; "called you to his eternal glory" in 1 Pet. 5:10).[35] Even more to the purpose of this study, there are numerous instances of a vocation to a church office ("called to be an apostle" in Rom. 1:1 and 1 Cor. 1:1; "God had called us to preach" in Acts 16:10).[36] One idiosyncratic occurrence, 1 Cor. 7:20 ("Everyone should remain in the calling in which he was called"), was used by early modern Protestant theologians as background for speaking of lay vocation, but few medieval or early modern Catholics followed this line of interpretation.[37]

These biblical concepts fed into the monastic tradition, which helped to normalize the idea that some adults were called from among the body of Christians to a particular state of life. Monastic writers did not always clearly distinguish between the call to salvation and the call to the monastery, for these acts of turning toward God were intertwined conversions.[38] Early texts by John Cassian (c. 360–435), Eucherius of Lyon (c. 380–449), and Caesarius of Arles (c. 469–543) all at times used *vocatio* to refer simultaneously to the call to salvation and the call to the monk's particular mode of life.[39] High medieval monks amplified this use of the word vocation to indicate the call to monastic life as a free act of salvific adult conversion, especially in the context of a twelfth-century decline in child oblation (the placing of children permanently in the monastery). After centuries in which most monks had entered religious life as child oblates, recruitment of monastics increasingly came once again from among adults, some of whom narrated their experience in terms of calling.[40] For example, monks wrote "vocation letters" urging their former associates in the world to heed God's saving call to monastic life.[41] After long usage with respect to monastic life, "vocation" was tentatively applied during the Middle Ages to the taking of clerical orders.[42] The term's application to lay commitments, such as marriage or a profession, was essentially an early modern development.

An equally important term used by early modern vocational reformers is "state" (Latin *status*; French état), which – along with its synonyms (such as *ordo*, *gradus*, *genus*, *conditio*, and *classis*) – was part of the medieval penchant for dividing and classifying members of Christian society into hierarchies.[43] Though as versatile in meaning as its modern English cognates of "status," "estate," and "state," status often denoted stable membership in a category of persons. Thirteenth-century Dominican theologian Thomas Aquinas, for instance, restricted the word status to identities that were not easily changed and that committed one to a set of clear obligations. He saw status as so binding and stable as to be analogous with slavery and freedom: to be in a state meant one was bound in certain ways and free in others.[44] Of course, many medieval sources used the term status with less precision. For example, collections of so-called *ad status* sermons were sometimes divided according to impermanent criteria, including the intended audiences' respective worldly professions.[45]

When used to indicate stable identities, medieval terms like status and ordo were integral to various hierarchically ordered social imaginaries, many of which have remained important through the early modern era. For instance, the tripartite division of *oratores* (those who pray), *bellatores* (those who fight), and *laboratores* (those who work) is well known because of its implications as the Three Estates of the realm in France.[46] Although this scheme remained important as a division of political authority, other systems were more important in theology and in pastoral care. Marital and sexual status, for example, provided a common tripartite division of widows and widowers, virgins, and married persons. But the system most frequently found in medieval sources was a division into the three orders: clergy (prelates); monks, nuns, and hermits; and laypeople.[47] This last scheme dominated the works of early modern Catholic vocational reformers, who often employed it by specifying three possible choices for a young person: the ecclesiastical state (for men only), the religious state, and the married state.

A final essential piece of the medieval inheritance, for the purposes of understanding early modern vocational reform, was the principle that decisions to enter a state of life were to be made freely. Around the twelfth century, a consent-based model for marriage and for religious vows became normative in canon law, such that both spouses entering a marriage and anyone professing religion ordinarily did so by way of individual spoken consent. Moreover, high medieval popes and canonists rejected parental desires as having any effect on a man or woman's ability to make vows after the age of majority. Specifically, the use of "force and fear" to gain outward consent would render marital vows and religious vows null and void.[48] These laws were not simply church disciplines that could be easily changed. Rather, they implied theological tenets to which the Catholic hierarchy would remain committed in ensuing centuries, despite many critics who favoured stronger parental control.

By the end of the Middle Ages, these concepts of vocation, state, and liberty of commitment were well established, but they had not yet been brought coherently together into a single system of beliefs and practices. Status and liberty of vows were especially well defined. Since the concept of status had been the subject of extensive theological debate, much had been written about its meaning and implications. Moreover, status was fundamentally an outward reality – associated with concrete institutions, rituals, and other markers – and hence it was normally easy to identify the state to which an individual belonged. Liberty of choice was enshrined in laws, even if its meaning in practice and its relationship to social and familial structures was complex. But the idea of vocation had been less clearly delineated. Was vocation still a matter only related to taking religious vows? In what way was salvation connected with vocation to a state? Did God call men and women interiorly, exteriorly, or both? Was vocation a one-time event, or was it a process? What were the signs that one was called? These sorts of questions were far from completely answered in medieval Christian society.

STRUCTURE: ANALYZING THE CATHOLIC REFORMATION OF VOCATION

This book's chapters seek to illuminate how early modern reformers, especially in seventeenth-century France, came to answer these questions, shaping for their own purposes inherited medieval beliefs and practices into coherent, comprehensive approaches to vocational discernment. The book's structure is more thematic than chronological, and so it is worth clarifying here the outlines of the development of vocational reform over time. Chapter 1 is concerned with the first phase of early modern Catholic vocational reform, which took place in the long sixteenth century, by considering especially the contributions of the Council of Trent, of Jesuit founder Ignatius of Loyola, and of bishop-in-exile of Geneva François de Sales. What resulted was the beginning of a Catholic vocational modernity that was intentionally distinct from the vocational modernity pursued by Protestants. The work of this first phase was the foundation of the more elaborate and rigoristic vocational reform that emerged later. The four remaining chapters are organized thematically, and each one analyzes one of the major characteristics (urgency, inclusiveness, method, and liberty) of French Catholic vocational reform in roughly the second half of the seventeenth century. Few ecclesiastics in the early decades of the seventeenth century offered a fully systematized vocational discernment process, and so few of the sources I analyze in the remaining chapters were published before the 1650s.

Chapter 2, on urgency, begins the book's analysis of how rigoristic reformers reshaped the vocational principles developed by men like Ignatius of Loyola and François de Sales. The choice of a state of life became a spiritual life-and-death scenario. It was this new vocational rigorism that drove reforming efforts to normalize and democratize good vocational discernment as an inoculation against a pandemic of sinful, worldly choices of state. Chapter 3 focuses on inclusiveness through an analysis of the ambiguous place of lay vocation in rigorist vocational reform. To say that a vocation was needed for marriage was not to affirm that the laity were equal in spiritual dignity to religious and clergy. Reformers emphasized rather that marriage, though good and holy, was the lowest state in the hierarchy, the state filled with the most spiritual perils. Without being called there by God, one was unlikely to resist the temptations of remaining in the world. Coexisting with this rigorism was a hope that God's grace of vocation, if accepted, would facilitate the transformation of lay Catholics. By living in accord with a new vocational social imaginary, the laity would play an essential role in the remaking of church and society.

If chapter 2 deals with the question of "why?" and chapter 3 with the question of "who?," then chapter 4, on the development and promotion of systematic methods of vocational discernment, especially addresses the question of "how?" These methods – usually framed around the three activities of prayer, counsel from one's spiritual director, and interior deliberation – ultimately expressed reformers' rigorist anxieties. Their advice tended to promote fears that choosing rightly was in fact very difficult. Imperfections in one's motives or one's deliberative process could be spiritually fatal. The final body chapter engages with vocational reformers' attempt to promote vocational liberty while also involving parents in the discernment process. In this effort, French clerics faced an uphill battle in terms of law and social custom, both of which favoured parental authority over their adult children's choices of marriage, clerical ordination, or religious vows. Since there was no use fighting royal edicts, reformers spoke directly to parents, drawing them in as participants in the discernment process. Even if vocational reform seems individualistic on the surface, the choice of a state of life was always embedded in wider social realities.

Analyzing and synthesizing seventeenth-century Catholic vocational reform ultimately expands our understanding of modernity, to which the book will return in its conclusion. Attention to these early modern sources helps us see their place in their own time, their long-term influence, and the ways in which they at once overlap with and diverge from other modern vocational cultures. Cultures of vocation – Catholic, Protestant, and secular – remain a feature of contemporary social imaginaries because modern people have continued to grapple with our individual and our communal identities. Vocation gives us a language that enables to balance our desire for individual autonomy with comforting certainties about our purpose and place in a larger whole. This historical study aims to help us discuss vocation in modernity with greater nuance and clarity. It may be hoped that such clarity will not only aid further scholarly engagement but may also aid the reflections of those for whom vocational choice remains a living practice of belief.

I

Before the Rigorist Turn: The Catholic Reformation of Vocation in the Long Sixteenth Century

In constructing their account of God's call and the choice of a state of life, seventeenth-century reformers did not start from scratch. Early modern Catholic reforms of vocational discernment took place in two major phases, the first of which ran from the middle decades of the sixteenth century through the early seventeenth century. Rather than attempting to comprehend all vocational reform from that first phase, this chapter analyzes three foundational sources for later efforts to promote vocational choice: the Council of Trent, Jesuit founder Ignatius of Loyola, and François de Sales. In response to Protestant challenges, Trent reaffirmed many aspects of medieval vocational culture and further developed structures and principles on the liberty to choose a state of life. Meanwhile, Ignatius of Loyola, in his *Spiritual Exercises*, focused new attention on the why and how of vocational choice. He believed that accepting God's calling could be a fundamental moment of individual conversion, and he offered concrete means to come to know God's will. François de Sales, the influential bishop-in-exile of Geneva, espoused a highly inclusive view of vocation and of the choice of a state of life. His account expressed, in a gentle manner, the results of sixteenth-century innovations, while providing a contrast to the more elaborate and rigoristic vocational edifices yet to come. Finally, this chapter will consider the continuing influence of Ignatian and Salesian vocational doctrines in early seventeenth-century French Catholicism, through a look at the examples of Jesuit Étienne Binet, Visitandine founder Jeanne-Françoise de Chantal, and Bishop Jean-Pierre Camus.

VOCATION AND THE COUNCIL OF TRENT

The Council of Trent, which took place in three separate periods between 1545 and 1563, had two main goals: responding to Protestantism and internally reforming the church, often respectively described respectively as Counter-Reformation and Catholic Reformation. The Council's efforts resulted in major contributions to a changing culture of vocational choice. First, in doctrinal declarations against the Protestants, Trent reinforced traditional distinctions among the states of life, reaffirmed the value of clerical celibacy and of religious vows, and upheld the doctrine that marriage was a sacrament. Secondly – and also partly in response to Protestantism – Trent's new laws and enforcement mechanisms sought to ensure greater freedom of individuals to take (or refuse to take) vows of marriage and religion.

Trent was responding to a revolution in vocational culture wrought by early Protestants, a revolution opposed to the medieval tendency to distinguish and rank Christians according to status. One of Martin Luther's first targets was the clerical state. Many early Protestants reiterated the basic claims of Luther's 1520 treatise *On the Babylonian Captivity of the Church*, in which he argued that all Christians were "equally priests" and that the institutional church set up a "detestable tyranny of clergy over laity."[1] Clerics' so-called priesthood was meant to be "nothing other than a ministry," principally of preaching the Word, and the role of minister was based on the consent and choice of the faithful.[2] All Christians had "the same power regarding the Word and all sacraments," even if "no one may use this power except by the consent of the community or the calling of a superior."[3] Ordination was thus merely an external commissioning by an authority. It did not bring about any interior change, such as the indelible sacramental character that Catholic theologians claimed was effected in the ordination rite. Luther's rejection of the sacrament of Holy Orders and his insistence on the equal priestly power of all Christians became a standard doctrine across early modern Protestant confessions. It ultimately proved to be one of the most important irreconcilable doctrinal divisions between Catholics and Protestants.

In another revolutionary move, early Protestants aimed to stamp out the religious state. Luther took up and extended late medieval critiques of religious vows in his 1521 treatise *On Monastic Vows*, to the point of delegitimizing religious profession altogether. Luther argued that, since the monk expected his asceticism and the dignity of his state to contribute to his salvation, religious vows were the prototypical example of seeking salvation by works. Furthermore, the monk made a vow to separate himself from the earthly work of loving the neighbours that Christ had given him – his true vocation, which came forth from his faith. Practically, moreover, very few Christians were actually able to live chastely in permanent celibacy, and so most in religious vows had promised the impossible without due deliberation.[4] The 1530 Augsburg Confession was rooted in Luther's thought and expressed the full development of Protestant anti-monasticism, condemning vows as "fetters" added to the original monasteries conceived as "free associations," decrying centuries of coerced monastic entries, even more strongly proclaiming that the ability to live perpetual chastity was rare, and finally lambasting the notion that religious life was a "state of perfection."[5]

This last critique resurrected medieval conflicts over whether the term "state of perfection" (*status perfectionis*) was an acceptable term for the state of religious vows. Usually, this conceptual debate had been part of a larger set of conflicts between secular and regular clergy over their respective privileges, conflicts only tangentially involving the laity. But in the late fourteenth and early fifteenth centuries, the debate was renewed and reinterpreted in light of the proliferation of "quasi-religious" laity such as beguines, tertiaries, and Brothers and Sisters of the Common Life. Jean Gerson, Chancellor of the University of Paris and one of the most influential theologians of that period, was the most able secular clerical critic of what he saw as an overly exalted view of the religious state. In several works from the 1390s through the 1420s, he undermined longstanding mendicant (especially Dominican) arguments that placed religious life at or near the top rank in the hierarchy of states. Some of his points were matters of emphasis that would have been readily acknowledged by the thirteenth-century Dominican theologian Thomas Aquinas, one of the chief expositors of the theological claim that religious life was the "state of perfection." Yet even though he followed Aquinas in substance on many points, Gerson was unsatisfied with the language that enabled excessive rhetoric from late medieval defenders of religious vows. Gerson preferred to identify religious life as a "state of *acquiring* perfection" and religious vows as aids toward perfection. He further emphasized the fact that Christian perfection was found abundantly among individuals from every state of life and that many in religious life were far from actual perfection. Even more controversially from the perspective of medieval mendicant theologians, Gerson struck a blow for his fellow seculars by insisting that simple parish priests were higher in perfection than regulars because of their role in sanctifying the laity. He fired back specifically at Dominican theologian Matthew Grabow, who had condemned the quasi-religious for refusing to take religious vows and accept a clearly defined *status*. Though he did not reject vows altogether, Gerson insisted that Christ was the model and source of perfection without having made vows, and that the "Christian religion" (*religio christiana*) was accessible to all without an "added-on religion" (*superaddatur aliqua religio*, *religiones factitias*). His playing with the term *religio* purposely downplayed one of its primary meanings as "religious order" and emphasized its potential inclusiveness.[6]

Gerson's interventions were polemical resources for both Catholics and Protestants in the early Reformation Era. The Augsburg Confession stated that "Gerson rebukes this error of the monks concerning perfection, and testifies that in his day it was a new saying that monastic life is a state of perfection."[7] In response, Johannes Eck and the other Catholic theologians behind the 1530 *Roman Confutation of the Augsburg Confession* responded by claiming Gerson for their camp and touting his phrase "state of acquiring perfection" as a helpful clarification of the original intended meaning of "state of perfection."[8] Early Protestant theologian Philipp Melanchthon's lengthy rejoinder to the *Roman Confutation*, the 1531 *Apology of the Augsburg Confession*, reiterated arguments against the monks' "false pretext of *religion*" (*falso praetextu religionis*) and said that the term "state of acquiring perfection" was a "prettily phrased" subterfuge, hiding the arrogance of the monks behind a sophistry: "If we follow this, monasticism will be no more a state of perfection than the life of a farmer or mechanic. For these are also states in which to acquire perfection. For all men, in every vocation [*vocatio*; *Beruf*], ought to seek perfection, that is, to grow in the fear of God, in faith, in love towards one's neighbor, and similar spiritual virtues."[9] In other words, all vocations were equally valid means of coming to perfection, and exalting any one of them was contrary to Christian liberty.

The second-generation Reformed Protestant theologian John Calvin echoed what these earlier Lutherans had argued. He rejected the narrow monastic meaning of *religio* in the very title of his *Institutes of the Christian Religion* (*Christianae religionis institutio*; *Institution de la religion chrestienne*). Later editions of the work included an extensive chapter condemning monastic vows in terms reminiscent of Luther and Melanchthon. He cited the absence of monastic vows in scripture, the blasphemy of setting up new burdens apart from God's law, and the inability of all but a few Christians to live chastely without marriage.[10] On the question of "perfection," he pulled no punches: "Why do they call their order the 'state of perfection,' keeping this title from all the vocations ordained by God? I am not ignorant of their sophistical solution: namely, that they do not call it this because it contains perfection in itself, but because it is the best for acquiring perfection ... This gloss is hidden, buried in a few books."[11] To Calvin, as to Melanchthon, all legitimate vocations (*les saintes vocations de Dieu*), such as those of the artisan or farmer, were equally states of acquiring perfection.[12]

These Protestant doctrines had direct and pervasive effects in the lived experience of Christians, especially many who had already committed themselves to celibacy, whether as male or female religious or as secular clerics. Early Protestants encouraged clergy and religious to renege upon their previous vows, since they had been made on the basis of erroneous doctrines. Indeed, many early Protestant pastors had once been celibate priests. A celibate life was said to be an unendurable burden for almost all Christians, except perhaps through a special revelation and gift from God. Hence, promises and vows to remain unmarried were almost always rashly made and therefore null.[13] By suppressing monasticism, undermining the distinct identity of clergy, and making consciously chosen celibacy rare, early Protestants undermined traditional distinctions among statuses and set up marriage as the ordinary, respectable Christian path.

Although they placed marriage at the centre of the Christian life, the reformers jettisoned much of the medieval theology surrounding that state.[14] As with clerical orders, Luther condemned the idea that marriage was a sacrament; however, it remained a means of sanctification. Luther lamented in 1522 that "marriage has universally fallen into awful disrepute," with the bad effect that children were enticed to enter celibate states likely to lead to their damnation.[15] Early Protestants argued that the medieval church had distorted the place of marriage in the Christian life and in the temporal order. For instance, the church's emphasis on the sufficiency of the couple's consent to contract a marriage, even against parental will, had had subversive and chaotic results, especially in disputed claims about clandestine marital vows. Reformers thus instituted significant changes to the legal framework around marriage and gave temporal authorities more control.[16] The reformers ultimately believed that holding marriage to be a sacrament had done nothing to help Christians see its true value as a Christian vocation (literally *vocatio* in many texts).[17] Sixteenth-century Catholic reformers, for their part, would themselves increasingly speak of marriage as a vocation, but without rejecting the notion that it was a sacrament.

The Tridentine response to Protestant challenges consisted both in reaffirming traditional theologies and in supporting widespread internal reform. First, the council upheld the spiritual value of freely chosen celibacy, whether for religious or for clergy. It was a matter of Catholic doctrine that it was "better and more blessed" to remain in virginity or celibacy than to contract marriage. More concretely, Trent taught that vows and promises of perpetual celibacy were binding, that such an affirmation was no attack on marriage, and that God would not deny the gift of chastity to those who had bound themselves to perpetual continence.[18] On the clerical state, Trent rejected Protestant theological levelling by reaffirming that priestly ordination was a sacrament, that it imprinted an indelible spiritual character on the soul that enabled the priest to perform certain sacred actions, and that the laity could not inherently perform the ministries of word and sacrament as if they were equally priests.[19] Marriage was also a true sacrament, instituted as such by Christ.[20] The brevity of these doctrinal statements belies their import in preserving the essence of the Catholic system of distinct, hierarchically organized statuses.

While opposing Protestant doctrinal revolutions, Trent embraced much-needed internal reforms on vocational questions, many of which simply sought to enhance clarity on and enforcement of existing church laws. In enacting these reforms, the council fathers ended up promoting freedom of vocational choice more vociferously – and on a different theological basis – than did their Protestant contemporaries. Several provisions of the council's *Decree on regulars and nuns* addressed coercion toward and against religious vows, which had remained a problem despite centuries of laws prohibiting it.[21] The minimum age of final profession of vows was set at sixteen for both men and women, and a year of novitiate after receiving the habit was required before final profession at any age.[22] Novices would be eligible to receive back their possessions if they left the monastery without professing.[23] Women were especially to be protected by a procedure wherein the bishop or his representative questioned every female candidate for the reception of the habit and for final profession, to determine whether she was doing so freely, with full knowledge, consent, devotion, and suitability for the monastery.[24] To put teeth into its efforts, Trent also augmented ecclesiastical penalties, bringing automatic anathema (the most severe form of excommunication) on anyone who forced or forcibly obstructed a woman's religious profession, or who in any way consented to or participated in such an act of coercion.[25] The gender specificity of these measures corresponds to prevailing perceptions that women were in greater need of protection, but early modern Catholic commentators held that coercion of men was likewise morally repugnant.[26] Both male and female religious who claimed that they had been coerced into vows "by force and fear" (*per vim et metum*), or who had professed under some other irregularity such as being underage, had recourse to various ecclesiastical tribunals, depending on the specifics of the case.[27] Trent likewise upheld a couple's freedom to marry, rejecting claims by Protestants and by some Catholic reformers that parental consent was needed. As a matter of discipline, anathema was imposed on those who forced a marriage or coercively prevented a marriage, and, as a matter of doctrine, anathema was imposed on those who taught that parental consent was necessary for a marriage.[28] These conclusions on marriage, incidentally, were especially galling to the French crown, which had encouraged the council's French delegation to lobby for required parental consent.[29]

The council addressed many other issues related to vocation, such as the formation of priests, but the issues considered above were the most relevant to vocational discernment reform. Against the Protestants, Trent reaffirmed the theology behind the three distinct statuses of clergy, religious, and laity. Furthermore, the official church supported more than ever before the freedom to choose a state. These Tridentine efforts ultimately preserved the medieval principles from which vocational reformers would construct a more coherent, comprehensive vocational worldview.

IGNATIUS OF LOYOLA AND THE CHOICE OF A STATE OF LIFE

The influence of the *Spiritual Exercises*, by Jesuit founder Ignatius of Loyola (1491–1556), on the question of vocational choice cannot be overstated.[30] Designed as a guidebook to the director of a four-week retreat, the text's style is simple and unadorned, consisting primarily of meditations, sets of "rules," and notes for the director.[31] Both as a text and as an activity, the *Exercises* far exceeded their original specific context as a retreat handbook, and it was used extensively as personal spiritual reading and as a seminal text for Catholic spirituality both inside and outside of the Jesuit order. Like other early modern reformers, Ignatius aimed not for originality but instead sought to present inherited medieval traditions more systematically and in new contexts. The *Exercises* were innovative not so much in their basic content, which had monastic roots, but in their adaptability for use by a wider spectrum of believers and in a variety of ways.[32]

For the purposes of later vocational reform, the text's section on "election" (Spanish *hazer election*; Latin *electionem facere*) – more helpfully translated as "making a choice" – proved essential.[33] This section came at the centre of the retreat, the end of the second of the four "weeks."[34] The first two weeks prepared the retreatant to make this choice, and the latter two strengthened his or her conviction in it.[35] The concept of *election* used here can be taken in more than one sense. At the highest level, it has been interpreted as a way of living, a continually renewed choice of God as one's end, and a continual discernment of God's particular will with respect to one's own life.[36] More basically, election was the choice of a permanent state of life. Ignatius repeatedly mentioned entrance into marriage or the priesthood as examples of what might be chosen, and he used the term *estado* ("state") in the Spanish text to refer to a potential object of this choice.[37] To those retreatants who had already chosen a permanent state of life, the *election* would focus on changing particular details of how one lived one's vocation.[38] Thus, one of the chief goals of the *Spiritual Exercises* was the choice either of a state of life or of "some reordering of the priorities" in one's current state.[39]

Ignatius wrote that making a good choice depended on right motives, "the praise of God and the salvation of my soul," and so one must never "subordinate the end to the means, but the means to the end."[40] Many Christians reversed means and ends in the choice of a state, by, for example, first choosing marriage or an ecclesiastical benefice for the sake of their lesser benefits, then secondarily choosing to serve God.[41] Many who thus entered a state of life claimed to be following a "divine vocation" (*vocacion divina*; *vocatio divina*) when they were simply following their own mixed motives and disordered desires, whereas "every divine vocation is always pure and clear."[42] At this point Ignatius exhibits a nascent principle of vocational inclusiveness. That is, "vocation" was already in his day a term applicable to any state of life – he specifically used marriage as an example – if that state could have God's glory and one's salvation as its ends. He commented further on inclusiveness when he instructed the retreat master not to push the retreatant toward one or another state of life. Outside the *Exercises*, it was meritorious to exhort Christians to consider religious vows, but, within the *Exercises*, the director must let God work as he pleases.[43] The director was especially to guide the retreatant away from making a rash choice of religion, for, in many a flighty soul, that attraction would come and go quickly.[44] Ignatius thus emphasized a key principle for later vocational reform, that a state was to be chosen not so much because it was more meritorious in itself, but rather because it was the particular state which God willed for the individual.

Given the possibility of choosing badly, that is, for the wrong ends, Ignatius offered concrete methods to aid discernment. He distinguished three occasions or "times" (*tiempos*; *tempores*) wherein to make a good choice.[45] The first was a direct attraction of the will to a state so that one would follow without hesitation, as had happened with St Paul and St Matthew.[46] The second was "when enough clarity and knowledge are received through experience of consolations and desolations and through the experience of discernment of various spirits."[47] This referred to the "Rules for the Discernment of Spirits," a guide for the retreat master to judge the meaning of various interior sensations and movements, especially concerning whether they were the work of God or of the devil.[48] By precisely analyzing interior movements of consolation and desolation – with respect to, for example, their timing, duration, and occasion – a wise director could guide the retreatant in responding to the movements and understanding how they related to God's will. Whereas the devil might incite feelings of desolation in order to derail a good choice made, God might do the same in order to divert the retreatant from a bad choice. Although discernment was tricky business, under the right circumstances and with the right guidance, it would yield "enough clarity and knowledge" to choose well.

The third occasion for making a good choice – to be used when the first two did not occur or were unclear – was based on discursive meditation and an active reasoning process. Ignatius' focus here helped to make concrete methods of rational deliberation a key feature of later vocational reform. The basic condition of this third occasion was a time without strong emotional movements, "when the soul is not agitated by various spirits and uses its natural powers freely and tranquilly."[49] Ignatius proposed two "ways," or methods of discernment, both of which would employ one's "natural powers" on this third occasion. The first way involved six steps: (1) to place before one's mind the choice to be made; (2) to focus on only the motives of the praise of God and the salvation of one's soul, and thereby to cultivate indifference to everything except those ends; (3) to pray fervently that God would show in one's mind and incline one's will toward what would best serve his glory, then to consider the choice with one's intellect according to this criterion; (4) to consider all the possible advantages and disadvantages of each possible choice, with respect to the praise of God and the salvation of one's soul; (5) to consider, after these ratiocinations, to which choice reason inclines, and to make a decision (*hazer deliberacion*; *electionem concludere*) based on motives of reason rather than of sense appetite; and (6) to pray fervently and diligently to God, offering him the decision and asking him to confirm it, if it pleased him.[50]

Whereas the first way of the third occasion was based primarily on reason, the second way relied more on the imagination.[51] The two ways could be used in tandem, and the imaginative methods of the second might clarify any confusion arising from the first. This second way was set out as four "rules" (Spanish *reglas*; Latin *regulas*). The first rule simply reiterated that any preference for one state of life or another must have love of God as its motive. The second rule asked the retreatant to imagine a total stranger and, desiring that man's "total perfection," to consider what that stranger should choose for God's glory and the perfection of his soul.[52] Then, one was to choose exactly as one would advise that man. The third rule required imagining what one would wish to have chosen, looking back from the moment of death. The fourth similarly required one to imagine standing before God at the Judgment and to think about what one would wish to have chosen. Disentangling the retreatant from lesser motives, these meditations would facilitate a choice in accord with the mantra of the *Exercises*, doing all things only for the proper ends of God's glory and the salvation of one's soul.

In the *Spiritual Exercises*, therefore, Ignatius offered a version of vocational reform that entailed inclusiveness, method, and liberty – three of the characteristics even more clearly present in later vocational reform. His vision was inclusive, both in the sense of promoting vocational discernment among more of the faithful and in the sense of accepting that one might discern a lay calling as the outcome of that discernment. Furthermore, Ignatius boiled down the process of choosing a state into clear rational methods. Later advice on discernment was often drawn from his discussion of the "third time," when deep self-examination through reason and imagination were most at play. His emphasis on liberty manifested itself in the core principle of individual "election" or "choice," as well as in his warnings against undue recruitment for religious vows. Seventeenth-century vocational reformers – including many who were outside of the Jesuit order – would build upon the inclusiveness, method, and liberty that Ignatius promoted. Their further elaborations in these areas, as we will see, depended on a component not as well developed in the Ignatian inheritance: urgency. Although Ignatius was concerned about the consequences of wrong vocational choices, his rhetoric and his conclusions did not reach the level of anxiety that would come with the seventeenth-century rigorist turn.

FRANÇOIS DE SALES AND THE DIVERSITY OF VOCATIONS

Whereas Ignatius wrote the urtext of early modern Catholic vocational discernment, François de Sales (1567–1622), bishop of Geneva (residing in exile at Annecy), further promoted discernment practices while shining a bright spotlight on lay vocation. He was one of the most effective proponents of vocational inclusiveness, and he continued the effort to package vocational discernment in systematic methods, available to wider audiences of the Catholic faithful. Though not a Jesuit, he had received a good Jesuit education and remained a friend of the order.[53] This helps account for the Ignatian style and substance of some of his counsels. That said, De Sales's thought was his own. His influence on spirituality in seventeenth-century France was pervasive, even as his gentleness (*douceur*) was overshadowed by the rigorist turn that took place in the decades after his death.[54] In his bestselling *Introduction to the Devout Life*, he wrote expansively and passionately on the accessibility of Christian holiness in every vocation. His specific advice on choosing a state of life is less well known, however, and his clearest statements on it are found in his *Treatise on the Love of God* and *Spiritual Conferences*. Ultimately, the flexibility and hopefulness of his simple discernment methods contrast to some degree with the dedication required by the *Spiritual Exercises* and to a much greater degree with the more elaborate methods that came later.

De Sales used the term "vocation" inclusively, applying it to the laity unequivocally, in a manner reminiscent of the early Protestants. In a letter from 1604, he wrote that "the means of coming to perfection are diverse, according to the diversity of vocations; for religious, widows, and married people ought all to seek this perfection, but not by the same means."[55] In his *Introduction to the Devout Life* (first published in 1609), he wrote that devotion was to be lived out "according to social status and vocation" by each different type of Christian, such as "the gentleman, the artisan … the widow … the married woman."[56] In this spirit, he commented on the debates over the term "state of perfection." Much like Jean Gerson, de Sales deemphasized (without altogether denying) this special claim for the religious life and wrote that poverty, chastity, and obedience – "the three great virtues proper for acquiring perfection" – were necessary and adaptable for all states of life.[57] Taking these three virtues as religious vows might bring many graces and place a person in the "state of perfection," but all Christians, with or without vows, were bound to live out these virtues.[58] Controversy over terminology, he implied, had obscured the most important issue from the standpoint of pastoral care, namely, helping all Christians in all states of life grow in holiness. While he praised religious vows, especially in other texts meant for more narrow audiences, and held that religious life was objectively superior to marriage, he also redirected his readers' attention to the subjective question of their own path to sanctity. Ignatius had laid the groundwork for this emphasis on the particular individual, de Sales developed it still more, and later vocational advice would maintain it as a fundamental principle of discernment.

The *Introduction to the Devout Life* was among the most influential Catholic spiritual books published during the seventeenth century, and it played a fundamental role in normalizing the concept of lay vocation. It was republished in dozens of editions and translations in its first few decades, and, despite some periods of declining popularity, it has remained an important spiritual handbook in France and elsewhere to the present day.[59] Yet despite this work's strong interest in the adaptability of devotion to each vocation or state of life, it contained no explicit advice on actually discerning one's vocation and choosing a state. Here we see a contrast with the *Spiritual Exercises*, wherein the choice of a state was one of the text's central interests. The *Introduction*'s series of Ignatian-influenced meditations culminated in a choice ("élection") not of a state of life but of the devout life itself, independent of one's state.[60] Reading the *Introduction* alone, one would be tempted to think that de Sales wished to downplay the importance of distinctions among states of life, but other works reveal a more nuanced picture.

De Sales's most systematic treatment of the choice of a state of life is found instead in book VIII of the *Treatise on the Love of God*. This work's core audience was narrower than that of the *Introduction to the Devout Life*, as it was directed towards readers more advanced in the spiritual life, including many religious in vows, as well as to clerics responsible for spiritual guidance. Book VIII addressed the means to conform oneself to God's will as "signified by his commandments, counsels, and inspirations."[61] Following medieval theology, de Sales distinguished between commandments – whose violation was sinful – and counsels – practices and commitments to which God "invites us without pain of sin," in order that we would be further perfected in charity.[62] Counsels included not only the traditional three evangelical counsels of poverty, chastity, and obedience, which were taken as vows by many religious; they also included commitments to more specific habitual actions, such as greater almsgiving, solitude, hospitality, or fasting.[63] Although no single counsel was ever strictly obligatory, taking up some counsels was integral to the Christian life well lived. Moreover, Christians could come to know which counsels God specifically desired each of them to take up, as most individually fitting.[64] Charity, writes de Sales, was the virtue God placed in charge of distributing the counsels among Christians: "She makes the martyrs redder than the rose, virgins whiter than the lily; to some she gives the fine violet of mortification, to others the yellow of the cares of marriage, employing the counsels diversely for the perfection of souls who are so happy to be living under her conduct."[65] But charity was not obliged to give an account to anyone of her reasons for giving some counsels to one and others to another.[66] As is evident in these examples, among the matters under charity's purview were choices among states of life. Although the word "vocation" itself only appears prominently in later chapters, this passage on charity implied that God called some to one state and some to another, for reasons beyond human prudence or understanding.

According to de Sales, God often expressed his will through "inspirations," transitory interior and exterior goads to some good action. The object of an inspiration could be a simple, isolated act of charity, or it could involve a long-term commitment, such as the choice of a state of life. Since the human heart and mind were subject to frequent and contradictory movements, inclinations, ideas, and influences, de Sales offered three marks that an inspiration was truly from God. These marks functioned like a simple, gentle Salesian version of the Ignatian Rules for the Discernment of Spirits. First, a true inspiration engendered "perseverance in one's vocation," rather than flitting about from one commitment to another. Though an inspiration could lead to a new vocational commitment, God would not ordinarily lead someone away from existing good commitments. Leaving the secular priestly state for religious vows, for example, could bring about the ruin of a virtuous priest's soul. Second, a true inspiration would yield "peace and gentleness of heart," rather than an interior storm. Third, such an inspiration would prompt a person to obey the church and other legitimate superiors.[67] Although de Sales admitted that there were extraordinary exceptions regarding these three marks, he nonetheless believed that few Christians would face such a contingency. His three tests highlight much about the nature of Catholic vocational culture, wherein calling was fundamentally about conforming oneself to something greater, rather than striking out as an individual. In choosing to accept God's guiding will, an individual chose to belong to an entity – a family, a diocese, a religious order – to be in relation to God through relations to others. And yet these external realities served the internal formation of the soul, which would grow in perseverance and obedience, ultimately experiencing spiritual peace.

De Sales concluded book VIII of *Love of God* with "a brief method for knowing God's will," his most concrete explanation of the actual vocational discernment process.[68] Most of the chapter is dedicated to warning against excessive discernment about minor decisions. Overthinking, especially in choices among small good actions, was a spiritual danger.[69] Only in momentous matters, such as "the choice of vocation," was one to "consider seriously what is most according to the divine will."[70] Yet even then, excessive discernment was harmful, and the will of God could not be found simply "by force of examination and subtlety of discourse," that is, by an unending and convoluted interior search, relying exclusively on one's own mind.[71] Rather, de Sales simplified right discernment to three steps: praying for the Holy Spirit's guidance, reflecting in search of God's good pleasure, and taking counsel from one's director and perhaps from two or three other spiritual persons. After that, one had to make a resolution and hold to it without wavering.[72] Apparent cause for doubting one's choice would come and go, but, by following this "brief method" in good faith, one could have the certainty needed to avoid unending discernment.

The last significant source for de Sales's teaching on vocational discernment is the seventeenth of his *Spiritual Conferences*. First given as a talk to Visitandine nuns in the spring of 1621, it discussed voting about candidates for entry and for final profession. Above all, a candidate needed to be "truly called by God," that is, to have a "good vocation," which de Sales defined as "a firm and constant will, which the person called possesses, to wish to serve God in the manner and place to which his divine Majesty calls her."[73] This need not be an emotional constancy but rather "a good will to amend their ways, to submit themselves, and to make use of the medicines proper to their healing."[74] Candidates with "strong passions" of anger, or who were "badly brought up," or who were of "crude and coarse nature" could "after much work, make great strides in religious life, becoming great servants of God and acquiring a strong and solid virtue, for the grace of God makes up for what is lacking."[75] Intention was more important than previous attainment.

If a candidate was not measured by her prerequisite holiness, neither was she measured by her initial reasons for entry, for God had "many means of calling his servants and handmaidens to his service."[76] An attraction to religion might be occasioned by preaching or spiritual reading, or the first inclination might come through "troubles, disasters, and afflictions" that led to distaste for the world.[77] Yet more surprisingly, a good vocation might come out of bad motives. De Sales recalled a holy Capuchin, for instance, who had originally joined as a joke to mock the friars. Others entered because a physical defect made them undesirable in marriage or unfit for worldly success. Many were coerced to enter by parents, on account of such physical defects or to preserve another sibling's inheritance. None of these motives disqualified a candidate: "God very often makes manifest in this the greatness of his clemency and mercy, using these intentions, which are not at all good in themselves, to make of these persons great servants of his divine Majesty."[78] De Sales even undermined the idea that one needed to be called at all: "[God's] liberality is so great that he gives these means [to live well in a state of life] to those to whom he has not promised them and to whom he has not obliged himself on account of not having called them."[79] In short, a sincere will to continue living in this state would render moot any imperfections in choosing to enter it.

As in his "brief method," de Sales warned against excessive discernment. He identified God's call as an inspiration to which one would respond and hold firm, not as a riddle to be endlessly pondered. One need not "wait until he speaks to us audibly, or until he sends us an Angel from Heaven to reveal his will to us." Nor was it necessary to have "ten or twelve doctors" of theology examine the inspiration to discover if it were authentic. After deciding, one needed to trust God's goodness with a firm and constant will, even amid second thoughts and feelings of distaste or coldness.[80] A good vocation was, by definition, that firm constancy in accepting one's place in God's plan. Firm constancy was not simply to be passively awaited; it was to be chosen and continually willed.

François de Sales's vocational discernment advice thus exemplified his gentleness and his consistent message of trust in God. He emphasized the simplicity of the decision and the abundance of God's grace, even if one ended up in a state of life for the wrong reasons. The choice of a state was thus a serious choice, but not the hinge on which all one's life and eternity depended; perfection was possible in every state, and God was generous to all who turned to him. It is perhaps because he lacked a rigorist sense of urgency about right vocational discernment that de Sales did not dedicate any portion of his most popular work, the *Introduction to the Devout Life*, to the topic.

IGNATIAN AND SALESIAN ECHOES IN THE EARLY SEVENTEENTH CENTURY

The spiritual legacies of Ignatius of Loyola and François de Sales helped to form the francophone Catholic world of the early seventeenth century, not least because those legacies respectively had powerful and prolific advocates, including the French Jesuits and the immediate disciples of François de Sales. Examples from the writings of three of those advocates – Étienne Binet, Jeanne-Françoise de Chantal, and Jean-Pierre Camus – illustrate the continued currency of Ignatian and Salesian vocational doctrines before the rigorist turn, while providing a contrast with the systematic detail and sense of urgency about vocation that was yet to come.

Étienne Binet (1569–1639), is one of many prolific French Jesuits whose Ignatian formation is evident in his discussions of choosing a state of life and who was not without Salesian connections. He was an acquaintance of François de Sales, first as a fellow student Sales at Clermont, the Jesuit college in Paris, and their interests and preaching styles overlapped.[81] Like de Sales, Binet was open to holiness in all states of life, and he wrote in a short treatise that the "principles and foundations of … perfection" could be practiced "according to one's state and profession."[82] He goes on to describe the beginning practices of perfection in a quintessentially Ignatian mode. As in the *Spiritual Exercises*, one of the first aims was to habitually possess "an entire and perfect indifference to all created things."[83] The next goal, as in the *Exercises*, was "to make a good choice of a state of life that is conformed to the will of God," or, if one was already committed, to adjust one's manner of living in a state to accord better with God's will.[84] At least in this text, Binet refrains from offering further advice on how to make that good vocational choice. He had imbibed these Ignatian principles from his own Jesuit formation, but he was too early to be part of the movement that made discernment methods far more systematic. For Binet and for many other early seventeenth-century French Jesuits, the *Exercises* were a touchstone, and perhaps a sufficient one.

Jeanne-Françoise de Chantal (1572–1641), the collaborator of François de Sales in founding the Visitation Order and the disciple whose work most directly incarnated his vision, promoted a Salesian culture of vocation among her spiritual daughters. In her own 1626 conference on voting to receive new Visitandine sisters and to advance novices to vows, she prescribed above all the reading of her co-founder's original talk on the subject, given a few years earlier. Her further injunctions, though mainly oriented toward practical matters, reveal a high spiritual doctrine rooted in Salesian gentleness. In considering and voting on a candidate's fitness, it was essential "always to act with charity" throughout this process.[85] She advocated a simple, focused voting procedure that avoided unseemly lobbying and long speeches for or against a sister.[86] Should a tearful novice, in fear of being rejected, inappropriately plead with a sister, no direct answer could be given but words of consolation were obligatory: "My dear Sister, Our Lord will not deny you his grace if you do not deny him fidelity, and you will have no reason to fear; it is necessary to have confidence in him; he never abandons those who hope in his goodness."[87] This principle of charity even demanded accepting a mediocre, but harmless sister, especially if returning to the world would endanger the young woman's salvation: "For, if she does no great good to the house, she will do no great evil to it."[88] Chantal's approach was therefore in full accord with the lack of anxiety de Sales had expressed about the fittingness of candidates. There was no need to seek out some hidden sign of vocation before allowing a sister to come or to stay. Rather, vocational discernment was an occasion for trust in God's own gentle, generous love.

As Chantal expanded on François de Sales's conference on the vocations of Visitandines, Jean-Pierre Camus (1584–1652) promoted a version of de Sales's principles for choosing a state of life. Consecrated bishop of Belley in 1609 by de Sales, Camus was in his own right one of the most prolific preachers and writers of the first half of the seventeenth century. Although scholars have disagreed on exactly how much Camus's writing and preaching accorded with that of his friend François de Sales, his six-volume *Spirit of St Francis de Sales* was an important vehicle for disseminating the Salesian vision well into the nineteenth century.[89] In that work, which Camus presents as essentially a collection of de Sales's sentiments, the section "on vocation" aims to reassure the reader with classic Salesian douceur. As de Sales had in *Love of God*, the text insisted that "the vocation to some state or condition" is only a counsel and hence not necessary for salvation, "since in all [states] one can be saved and in all one be lost."[90] Moreover, attaining certainty about the state to which one was called was difficult, and so Camus's text again echoed *Love of God* in warning against excessive discernment:

"There are some ... who break their heads and rack their brains by force of meditating and consulting on what kind of life they should embrace, whether celibacy, or marriage, or the cloister, or some occupation in the world."[91] Although one who followed a call to a particular state did well and would be "crowned with mercy" in a special way, by no means was doing so essential.[92] Camus's de Sales seems more indifferent to vocational discernment than is evident in the texts mentioned above from the *Love of God* and the *Spiritual Conferences*. The Salesian disciple did, however, temper this seeming indifference by recommending the chapter of *Love of God* that includes the "brief method for knowing God's will," and thus Camus implied that vocational discernment could and should be done well.[93] Whatever variations in emphasis we find between the two bishops, both highlighted the gentle love of God, who wished the choice of a state to be a means of greater sanctification, rather than a perilous stumbling block on the road to salvation.

CONCLUSION

By the early seventeenth century, Catholic reformers had reshaped medieval materials into more coherent visions of vocational discernment. The early Protestants were not alone in extending the notion of "calling" to life in the world. But Catholics had a different understanding of what that calling meant, above all in that they retained traditional distinctions among the three major states of life (ecclesiastical, religious, and lay). Moreover, Tridentine assertions of individual freedom to make vocational choices helped enable later rigorists to assert that all were obliged to make individual vocational choices. The teachings of Ignatius of Loyola and François de Sales expanded interest in both vocational inclusiveness and systematic discernment methods. It would not be a far step to more rigorist vocational reforms. If, as Ignatius and de Sales implied, God had a calling for each person, would there not be consequences for failing to discern or to obey that call? According to Ignatius, much depended on the motives by which one made one's choice. De Sales, knowledgeable as he was about Jesuit spirituality, may have purposefully offered a more optimistic view. His discernment method demanded less precision than did the *Exercises*, and he emphasized fidelity to one's choice as an antidote to fears of choosing wrongly. Despite their differences, both writers, especially given the chronological gap between them, successfully planted the idea that vocational discernment could be a normal part of a Christian life well lived. Vocational discernment might be taken up in due course by any devout Catholic, including those whose life's path would be marriage. The result of discernment was not necessarily the monastery or the clerical tonsure. Although vocational discernment was not yet a widely known practice in early seventeenth-century France, it had already entered the culture of devout elites and was further spread by figures such as Binet, Chantal, and Camus. Later French reformers would find that level of diffusion insufficient, and so they would reinterpret again this new culture of vocation and bring it to more audiences, in more systematic forms, and with a greater sense of urgency and anxiety.

2

Urgency: Vocational Rigorism and the Dangers of Choosing Poorly

In his late seventeenth-century "Instruction on the Choice of a State of Life," the Jesuit Louis Bourdaloue advised "a young person of quality" as follows: "There is nothing on which salvation depends more than to choose well the state in which one should live, because it is certain that almost all the sins of men come from the engagement of their state ... For what will be if you should come to make a mistake in this, and take another way than that wherein God has prepared for you graces to make your salvation?"[1] Here "the king of preachers and preacher of kings" expresses succinctly the phenomenon I call "vocational rigorism."[2] Rigorism is a slippery word – often a term of abuse – which is in the eye of the beholder. "Vocational rigorism," as I use the term, primarily denotes the belief that salvation was virtually conditional on choosing the state to which one had been called by God. Vocational reform could also be rigorist in other ways, such as in a demand for purely spiritual motives in the choice of a state or for the use of a precise discernment method. These latter forms of vocational rigorism will be addressed more extensively in later chapters.

This chapter explores the rigorist sense of urgency that became the chief driving force behind a new phase of comprehensive vocational reform in France. The tradition of vocational discernment that had been brought into its early form by men like Ignatius of Loyola and François de Sales was reinterpreted in the rigoristic church context of the mid– to late–seventeenth century. Reformers of the latter era made vocational discernment into a (spiritual) life-or-death scenario. They consequently attempted to normalize and democratize good vocational discernment as an inoculation against the pandemic of rash, worldly choices of state. The second-wave reformation of Catholic vocation thus emerged from a milieu that imprinted a lasting rigorist character on Catholic culture.

THE RIGORIST TURN IN FRANCE

Vocational rigorism was but one expression of a wide-reaching "rigorist turn" in French Catholicism that took place in the middle decades of the seventeenth century. This rigorism was by no means limited to the doctrines, texts, persons, and institutions associated with the Jansenist movement, which is only part of the story. Recent scholarship has made clear that Jansenism was both an effect and a cause of increasingly rigorist approaches to the Christian life in mainstream French Catholicism.[3] Moreover, for the purposes of contextualizing the effects of rigorism on vocational culture, we should look for rigoristic approaches to pastoral care, rather than for formal adherence to Jansen's (alleged) doctrines on grace or for friendship with Jansenistic institutions such as the Abbey of Port-Royal. Rigorism was not, moreover, always an integral worldview, and an individual or a text could be rigorist in some respects but not in others. For this reason, an overview of the development of rigorism in concrete Catholic practices in seventeenth-century France will help us to understand the precise character of vocational reform.

Early modern Catholic rigorism was most clearly manifest in pastoral approaches to the sacraments of confession and communion. Some historians define seventeenth-century French rigorism as typically marked by the following confessional practices: "The delay or the refusal of absolution, in particular to *habitudinaires* [those who repeatedly returned to the same sins] and to *occasionnaires* [those who repeatedly returned to the same occasions of sin], the practice of rigorous – and public, if necessary – penances, and an inquisitorial practice not only regarding the confession itself, but also regarding its spiritual motivations, by the pursuit of a real discernment of the degree of the penitent's contrition."[4] In other words, rigorists believed it was very difficult to make a valid confession and thus to be truly absolved of sins. Furthermore, one needed to be very well prepared and cleansed of sin before receiving the Eucharist. Hence, communion was to be an infrequent affair for most Catholics.

Starting in the middle of the seventeenth century, contentious debates over rigor in confession and communion rocked the church in France. Seeds of this conflict were planted long before Jansenism arose. Early divisions among the *dévots* – that broad range of Catholics who pursued and promoted the renewed spirituality of the time – led to wider and more formal fissures later on. Devout spirituality in France can be symbolized in two divergent models of saintly bishops. Carlo Borromeo of Milan represented a more rigorist approach to pastoral care, whereas François de Sales represented greater flexibility.[5] As of the 1610s, some church luminaries were still debating a principle affirmed by the Council of Trent, that attrition (rather than perfect contrition) was sufficient for sin to be forgiven in the sacrament of penance.[6] Attrition, also called imperfect contrition, could involve fear of divine punishment as a motive, but it had to include a rejection of one's sins with the intent not to sin again. Perfect contrition meant sorrow for sin arising entirely out of love for God, rather than lesser motives. In effect, if a rigorist, "contritionist" approach was right, then assurance of forgiveness was harder to come by. Added to this debate was the oft-maligned, Jesuit-promoted science of casuistry, in which ethical questions were evaluated by posing hypothetical cases and applying principles to determine possible moral courses of action. It was frequently alleged that Jesuit casuistry led to laxity, in the confessional and in spiritual counsel, on questions such as usury, duelling, and even regicide.[7] Conflicts over confessional practice fed into conflicts over Holy Communion. Since being free of mortal sin through confession was a prerequisite for receiving the Eucharist, many who doubted the validity of most confessions also rejected the possibility of frequent communion, especially for the laity. The high level of ecclesiastical support given to the publication in 1643 of Antoine Arnauld's *Frequent Communion* – which might have been better entitled "Against Frequent Communion" – underlined the pre-existing conflict.[8] Many churchmen thought that easy confession in tandem with frequent communion built up a self-complacent laity, lacking any true conversion of heart.

Likewise at issue in seventeenth-century French rigorism were theoretical questions of how human beings cooperated with God's grace and thus how individual salvation occurred. Cornelius Jansen's *Augustinus*, posthumously published in 1640, intensified academic disputes over these perpetually unresolved theological questions.[9] Following on the furor over doctrines of justification and salvation espoused by Protestants, intra-Catholic disputes on God's grace had arisen in the late sixteenth century, mainly between Jesuit Thomist and Dominican Thomist theologians. At the heart of that debate were questions about predestination, God's "efficacious grace," and the doctrines of the Jesuit theologian Luis de Molina. The latter's Molinism – the quasi-official position of the Jesuit order – emphasized free will, the abundant availability of grace, and, hence, a certain ease in attaining salvation.[10] French theologians had been little involved in this debate, which ended inconclusively. In 1607, Pope Paul V permitted both the Molinist and Dominican positions to be taught, while forbidding both sides from condemning the other as heretics, or even from publishing new works on the subject.[11] The *Augustinus*, published posthumously through the efforts of Jansen's long-time friend Jean Duvergier de Hauranne (known as Saint-Cyran), implied a scathing critique of Molinism and the Jesuits, based primarily on an exposition of Augustine's doctrines on grace. Over the rest of the seventeenth century and into the early eighteenth century in France, controversy – involving popes, *sorbonnistes*, the king, laymen, nuns, priests, and many others – raged over the orthodoxy of the *Augustinus* and of various positions on grace. Although not all rigorism was Jansenist, Jansen's name provided a derogatory label that the less rigorous could use against the more rigorous. Rhetorical framing was central to these disputes. The Jansenist-aligned polemicist Blaise Pascal, for example, could present his position as the Augustinian Catholic mean between Calvinism and Molinist Pelagianism, while others who rejected both Molinism and Jansenism could present their views as the Catholic mean between those two extremes.[12]

Without further belabouring the history of these *querelles*, which were fundamentally about how easy it was to live the Christian life, we can begin to see their implications for the history of vocational reform. Debates over rigor and laxity, whether manifested in abstruse theological disputes or in the experience of sacramental administration, shifted the pastoral conversation in France toward an emphasis on sin and how to avoid it. Jean Delumeau classically highlighted this phenomenon in *Sin and Fear*, published in 1983. He argued that late medieval and early modern Christianity exhibited a tendency toward "'culpabilisation' ('guilt-ification')," defined as "the arguments that inflated the dimensions of sin over and against those of forgiveness."[13] Even if, as critics contended, Delumeau insufficiently contextualized his sources, excessively psychologized about early modern people, and generally overextended his argument, such "guilt-instilling" discourse was clearly a prominent experience of many early modern Christians. The balance was not always and everywhere the same, but the scales certainly tipped in mid- to late seventeenth-century France toward the fear of sin and of the consequences of sin.[14] This emphasis on sin became an essential ingredient in the vocational rigorism that developed during the period, such that vocational reform was envisioned primarily as a remedy for sin.

This exploration of vocational reformers' anxious sense of urgency underscores the complexity and pervasiveness of France's rigorist turn. It was not the closest allies of Port-Royal or of other Jansenist-leaning institutions who will appear most frequently in this chapter or those that remain, because those most easily labelled as Jansenists – however we define the term – were not the chief systematizers of vocational reform. This is not to say that Jansenists did not espouse some of the same principles. Saint-Cyran, for example, shows himself part of this phenomenon when he insists on right discernment of God's call as the "root" of all the good one might do in life.[15] But the staunchest Jansenist partisans seem less likely to take up vocational reform in its most systematic versions, which were ultimately tied to Jesuit spirituality. The influence seems to go more in the other direction: even those grounded in the seemingly world-affirming vocational principles of Ignatius of Loyola or François de Sales were caught up in the rigorist spiritual currents prevalent in later seventeenth-century France. A significant number of those identified here as vocational rigorists were Jesuits. This does not mean that the whole French church was equally rigorist or was rigorist on every question. Nevertheless, the concept of "vocational rigorism" captures how rigorist approaches to sin and grace determined the evolution of vocational reform in this era.[16]

SINS, GRACES, AND THE CONSEQUENCES OF VOCATIONAL CHOICE

In keeping with their rigorist milieu, seventeenth-century vocational reformers framed the choice of a state of life chiefly in terms of sin. To choose a state without being called there was itself a sinful rejection of God's will. More importantly, the fundamental consequence of wrongly choosing a state would be an inability to fulfill one's duties without frequently falling into sin. Such a life would be anguished on earth and would likely lead to eternal damnation. To ignore God's calling was an act of contempt and of spiritual suicide. A deeper look at these reformers' arguments shows that their convictions involved a rigorist theology of grace – a theology that saw grace primarily in its relationship to temptation and sin. Above all, reformers sought to convince young Catholics and those who shaped the lives of young Catholics that right vocational choice was one of the most urgent pastoral matters facing the Church.

One of the most extensive mid-seventeenth-century accounts of vocational discernment was the fifth part of Charles Gobinet's *Instruction of Youth in Christian Piety*, which first appeared in 1655. He culminated his advice to young Catholics by highlighting "the importance of choosing well a state of life, and the means of doing so properly, which is a subject little known by young people, and even less practiced."[17] A doctor of the Sorbonne and the principal of the Collège du Plessis-Sorbonne for over four decades, he developed the treatise in his first years of directing young men at the collège.[18] Gobinet exemplifies the fact that a churchman might be more rigorist on some questions than on others. His voting record as a *sorbonniste* shows him an enemy of the Jansenists, and his overall orientation was indebted to the gentle François de Sales, even if he was slightly more cautious on confession and communion than the saintly bishop had been.[19] According to Gobinet, vocational discernment was the single most important issue in the education of youth, and "the disorders which we see in each state" resulted from the fact that most people had entered their state of life "lightly, without examining whether they are fit for them, or whether they are called by God."[20] On the choice of a state depended "all the good of man, both for this life and for eternal salvation."[21] Such affirmations did not originate with Gobinet. In 1638, the Jesuit Bernard Dangles (c. 1585–1658) similarly warned: "On this choice depends, for the majority of people, the good or bad life, the happy or unhappy death, and the eternal salvation or damnation of each person."[22]

Tropes about unhappiness in this life appear frequently. According to Gobinet, there was "no condition more miserable" than to have entered a state ill-chosen: "The displeasure of seeing himself engaged against his inclination, joined with the difficulties he suffers in satisfying his duties, casts him into grief and into a melancholy that incessantly gnaws at him; it renders him insupportable to others and to himself."[23] The poor vocational choice left the soul without peace, because it entailed obligations for which one had neither the attraction nor the preparation. Similarly, François Nepveu (1639–1708), a Jesuit writer of many devotional and moral works, compared one who entered a state of life "without consulting God, without a vocation," to a "dislocated bone" that "suffers much and makes the whole body suffer."[24] What emerges is a principle that there could be only one right choice. God had determined but one calling for each person, and the choice of any other would be disastrous.

Graver than the consequence of suffering on earth was that of eternal damnation, and in this we see more clearly an underlying rigorist theology of grace. Grace was understood in Catholic theology as an interior, supernatural gift from God, and living the Christian life required the help of God's graces. The rigorist milieu of seventeenth-century France had narrowed these reformers' theological and pastoral focus. That is, controversies over grace in terms of rigor and laxity had obscured the positive aspects of Catholic theologies of grace. Hence, vocational rigorists addressed the multifaceted theological concept of grace largely from one perspective, its relationship to sin. They painted a picture of human life as a string of temptations. The role of grace was primarily to help one evade those temptations or to face them without falling into sin.

Vocation, in this rigorist context, became the means by which God determined the graces particularly needed by each person. Choosing the wrong vocation would be to reject the graces needed for one's particular state. Hence Gobinet: "With what pains must he make his salvation, in a state wherein he has neither ability nor a vocation from God? The lack of these two things will lead him to commit an innumerable number of sins, which he would not have committed in another state. The defect of capacity makes him find continual difficulties in satisfying his duty and the particular obligations of his state. The defect of vocation is the cause for which he lacks many graces he would have received in another state."[25] Similar is the quotation from Louis Bourdaloue that opens this chapter, wherein he speaks of one's calling as the "way … wherein God has prepared for you graces to make your salvation."[26]

Vocation itself was sometimes conceived of as a grace on which all other graces were dependent; in Nepveu's words: "The grace of vocation is an important grace, a critical grace, a universal grace, which incorporates an infinity of others. If you lack the vocation, you will lack all these graces."[27] Emanuel de la Croix

(1611–1671) – a Discalced Carmelite whose brother was the controversial Jesuit Louis Cellot – affirmed the same principle in his 1667 work *The Good Choice, or Instruction on Choosing Well a State of Life*: "After the grace of Baptism, which begins our salvation, and the grace of a happy death, which achieves it, the grace of choosing well a state is the most important, and the most necessary for the whole course of life, because it is like the middle and the link that joins the grace of Baptism to the final grace."[28] Jean Richard (1639–1719) – known as Richard l'Avocat – a layman and lawyer who wrote and published many model sermons, stated in a sermon on marriage that the graces needed in one's state depended "on one first grace which is the grace of vocation, the grace by which God calls us and we call him, the grace by which we go the way that we ask him to show us, the grace indeed that has, as it were, a general influence on all the others."[29] Bourdaloue concluded an intimidating account of the duties of the married state with an assurance of God's grace for those called to it: "The thing is impossible for men, but it is not impossible for God. It is impossible to those who enter of themselves into marriage and without the grace of vocation, or who, having this grace, do not make the use of it that they ought. But to those who are faithful to it, all becomes possible."[30] This grace of vocation informed and determined not *one* particular realm of life but *every* particularity of one's life. Every grace, that is, every supernatural help from God to live well, revolved around the choice to follow his will for one's state of life. One's état gave the context for every action, and God's grace was needed at all times for actions to be both morally good and eternally salvific. Vocation was thus to be at the very heart of the life of Christians.

Some vocational reformers conceded that God would not deny "ordinary" graces to those who had chosen their states against his will, but they asserted that salvation demanded more than "ordinary" graces. For instance, Claude Joly (1610–1678), the bishop of Agen whose record places him in the rigorist camp on sacramental questions, asserted this position in a sermon "on the means of sanctifying oneself in one's state": "Although God gives ordinary, common, and sufficient graces to those who have chosen for themselves a state of life without his participation, it is to be feared that he will refuse them the extraordinary and chosen graces to which their salvation is attached ... You have stopped your ears when God has called you; you will have common and sufficient graces, but do not rely on having extraordinary graces; you have not responded to the grace of your vocation, perhaps God will again give you another one, but, if he does not, how will you save yourself?"[31] In other words, "sufficient grace" (a technical term in theological controversies) was not actually sufficient. The graces God gave for the Christian life in general would not enable a Christian to live well in a particular state. The teaching of Emanuel de la Croix rested on a similar premise:

> God, by his particular providence, having resolved … to call and to save … some by one particular state and others by another, has also attached his singular graces to one particular state and not to another … He who will follow the state to which God calls him will receive there a great abundance of extraordinary graces. These graces will make easy for him all that which he could have found in that state to be difficult to do and harsh to suffer … In a word, they will wonderfully facilitate the practice of the highest virtues and victory over the most entangling vices. But if, by his bad will, or out of human respect, he engages himself in another state than the one to which God calls him … he will have enough ordinary graces, with which he can make his salvation, but he will not have this abundance of graces, nor these victorious and triumphant graces that God would have given him in the other state, where he had called him. And thus, lacking these abundant and extraordinary graces, he will succumb to the least temptations. It will be for him almost as if all dangers are mortal dangers.[32]

Although Emanuel's rhetoric was slightly more optimistic than Joly's – perhaps partly on account of the Carmelite friar's Jesuit influences – the substance of their vocational rigorism was nearly identical.[33] Emanuel may have written of "triumphant" and "victorious" graces, which made resisting the gravest spiritual dangers an "easy" task. Yet despite that positive spin, he remained doubtful about the possibility of salvation when a wrong vocational choice prevented those extraordinary graces from being given.

When we consider how Joly and Emanuel downplayed the saving power of "ordinary" graces, we see in high relief the impetus behind seventeenth-century vocational reform. In view of these reformers, "ordinary" Catholics, who had access to all the usual opportunities for receiving God's grace – prayer, the sacraments, and good works – were far from living the Christian life well. Something more was necessary, namely, right discernment of the grace of vocation and the right choice of a state. In a dangerous world of temptation and sin, only extraordinary graces would suffice, and those extraordinary graces came only to Catholics who accepted God's call.

SECOND CHANCES

If the receipt of needful graces so depended on the right choice of a state, then what would become of a soul who learned this too late, having chosen a state not intended by God? Permanence and irrevocability – at least after some point of no return such as marital vows, final profession, or sacramental ordination – were essential to the medieval definition of a status or state of life assumed by many vocational reformers. Advice varied, but at least some reformers believed that the prodigals might return for a second chance at grace.

As in other matters of vocational discernment, Ignatius of Loyola initiated the discussion in the *Spiritual Exercises*. He had made a clear, if passing, note that those who had wrongly chosen a state could repent of their poor manner of choosing and seek to live well in it. For them, as for those who had already chosen their state in a good way, the "election" would focus on arranging the details of how one lived out one's calling with an eye toward God's glory and one's eternal salvation.[34] Even less restrictive and more hopeful was François de Sales, who taught that one might enter a state without having been called and still receive the graces necessary to live well.[35] Both assumed that God called each person to a specific state, but they were confident about the availability of God's grace when someone turned to him after unwisely making a solemn commitment.

Few among the later reformers were willing to voice such a hope, especially to audiences of young people. These clerics feared that talk of future repentance would undermine their urgent claims about the consequences of choosing wrongly. Why not instill the principles of right discernment the first time? Most vocational texts spoke to this issue only from their silence. Hearers and readers could not assume there were second chances if none were mentioned. Charles Gobinet, speaking only to the young, exemplified this silence. His 187 pages on choosing a state of life contained nothing about later repentance for a wrong choice and much on the unfortunate fate of one who would make such a choice.

Some reformers, however, reshaped their message about second chances for different audiences. Louis Bourdaloue's instruction on the choice of a state of life, addressed to "a young person of quality," omits mention of second chances, just as Gobinet had done when he wrote for youth.[36] Bourdaloue's Sunday sermon on marriage, however, says that one who had entered that state without a vocation could, through repentance, "have recourse to God to obtain his second graces; for God has second graces to supply for the lack of the first, and it is on these second graces that you must place your confidence."[37] Addressing in this latter text a mixed Sunday sermon congregation, Bourdaloue presumed that many of his hearers would need to hear a message of mercy. As a Jesuit, he was simply elaborating on Ignatius's position on repentance from a wrong choice. This discussion of God's mercy came, however, after he had already vehemently stressed the necessity of following God's vocation in the first place. He could not neglect that basic vocational rigorist principle, since his sermon audience would also have included many young, uncommitted persons whom he did not wish to make complacent.

Bishop Claude Joly likewise crafted different messages on repentance for distinct occasions. In a general sermon on sanctifying oneself in one's state of life, Bishop Claude Joly expressed grave doubt about the possibility of repenting and receiving the graces needed for a state wrongly entered: "Nothing is more to be feared than not having responded to the vocation of God, who does not always call many times."[38] Citing the parable of the workers in the vineyard (Mt. 20:1–16), he denied the possibility of a second vocational chance: "In our whole Gospel reading, I do not see that the father of the family has called the same persons twice."[39] By contrast, in a sermon on marriage, which he says is addressed primarily to those already married, he expressed more hope for those who had entered without a vocation: "God can grant you a miracle like the one he worked at the wedding of Cana, and you can make reparation for this fault by leading a holy life in your state."[40] He was therefore open not only to the sinner's repentance but even to the possibility of "a holy life" for one who had made the wrong commitment.

An outlier among his more rigorist contemporaries was the Oratorian François de Clugny (1637–1694), who expressed still more hope. In his *Catechism of Devotion*, he adapted the teachings of François de Sales into a straightforward format for "simple" persons.[41] He wrote that the vocation to a state of life "was not such a strict obligation" and was, as de Sales would say, "rather a counsel than a commandment."[42] Nevertheless, Clugny also agreed with François de Sales that one's salvation was endangered if one had rejected God's counsel as an act of contempt for the counsellor.[43] Clugny therefore advised penance and "the exercise of true devotion" as "the whole secret to drawing profit" out of a state to which one had not been called.[44] A missed vocation was no trifle, even if, in Clugny's eyes, it was not the gravest of spiritual dangers.

CONCLUSION: VOCATION AND THE COMMON GOOD

Whatever the possibilities of later repentance, these reformers fundamentally agreed that God's calling was necessary for right entrance into a state of life and that the consequences of wrong choices were often disastrous, both for the individual and for Christian society. Gobinet had called the bad choice of a state "the cause of the disorders which we see in each state."[45] Since those who had chosen wrongly would not be equipped to fulfill the duties of their respective states of life, the needs of others would be unmet. As Clugny, for example, explained in Pauline terms, good vocational choices enacted God's providential plan for a church composed of various members: "The diversity of states and the variety of kinds of life make the church subsist and give it its beauty. If a body had nothing but eyes or feet, it would be monstrous. We are all members of a Body, of which Jesus Christ is the Head."[46] When Christians failed to follow God's call, they were rebellious members of Christ's body, like a foot trying to be an eye. Especially worrisome in the post-Tridentine era of clerical reform was entrance into the priesthood without a vocation. Hence Claude Joly's catechism warned that parents who forced their sons to be clerics would have to "answer before God for the scandal that their children give to the whole Church."[47] Right vocational choices were therefore no private matter, between God and the individual.

Rigorist vocational reformers hoped not only that more individuals might be saved, but that the body of the church might be healed. Bad priests led Christians into sin more readily than anyone else. Bad religious and laity were no help, either. If no priest, religious, or lay person could be good without the grace of vocation, then ongoing Catholic reform demanded that young Catholics learn to discern rightly God's will for their lives. Catholic vocational culture in France needed to be remade. Rigorist vocational reformers therefore sought to normalize vocational discernment, and one of the biggest challenges in doing so was the effort to instill the idea that each person was called to a state of life, including all laymen and women. Vocational rigorists sought to leave no space for a mediocre laity, and so they offered an inclusive framework for lay vocation, which will be explored in the next chapter.

3

Inclusiveness: Lay Vocation in a Rigorist Framework

By the latter half of the seventeenth century, many Catholics had come to employ the language of vocation inclusively, that is, in reference to worldly states of life, rather than restricting vocation to religious and clerical life. Consider the following examples. In a funeral oration for Éléonor de Bergh (1613–1657), duchess of Bouillon and princess of Sedan, the Cluniac-Benedictine priest Jacques Biroat (d. 1666) noted that marriage was established by God "for the particular good of *those whom he calls to this state*" and that the duchess's marriage had been "concluded in heaven before [it was] made on the earth, since it served as the occasion and means for the sanctification of both spouses."[1] Jules Mascaron (1634–1703), Oratorian and then-bishop of Tulle, in a funeral oration for Henri de la Tour-d'Auvergne (1611–1675), Viscount of Turenne and Marshal General of France – as well as brother-in-law to Éléonor de Bergh – took pains to defend the military vocation: "All of you whom birth *and even the vocation of heaven calls* to this glorious profession, which is the defense of the altars of God, of the authority of your prince, and of the security of your homeland, do not consider it a formal obstacle to your salvation and to your Christian glory."[2] An obituary notice for Visitandine nun Françoise Agnès Descomps (d. 1714, age eighty-three at the order's monastery in Agen), written by a nun of her monastery, praised the deceased's mother for not attempting to "inspire the choice of a state, being persuaded that this was the Holy Spirit's business." Instead, this good mother gave Françoise an education as a boarding student in the convent, where she learned "all that a girl needs to know in order to live in a Christian manner *in whatever state to which God might destine her*."[3]

These quotations urge us to rethink our history of lay vocation in Catholicism. These early modern authors – a Benedictine monk, an Oratorian cleric, and a Visitandine nun – had all internalized inclusive understandings of God's call. We can see serious discrepancies between this evidence and generalizations that are still often repeated, exemplified in these words by the editor of an anthology of Christian writings on vocation: "For most of the centuries after the Reformation, Protestant and Catholic thinking about vocation diverged dramatically. Catholics retained the medieval idea of 'vocation' as a call to be a priest, a nun, or a monk; Protestants insisted that *any* job could equally be a vocation." He goes on to say that twentieth-century statements from the Second Vatican Council and Pope John Paul II "would previously have seemed obviously Protestant" on account of their affirmations of lay work in the world.[4] But *to whom* – and *when precisely* – would lay vocation "have seemed obviously Protestant"? To be sure, many pre-Vatican-II Catholics would have found lay vocation an unfamiliar idea, as is evident from a New York priest and seminary professor lamenting in 1942 that ordinary Catholics held the "impression that vocation is something reserved for priests or nuns."[5] His critique reveals that Catholics did indeed already had a tradition of lay vocation, but that, in his view, that tradition was insufficiently diffused among the laity of his day.

As we have already seen, seventeenth-century vocational reformers in France promoted the concept of a call to the lay state – especially to marriage. This chapter analyzes in greater depth how reformers conceived of lay vocation, with special attention to their infusion of the concept of vocation into traditional notions of ranked states of life. Beginning with Pauline biblical tropes about the one body with diverse members, Christians had held that God, in his providential wisdom, had distributed various roles in the body of Christ and the body politic, so that all necessary tasks could be fulfilled. Seventeenth-century reformers transformed this trope by insisting on the need for an explicit choice to enter a state, rather than merely passive conformity to one's place in the world. Even remaining a layperson in the world was to be done in answer to a discerned call from God.

This assertion that vocation was needed for every state of life was a double-edged sword, entailing simultaneous affirmation of and suspicion of the lay state. In many respects, early modern reformers drew from and augmented a long spiritual tradition that exalted the married life. Many high medieval Franciscan and Dominican model sermons, for instance, claimed that marriage was the highest of all religious orders, having been instituted by God himself in paradise, rather than by a saint in later times.[6] But to treat the married state as a vocation in the strict sense, requiring an explicit call from God prior to taking vows, seems to be a theological step not taken before the early modern era.[7] This added ingredient, so important in the exhortations of seventeenth-century vocational reformers, made marriage conceptually more akin to religious life and the priesthood than ever before. Yet in the rigoristic milieu of seventeenth-century France, reformers began to emphasize the *necessity* of being called and the *danger* of remaining in the world without a calling.[8] The rise of lay vocation, therefore, existed within a constellation of beliefs and practices, some of which were medieval inheritances and some of which were early modern innovations. The complex picture that emerges shows that there were indeed important divergences in vocational culture between early modern Catholics and Protestants, but not exactly in the ways often assumed.

PROVIDENCE AND THE DIVERSITY OF VOCATIONS

Seventeenth-century vocational reformers inherited from the Middle Ages – and ultimately from biblical exegesis – the tendency to rank the states of life according to degrees of perfection. All states were good; all states were necessary; but all states were not equal in dignity. Pauline texts, especially 1 Corinthians, had provided the main conceptual tools. "Varieties of gifts" were given by the "same Spirit," such that the body had "many members," not one of which could say to another, "I have no need of you," regardless of which members were "weaker" or "inferior" (1 Cor. 12). The same letter finds Paul arguing extensively for the superiority of celibacy to marriage, and he summarized his point near the end of chapter 7: "He who marries his betrothed does *well*; and he who refrains from marriage will do *better*." Texts such as these facilitated the longstanding Catholic belief that the lay state of life could be lower in dignity without being evil or unnecessary.

These principles raised the further question of how God chose who would belong to one state or another, to a higher state or to a lower one. Biblical texts had long provided material indicating that God had planned the arrangements. Paul's "each has his own special gift from God" (1 Cor. 7:7) fit well with Jesus's "not all men can receive this saying, but only those to whom it is given" (Matt. 19:11). But why and by what means did God give the gift of a higher state to some and not to others? Many interpreters had treated this as a mystery of divine providence, accessible in its outlines but never fully fathomable. Others were inclined to say that the highest states of life were open to almost all. Thirteenth-century theologian Thomas Aquinas, for example, ended his treatment of the religious life in the *Summa Theologiae* with an uncharacteristic ferverino urging readers to take the habit. Sufficient reason *not* to enter religion was, apparently, rare.[9] Many thinkers thus emphasized the individual's free decision-making, but how exactly providence and freely willed choices interacted was never easy to describe, in this context or in any other.

Seventeenth-century vocational reformers tackled these mysteries by making God's act of calling into a point of intersection between providence and human choice. Accepting God's providential will was a matter neither of passively conforming to circumstances nor of freely taking up any state one desired – even if it might be the objectively highest state. Although God did sort Christians into the various states, young Catholics were now said to have the responsibility of interpreting the subtle signs of what his wisdom had ordained. God's providence was exercised through an individual, discernible call, and thus the right choice for one was not the right choice for another.

Some reformers, in employing this vocation-infused providentialism, downplayed the ranking the states of life and encouraged a high view of the lay and married states. In other words, if God actively called *every* person to a state, then it was a praiseworthy spiritual act to follow his will and so remain a layperson. The laity were not in a "default" state or *lacking* a vocation, particularly if they had taken marital vows. Rather, if they had chosen rightly, they had actively accepted God's will, or, as Louis Bourdaloue put it, "the views and designs of his providence."[10] Conformity with one's calling was of the first importance. Charles Gobinet, for example, advised the young that "although all the states are good, not all are nevertheless good for all persons," because "God, who has established by his providence the diversity of states and employments of man's life, distributes them differently according to his wisdom, destining some to one employ and others to another." These destinies were manifested in each person by God's endowment of "different inclinations, and diverse natural abilities, both corporal and spiritual," and above all of different graces, "according to the diverse needs of the respective states to which he calls them."[11] Emanuel de la Croix similarly based vocational discernment on the fact that "God, in his particular providence," had "resolved in his eternal decrees to call and to save in time, some by one particular state and others by another."[12] One's vocation – including a vocation to the lay state – was an eternal decree of providence, a particular means of salvation to which God actively had given a calling.

These principles implied a partial spiritual levelling that made great holiness accessible to all Catholics, irrespective of their states of life. Bourdaloue, in a Sunday sermon, concluded that "what contributes more to our salvation is not in fact the holiness of the state, but the fittingness of the state with the designs and views of God, who has set it out for us, and who makes us to enter there."[13] This enabled him to teach that paths to holiness were individual, while subtly holding to the traditional principle, reaffirmed at Trent, that the states of life were ranked according to spiritual dignity. One of the most sanguine commentators was the Salesian-minded Oratorian François de Clugny. He wrote that "the diversity of states and the variety of kinds of life make the Church to subsist and make it beautiful," and that "diversity and inequality" were both necessary in the body of Christ.[14] Yet individual holiness was not determined by that inequality: "The perfection that is acquired by devotion does not depend on the state or condition in which one is, but on the fidelity to the practice of the virtues fitting to him … The perfection of a traveler does not depend on the way, but on the swiftness with which he walks there … The virtues can be found equally perfect in two persons who are in two states of life unequal in excellence."[15] Like his inspiration François de Sales, he did not deny that states were to be ranked. That ranking, nevertheless, was irrelevant to the individual young person's discernment calculus.

On the basis of these principles, vocational rigorists were often willing to dissuade young men and women from entering the clerical and religious states without being called to them. This tendency manifested, in a new way, centuries-long reform efforts aimed at weeding out worldly clerical and religious candidates. Gobinet emphasized that right motives – "the sanctification of your soul and the salvation of your neighbor" – were the key indicators of a clerical vocation. One had no calling who hoped as a cleric "to live more at ease ... to find repose, idleness, and delights; to amass riches; to be honoured and esteemed by men."[16] His account of motives for a religious call was similar: "The intention needed is to withdraw from the world to do penance and to sanctify oneself interiorly by the practice of the Christian virtues ... For if another motive brings you to this state, then your design is not of God."[17] These reformers saw in their vocational theology a way to higher quality clergy, rather than to greater numbers of clerics. Hence, a catechism for the diocese of Meaux, produced under bishop Jacques-Bénigne Bossuet (1627–1704), stated that "the principal disposition" for receiving tonsure was "to be called by God."[18] One seeking a clerical benefice simply for the sake of the income itself need not apply.

Ironically, therefore, the core principle of vocational rigorism – that entry into a state of life required a vocation – enhanced the spiritual dignity of the lay state, and especially of marriage. It did not matter that the religious life was the "state of perfection" or, as late medieval thinkers modified it, "the state of acquiring perfection," because to choose it without being called there would be to jeopardize one's soul and those of one's fellow Christians. Likewise, to become a cleric without a calling would be to seek a life of material ease ending in eternal damnation. Further, to reject a calling to marriage would be to hold God's providential will in contempt. The way to a holy life and eternal blessedness was indeed open to every Christian who had entered his or her state in response to God's providential calling. Hence the Jesuit ascetical writer and missionary Claude de la Colombière (1641–1682) wrote of marriage that, "like in religious life ... one tastes continual delights there, when one is called there by God."[19]

LAY VOCATION AS REMEDY FOR A DANGEROUS STATE

These world-affirming aspects of vocational reform symbiotically coexisted with equally world-denying, rigorist warnings about the dangers of the world.[20] Overshadowing the doctrine that God positively called men and women to marriage was the claim that remaining in the world without that call was a grave spiritual danger. Traditional tropes about the perils of life in the world punctuated vocational reformers' arguments that one needed a clear sense of calling to commit oneself to such a dangerous state. In practice, therefore, later seventeenth-century discernment advice turned on its head the ennobling potential of lay vocation. Not so much a robe of glory, God's call was rather a haz-mat suit necessary for survival in a spiritual toxic waste dump.

This pessimistic side of lay vocation is especially evident where reformers contrasted marriage with religious life. Despite asserting that God distributed vocations in his wisdom, with holiness available in the state to which one was called, vocational reformers often employed traditional strong rhetoric in favour of the religious state as the "state of acquiring perfection" par excellence. Since they understood the state itself to be inherently ordered toward *becoming* holy over time, they made it seem as if prerequisite strengths or even the grace of vocation itself were unnecessary to one entering religion. Life in the world, by contrast, was so full of dangers that many special graces were required for Christian living. Jesuit Bernard Dangles thus warned: "It is necessary to have many more signs that God calls you to the secular state … than for the religious state, because Our Lord has … declared to us that the secular state carries all sorts of dangers for eternal salvation, and that, to the contrary, the religious state is an assured path to paradise."[21] Although God actively called young men and woman to vocations in the world, it was easier to know God's call to the safe harbour of religious vows. Louis Bourdaloue's instruction on choosing a state of life reveals similar ambivalence. Having initially emphasized the importance of accepting whatever state "which God has prepared for you with graces to make your salvation," he offered a final exhortation in favour of the religious life. But he concluded this latter statement with some backpedalling: "I will speak to you no more of it. It is for the Lord to explain himself, and you will always be well anywhere you go under his conduct and by his vocation."[22] Well aware that his general advice about discernment was in tension with his specific commendation of religion, Bourdaloue left the tension logically unresolved.

Emanuel de la Croix similarly struggled to reconcile his sense of the proper ranking of states with the fact that God called many to be laypersons. He treated in succession the lay, clerical, and ecclesiastical states, moving from lowest to highest. The number of those who served God rightly while living in the lay state was far fewer than the number of those who were damned there, he wrote, whereas religion was "the surest, easiest, and shortest way to reach heaven."[23] Most of his section on the lay state consisted of an account of the corruption of worldly people and of the many spiritual dangers to which both good and evil people in the world were constantly exposed.[24] He justified his account as a realistic preparation for spiritual battle: "What I have said should not nevertheless keep you from remaining in the world, if you are certain that God calls you there; I say this only so that you will take careful measures and seek safeguards, to live there in fear and to make your salvation there with trembling. Strongly prepare for so many enemies, whose perpetual attacks will make your salvation very difficult. But if you do not feel that God calls you to the world, bless him a thousand times for willing to take you from this place that is so slippery and full of precipices, in order to place you in a safer condition of life."[25] Presented this way, a call to remain in the world was a burden, indeed almost a curse.

Having laid out this melancholy view of life in the world, Emanuel followed it with a glowing account of religion as the best and easiest way to salvation. For both the lay and ecclesiastical states, he had warned of many dangers, but for religion, he enumerated not one danger but rather highlighted its "infinite advantages."[26] He wrote that "religion *delivers us from all the impediments to our salvation*, which are riches, intense pleasures, pride, bad company, our own will, our own judgment, and generally all occasions for offending God."[27] Taking his account at face value, religious life involved no occasions of sin whatsoever. No wonder he concluded his section on the lay state by saying a young man or woman should "bless God a thousand times" if *not* called to remain in the world. Yet he closed his section on the religious life with an affirmation of a higher order, that being in religion was "a mark of predestination so sure that, absent a particular revelation from God, it is not possible to have a more certain testimony of it."[28] Emanuel's rhetoric here is difficult to square with his emphasis elsewhere on the particularities of vocation and of God's providential plan for each individual. On the one hand, if the ultimate goal of Christian life and vocational discernment was salvation and if taking religious vows removed virtually all dangers to salvation, why then would one choose anything else? On the other hand, if one could only enter the state to which one was called, why push the reader so hard toward religious vows?

It would be reductionistic to say that Dangles, Bourdaloue, and Emanuel, all members of religious orders (two were Jesuits and one a Discalced Carmelite with Jesuit connections), were simply puffing up and recruiting for their own state of life. To be sure, they hoped to attract good candidates to their respective orders, but the tensions in their works between the objective hierarchy and the particular vocation had deeper roots. All three of them taught a systematized and universalized vision of vocations and of discernment, in which God in his providential wisdom gave a calling to each Christian. All three of them believed that God gave graces of vocation by which he directly called young men and women to marriage and to life in the world. Nevertheless, they also thought and worked in a theological tradition that upheld the inequality of the states of life, especially the superiority of vows of celibacy. To deny that inequality, in their view, was to deny the teachings of not only the Council of Trent, not only popes, not only fathers and doctors of the church, not only the Pauline scriptures, but even the very words of Jesus in the Gospels (e.g., Matt. 19:12; Luke 18:29–30).

Furthermore, these reformers were heirs not only of the relatively recent Ignatian principles of individual vocational discernment but also of the still-influential Thomistic teaching that virtually all Christians were invited to the religious life, the "state of perfection" par excellence. For, in this state, even great sinners, with little aptitude but with a willing heart, might be brought toward Christian perfection.[29] Even the more recent influence of Ignatius was not unambiguous on this point. To be sure, he forbade priests leading the *Spiritual Exercises* from pushing retreatants toward religious life, but he added that "outside the Exercises … we may lawfully and meritoriously urge all who probably have the required fitness to choose continence, virginity, the religious life, and every form of spiritual perfection."[30] Hence, seventeenth-century reformers like Bourdaloue who inherited Ignatius' innovations also carried on his traditionalism. Inspiring young people to enter religion remained for them a high priority and indeed a great act of love and devotion. Even François de Sales, champion of the concept of lay vocation, had not wholly abandoned this objective.[31] The later reformers we have been considering followed suit, attempting both to entice entries into religion and to teach right vocational discernment in general. Rather than give up one or the other goal, they permitted ambiguity. Even if they resolved this tension in their own minds, their two-sided advice to young men and women failed to explain any such resolution. Old habits, especially religious habits, die hard.

The Jansenist luminary Saint-Cyran serves as a point of comparison here, as he espoused a vocational rigorism grounded more in Augustine than in Aquinas, Ignatius, or de Sales. In advice to a young princess interested in monastic life, he cautioned that the Holy Spirit's act of calling was an absolute prerequisite for entering and for doing well in that state, and thus he asserted the most basic principle of vocational rigorism.[32] And like the reformers already mentioned, he was often a cheerleader for religious vocations, as in a letter to a young lady, congratulating her in her desire for religion over "the rough yoke of marriage."[33] But he ultimately was less inclusive, less willing to see marriage and the world as viable options for most. Remaining in the world was to be avoided whenever possible. In another interesting letter, he contradicted certain counsels that his recipient received from someone else on how to choose a state of life. This unmarried gentleman had been led, presumably by a more Ignatian or Salesian spiritual guide, into thinking that marrying and remaining in the world might be a good path. But, argues Saint-Cyran, the man's spiritual awakening occurred before he was married, and so it would be folly to sacrifice his spiritual freedom: "Since God finds you free and disengaged from marriage (which is one of the great obstacles to the good life for penitents), you are obliged to humble yourself more to obtain the grace to live well and to take up the practice of many means to your salvation which are forbidden to married persons, for whom for this reason salvation is more difficult."[34] Vocational rigorism thus need not bear the stamp of the innovation of inclusiveness, and a writer like Saint-Cyran might reinforce one aspect of vocational reform while undermining others.

Even among the less purely rigorist, the central contention of seventeenth-century vocational rigorism – that a discerned calling was a *requirement* for entering a state of life – became fuel for guilt-instilling rhetoric surrounding lay vocation. To pursue marriage for mere lack of interest in other states was insufficient, since marriage was arguably the most dangerous state of all. A discerned vocation to marriage, with protective graces attached, was compulsory for one who would have to live with the temptations inherent in such a worldly, fleshly state. This lay-oriented vocational rigorism was another manifestation of how later thinkers reconfigured Ignatius of Loyola's doctrine that one must not choose a state of life without being called to it.[35] He had mentioned the vocation to marriage, but it was left to the rigorists of the seventeenth century to make the eternal salvation of married persons dependent on being called. These later reformers made Ignatius' basic vocational principle into an absolute by combining it with the pessimistic theology of grace that prevailed in their time. When deployed in conjunction with intense rhetoric about the world's spiritual perils, the idea of lay vocation was intended to produce more fear than consolation. Theoretically, that fear was oriented toward right discernment of God's particular will, such that the grace of vocation would remedy any spiritual dangers inherent in the lay state. Yet, in practice, it could also serve the more traditional purpose of promoting religious life as a safe harbour.

LAY VOCATION AND THE REFORM OF THE CLERGY

If traditional rhetoric about the religious state was one obstacle to building a culture of lay vocation, the urgency of reforming the clergy was another. While some vocational rigorists made it clear that a call from God was required for entering any state of life, others only took an interest in God's call to the secular priesthood. Well before the rise of Protestantism – indeed, in every major era in church history – Catholic reformers insisted that reform of the whole church depended on rooting out clerical corruption. This work was taken up in earnest in the post-Tridentine period generally and especially in seventeenth-century France. Seminaries and other tools of priestly formation sprang up throughout France in the decades after the Wars of Religion.[36] Bishops, seminary instructors, and others involved in priestly formation helped promote a clerically-focused vocational rigorism, which took little interest in the religious and lay vocations. This narrower expression of vocational reform asserted that corruption in the church came from the fact that so many clerics had entered their state without being called it. This was a version of the "clerical anticlericalism" pervasive in early modern Catholic reform, then infused with the vocational doctrines of seventeenth-century French rigorism.[37] In this way, clerically oriented vocational rigorism often overshadowed the promotion of the married and religious vocations.

A figure who exemplified clerical vocational rigorism was Louis Tronson (1622–1700). Third superior of the Sulpicians and a notable theorist of the priestly vocation, he had little to say about other callings. He helped solidify the exalted vision of the priesthood that was a central component of the French School of spirituality, and he was a vocational rigorist, insofar as he was uncompromising on the necessity of a vocation for entry into the priesthood. And yet, as leader of one of the most important reforming institutions for priestly formation, he felt little need to comment on vocations to the religious life or to the lay state. Partly at issue was the centuries-long tug-of-war between secular clerics and regular clerics over claims about "perfection," and Tronson's Sulpicians favoured the seculars. While Tronson is known to have used the term "vocation" in reference to religious vows, he questioned the absolute necessity of a call from God for one who entered. Although some promoters of religious vows made a similar move, on the claim that religious life was the best means of perfection, Tronson did so as a way of placing religious life lower than the secular priesthood in the hierarchy of states. And when Tronson infrequently referred to lay professions as "vocations," he did not attach as strong a theological meaning to the term. In his view, the priesthood was too high a state to be entered lightly, without a vocation. Vocational rigorism was integral to the area of reform in his purview, priestly formation, but vocational rigorism in other spheres was unnecessary and uninteresting to him.[38]

Many catechetical texts exhibited the same priorities by deploying vocational language in service of clerical reform. A Bourges archdiocesan catechism, not-coincidentally written by the curé of St-Sulpice (Joachim de la Chétardie, 1636–1714), repeatedly highlighted the necessity of having a well-examined vocation before seeking the clerical state, but it omitted vocational language in the immediately following sections on marriage and celibacy.[39] So also with the Meaux catechism produced under Jacques-Bénigne Bossuet, which stated that "the principal disposition" for becoming a cleric was "to be called by God": "Do they offend God who seek tonsure for themselves or for their children only in order to possess benefices? / Yes, they offend God grievously, for this vocation should come from God, and not from them."[40] Even a 1669 *Catechism in Verse*, by Louis le Bourgeois d'Heauville (c. 1620–1680), included a rhymed sestet explaining how Christ instituted the sacrament of holy orders for "those whom his vocation / Pledges to this function," but it refrained from mentioning a call to marriage.[41] As progeny of the *Roman Catechism* produced after the Council of Trent, all these catechisms advanced the clerical focus that often trumped other aspects of post-Tridentine reform.

Yet not all secular clerics were averse to promoting the newer, more inclusive view of vocation. The Oratorian Charles Gonsin (c.

1635–1693) noted in a catechism for the diocese of Amiens that vocational discernment and spiritual direction were important for one choosing marriage, "because the vocation of God is necessary for every state."[42] Similarly, Bishop Claude Joly, in his catechism for the diocese of Agen, stated that the first disposition necessary for marriage was "to have consulted God to know if one has been called to it."[43] He even exhorted parents to think vocationally about their children's future profession in the world: "Q. What should fathers and mothers do before engaging their children in a profession in life? A. They should pray and consult God, in order to know whether their children are called to it and to make known to them the obligations of their state."[44] Through such catechetical texts, even children in rural French villages were exposed to vocational reform that included the laity.

Moreover, although some clerically-focused reformers tended to downplay, ignore, or deny the idea that a vocation was necessary for non-clerical states, others promoted vocational inclusiveness among future priests. Mathieu Beuvelet (1620–1657), priest of the Parisian seminary of Saint-Nicolas-du-Chardonnet, wrote in a 1655 formation text for seminarians in a spirit like that of Tronson's Sulpicians, espousing a high view of the secular priesthood over and above religious vows. Whereas religion was "a state … of penitence," the priesthood was "a state of perfection."[45] Like so many other reformers, he believed that entry into the priesthood without a calling was among the gravest sources of spiritual peril for the individual and for the church. But Beuvelet also taught seminarians to be inclusive vocational rigorists, claiming that a call from God was needed even for entry into one or another secular profession.[46] In a book on the sacraments, written both for clerical and lay readers, he asserted that a calling was needed not only for "marriage in general" but that "this vocation includes such or such person in particular whom one ought to marry."[47] Many other formators, such as Pierre de la Font, in charge of a seminary in the Uzès diocese, likewise insisted on the same basic principle: an equal need to be called before entering either marriage or the clerical state. Vocational rigorism with respect to marriage had thus become a commonplace in many priests' education and in the model sermons that aided their preaching.[48] And so, the reform of priestly formation was often also a locus for promoting lay vocation.

These examples suggest that interest in lay-inclusive vocational discernment varied significantly among seventeenth-century reformers.

The same basic language about the necessity of a vocation for living well (and ultimately being saved) in one's state was applied by some only to the clerical state, and by some to every state. But if clerically-oriented vocational rigorism was more common than vocational inclusiveness, it was because early modern Catholic calls for reform had always focused on the reform of clerical corruption, as the central means of reforming the church at large. And yet many formators of priests bought into the larger vision of rigorist vocational reform. When occasion arose, a Joly, a Gonsin, or a Beuvelet could speak with just as much conviction about the married vocation as they did about the priestly vocation. These were the true believers who made lay-oriented vocational rigorism into a commonplace.

CONCLUSION: LAY VOCATION IN THE REPERTOIRE OF CATHOLIC REFORM

Lay (especially married) vocation in seventeenth-century French Catholic reform was a concept pushing in at least two directions, since it both exalted the lay state and enhanced suspicions about it. While marriage and secular professions could be means of holiness (if not "states of perfection," in the technical sense) for those called to be in the world, they were sites of damnation for all who lived in the world without being called. Moreover, inclusive vocational reform coexisted long-term with more exclusive approaches that reserved the concept of vocation to clergy and religious. These ambiguities help explain why twentieth-century ecclesiastics and scholars alike believed that Catholic lay vocation was virtually unknown prior to their own time. As so many commentators of the past hundred years have said, Catholic and Protestant cultures of vocation did in fact diverge during the early modern period. But, contrary to what we are commonly told, that divergence did not consist in an absence of lay vocation from Catholicism, a lacuna to be filled only with Vatican-II-era rethinking. Rather, the main divergence stemmed from the fact that Catholic reformers retained hierarchical distinctions among states of life, held to be unequal in spiritual dignity. This was no static retrenchment but rather a dynamic attempt to integrate innovative inclusion of the laity with the traditional distinctions among states of life.

This stratified form of vocational modernity – quite distinct from the apparent spiritual levelling sloganized as "the priesthood of all believers" – was also more open to rigorism than were Protestant vocational cultures. Maintaining notions of higher and lower states allowed Catholics also to maintain notions of respectively safer or more dangerous states. Adding in the core principle of vocational rigorism, that the grace of vocation was needed for Christian living, made the choice of a state quite urgent, as shown in the previous chapter. This rigorist theology of vocational grace could thereby serve to promote fear about the lay state as the most dangerous of all possibilities. The fearful rhetoric employed by many reformers sometimes undermined the consoling claim that protective graces came to one who was truly called. None of these questions could arise in the same way within the theological, pastoral, and social cultures of Protestantism.

Ultimately, while lay vocation became an important theological and pastoral tool in early modern France, Catholics used this tool in ambivalent and inconsistent ways, as circumstances dictated. Vocational inclusiveness was simply not the most useful pastoral tool or highest pastoral priority for every context. That is, lay vocation, even if it was a commonplace, could still be safely forgotten. This inconsistent use was enabled by the relative newness of lay vocation, which was one way among many of speaking about the various states of life. Though drawn from older practices and beliefs, seventeenth-century reformers' vision of comprehensive, inclusive vocational discernment was an innovation. The elements that distinguished this vision from that of earlier Catholic eras – especially the core idea of the necessity of a vocation – were not mandated by official church teaching or Tridentine reform decrees. Hence there would always be higher priorities, especially the rooting out of corruption among the clergy. Lay vocation was sometimes lost in the shuffle, and even its strongest advocates sometimes defaulted to more limited uses of vocational language in reference to clerical and religious life.

This inconsistency is apparent in some of the biographical texts mentioned at the beginning of this chapter. Life-writing was always simultaneously descriptive and prescriptive, but it could never be quite so systematic in its prescriptions as the catechisms, sermons, and treatises considered above. Biographies reveal the concepts and tropes that authors and, at times, their subjects used to narrate lived experience. Lay vocation was mentioned in passing in the obituary written about Visitandine nun Françoise Agnès Descomps, because lay vocation fit the story the memorialist wished to tell. Yet, looking at a larger sample of Visitandine obituaries, we find that lay vocation rarely entered into the sisters' rhetoric. Rather, death notices served the ongoing formation of sisters by emphasizing the traditional notion of religious life as the fruit of a special, high calling. Since there was usually no reason to mention other possible callings, sisters continued to associate vocation primarily with their own monastic state.[49] Lay vocation was simply not a frequently needed tool in the sisters' vocational social imaginary. It was thinkable but not often thought of. By contrast, the funeral orations of the eminent aristocrats Éléonor de Bergh and Henri de la Tour-d'Auvergne were perfect occasions for construing their lives in terms of divine callings to marriage and to military life, respectively. In such contexts, the commonplace of lay vocation served the preachers' purposes.

The fact of inconsistent attention to lay vocation among seventeenth-century Catholics helps us begin to measure reformers' success in planting a new vocational social imaginary. As with all other aspects of early modern reform, it can be misleading to take the reformers' own ideals as absolute barometers of change. It is more useful in this case to consider that lay vocation became an important and lasting part of the Catholic conversation. This concept was a solid part of the spiritual Catholic repertoire of later seventeenth-century France. French Catholics were "thinking with" vocation in ways scarcely imaginable in earlier eras. Lay vocation could be taken for granted, as an unexceptionable concept, and it could also be ignored as inconvenient conceptual clutter. And depending on the needs of a given preaching or teaching moment, reformers might use it to emphasize the dangers to salvation inherent in marriage, or they might stress the glories of matrimony for one who was truly called to it. They might push for entry into religion as the safest state, the "state of perfection" par excellence, or they might, in the spirit of François de Sales, stress that perfection can be attained in any state. And since Christian preaching has often thrived on paradox, a preacher might try to balance these two sides of the story in a single sermon.

In the end, this new vocational culture would not have been so widely diffused in Catholic France without the work of those clergy who made it their mission to promote the right choice of a state of life. We have thus far considered how the first early modern Catholic reformers created from a medieval inheritance the core of a new set of ideas about vocation and how rigoristic reformers in seventeenth-century France further revised those ideas. The result was the claim that all Catholics, including the laity, needed to discern and choose the states of life to which God had called them. The consequences of ignoring God's call would be grave, regardless of whether one might be called to religion, to the clergy, or to marriage. And, the reformers lamented, precious few French Catholics made any effort to seek out God's will for their vocational choice. This is the urgent problem they believed they had identified. What remains in the next two chapters is to analyze their attempted solution, which was to offer systematic methods by which right discernment might happen, even amid the challenging social realities of Old Regime France.

4

Method: Systematizing the Discernment Process

The vocation story of Madelene Myron, described in the 1673 *Chronicles of the Order of Ursulines* by Marie de Pommereuse, was almost an ideal exemplar of the vocational discernment process advocated by seventeenth-century reformers. Madelene was the daughter of the king's ambassador to Switzerland, and her parents placed her at age eight as a *pensionnaire* in Paris's primary Ursuline convent, where she showed herself studious, amiable, and full of life.[1] More to the point, she was full of religious devotion and took great care in preparing herself for her first Holy Communion, "distancing herself from trivial and childish things, in order to bring herself to serious and solid things."[2] When receiving that first communion, "she conceived her first desires to be a religious, which grew ever after."[3] Over the next few years, she advanced in holiness, talent, and virtue – without a hint of self-importance – and her personality blossomed: "Her humor was easy, sweet, and balanced, and her conversation was agreeable and obliging."[4] The account of her childhood and youthful traits concludes: "In short, she had all the qualities proper to make a perfect Ursuline."[5]

Yet despite being a strong fit for Ursuline life, Madelene made no rash decisions, and it is in describing her process of reflection that her biographer Pommereuse – consciously or not – reinforced the principles of seventeenth-century vocational reformers. Madelene embraced the religious state "with mature deliberation" at the age of fifteen – that is, several years after experiencing those first desires for religious life.[6] Madelene did everything needful to prepare her to hear God's call. She had grown in holiness from a very young age, using all the means at her disposal, especially the religious formation given her by her parents and the sisters. She fled worldly attachments and made good use of the sacraments. Her desire to become a nun at her first communion would have been a very good sign.[7] But most importantly, she could be certain that her motives and aptitudes for her chosen state of life were impeccable, having examined her call over several years until the proper age of reception. Vocational reformers taught that these were the practicalities – motive, preparation, and deliberation – upon which the spiritual integrity of choices of state ideally turned.

Vocational reformers asserted that young people who discerned with great care and deliberation, as Madelene had, were the exception that ought to be the rule. As Charles Gobinet put it, "the importance of choosing well a state of life, and the means of doing so properly … [was] a subject little known by young people, and even less practiced."[8] To provide a solution to this problem, reformers sought to normalize, or democratize, vocational discernment; they attempted to make it a staple of Catholic culture in France and elsewhere. In this chapter, I will analyze their attempt to inculcate precise, systematic discernment practices meant to enable all young Catholics to come to know their calling. Although they drew on earlier traditions, especially the discernment methods developed by Ignatius of Loyola, they reconfigured those traditions in rigoristic ways. Their methods, though intended to be used by all, became convoluted, demanding, and full of room for second-guessing. The new vocational culture was therefore rigorist in two senses. First, as we have seen, good vocational choices were considered virtually necessary for salvation. Secondly, such choices were extraordinarily difficult to make rightly. Both of these aspects of vocational rigorism – anxiety over wrong choices and anxiety over the process of choosing – expressed a fundamental distrust of the world and of the sinful Catholics who populated it.

THE GREAT PITFALL: WORLDLY MOTIVATIONS

The discernment methods enjoined by vocational reformers centred on Ignatius of Loyola's principle of right motives, that one must choose a state of life only "for the praise of God our Lord and for the salvation of my soul."[9] The biggest danger in choosing a state was to do so for the sake of some worldly good, such as wealth or pleasure; consequently, a major part of the discernment process was contemplating and purifying one's motives. Ultimately, rigorist reformers taught that the only good reason to enter a state of life was because one was called to it by God, but this raised the question of how one might hear this call. How could one know God's will? In this context, motives were simultaneously a means and an end: knowledge of one's motives would point to what God's will might be, and the result of good discernment would be a choice made with good motives.

Vocational reformers pointed toward good motives by elaborating extensively on bad motives, so that the latter might be easily recognized and avoided. With this *via negativa*, they offered an account of how sinful and unchristian living was perpetuated in Christian societies. Since right living depended so much on being in the right state of life, and since the principles of vocational discernment were little known, most adults were in the wrong states of life and so exhibited the moral and spiritual failures of life without the grace of vocation. The young would imitate their elders' folly, both in failing to discern their callings and in consequently failing in their duties in life. Those young people would then influence the subsequent generation to do the same, and so on. If, however, young people could choose rightly, they would break that sinful cycle and transform Christian society. For the reformers, then, a major step toward that transformation would be pointing out exactly what was wrong with the world's methods of vocational decision-making.

At many points, reformers sharply contrasted worldly motivations with spiritual motivations in the choice of a state. Gobinet summarized the problem thus: "Some consider in a state they wish to embrace the sweetness and ease of the life; others riches and advancement; others honour and reputation; and, in a word, all consider temporal goods and the present life; but few set before themselves virtue and eternal salvation, which is what they ought to consider in this matter first, before all things."[10] Calling attention to eternity, he reminded his young readers to make God the chief end of this choice, which would determine so much of their future spiritual life. Bourdaloue similarly lamented that so few entered their state for reasons other than "interest … ambition … passion … or to seek therein the advantages of fortune."[11] According to Emanuel de la Croix, the chief "mark of a bad choice" of state was that it came from motives that were "evil, or temporal and earthly, or useless for salvation."[12] Such motives included "to choose on a whim or fancy, to have one's pleasures, conveniences, diversions, or to have honour and riches; to please one's parents and to content their inclination; to make a fortune, to enlarge one's household, to elevate one's family, or to live with greater liberty."[13] From such examples, we can see that reformers particularly set their sights on pecuniary motivations, especially the familial inheritance strategies that were at the centre of France's political economy.[14] Greed itself, in the eyes of the reformers, was the true inheritance that captured generation after generation.

Such avarice was but one of the obstacles to hearing God's call, and many otherworldly passions also led to wrong vocational choices. Hence François de Clugny believed that Christians chose wrongly primarily by "allowing themselves to be carried away by their passions, which the majority of men obey."[15] This included lust, greed, desire for ease, and prideful ambition. Gobinet, focusing on lust, wrote that many entered marriage from "no other end … than sensuousness and the enjoyment of the pleasures they hope to find there, and which they imagine to be wholly other than what they actually are."[16] The Jesuit preacher Claude La Colombière warned against several types of passion-driven motives for marriage: "They marry for ambition, for avarice, for amorousness, and so they do in passion that which demands more dispassionate sense than anything else in the world: they do it, I say, in passion, and for passion."[17] This was not to deny the goodness of marriage per se, since it was a true vocation, and the grace of vocation was powerful. Thus La Colombière taught (in the same sermon) that in marriage, "like in religious life … one tastes continual delights there, when one is called there by God."[18]

But it was not only marriage that might be sought for worldly reasons; no state of life was exempt from abuse. Gobinet, quoting Augustine of Hippo, wrote the following of the ecclesiastical state: "There is nothing in this life … more easy, more light, and more agreeable to men than the office of a bishop, of a priest, and of a deacon, when one discharges it with negligence and self-flattery; but there is nothing more miserable, more sad, and more damnable before God. Moreover … there is nothing in this life … more difficult, more painful, and more dangerous, than the office of a bishop, of a priest, and of a deacon, if one discharges it as one ought and according to the will of our Master; but also … there is nothing happier before God."[19]

Here Gobinet simply echoes the widely held reforming mentality that the priesthood was too important to be taken up for the sake of worldly ease or temporal gain. The dangers of the religious state, Gobinet adds, were not quite as threatening as those of the married or ecclesiastical states, but having the right intention remained an essential part of a true vocation: "The intention needed is to withdraw from the world to do penance and to sanctify oneself interiorly by the practice of the Christian virtues ... For if another motive brings you to this state, then your design is not of God."[20] By way of contrast, we can consider the advice of François de Sales from the seventeenth *Spiritual Conference*, discussed earlier. De Sales had been little concerned about the manner of entry into the religious state. He believed that bad candidates would easily be weeded out before final profession and that good vocations often in fact began badly, even from the lowest and most worldly motivations.[21]

Some reformers explicitly allowed a subordinate place for temporal concerns when choosing a state of life. Gobinet, as noted above, wrote that one must consider virtue and salvation "*first*, *before* all things," and that "temporal motives do not enter into this deliberation except *after* this first and principal end" of serving God and attaining eternal salvation.[22] Bourdaloue offered similar, more expansive advice: "It is not that it is absolutely evil to consider all those things. There is a human prudence, which is not at all contrary to evangelical wisdom, provided that the former is subordinated to that latter. But the abuse is to listen only to that prudence of the world, to behave only according to the principles of the world, to regard only the things that connect to the world, and to determine ourselves only as far as the considerations of the world bring us."[23] Human and temporal prudence were thus not evil in themselves. Rather, they were secondary goods – even secondary indicators of God's calling – always to be considered hierarchically, subject to the primary goods of virtue and salvation. Attention to secondary motivations was often present, for example, in advice about choosing a particular spouse, once the vocation of marriage in general had been chosen. For instance, the Jesuit Jean Cordier (1597–1673) strongly advocated "an equality of birth, condition, humour, age, body, and spirit."[24] When these writers suggested that discernment include consideration of temporal goods, they acknowledged that vocational choices did not take place in a vacuum. Vocation necessarily involved concrete human circumstances. Rather than denying that reality, they sought to place the human in a divine context, within an interpretation of God's providential will. The temptation to consider worldly motives alone would always be present, and so teaching the primacy of spiritual motives was essential to these systematized vocational discernment methods.

PREREQUISITES TO GOOD DISCERNMENT

Good vocational discernment was never meant to be an isolated event. Many vocational reformers highlighted the need for pious living, long before the time came to make a choice of state. Although the prime time for serious discernment was understood as the period between adolescence and age twenty, reformers thought the process would likely fail if habits of holiness had not already developed.[25] Lacking such habits, selfish motives and unquiet passions would drown out wise counsel and the fruit of prayer. Preparing to choose a state of life therefore had to begin in childhood, before sin and indifference took root.

As Gobinet put it, many would choose their state badly, contrary to God's calling, because of "the dissolute and sinful life they lead when they are young."[26] The devil misled in the choice of a state those who "have given their first years" to him, and so Gobinet advised vigilance against sin from an early age, as a remote preparation for later discernment.[27] He reinforced this point through the overall structure of the *Instruction for Youth*, which first discussed general means of Christian sanctification for the young before treating the choice of a state of life as a capstone to youthful holiness.[28] With the selection of a state, a young person would make the transition into Christian adulthood.

Like Gobinet, Emanuel de la Croix taught that sin at a young age brought "shadows into the sinner's intellect and coldness into his will," preventing the young person from later receiving God's inspirations and acting on them.[29] He devoted a chapter of his manual to the "remote dispositions" needed for vocational discernment, dispositions to be formed during childhood and youth through conventional means of sanctification: prayer, almsgiving, fasting, fleeing occasions of sin, corporal mortification, sacraments, spiritual reading, prayerful meditation, and so on.[30] In order to follow God's calling as an adolescent, Emanuel asserts, one needed to live and grow in holiness long beforehand – even from the baptismal font, since the grace of vocation was the "link" between the grace of baptism and the grace of a happy death.[31]

François de Clugny likewise traced God's act of calling to the very beginning of life, and he offered a peculiarly sanguine account of God's providential care in the choice of a state. He envisioned God conducting souls to their vocations throughout childhood and youth, if they chose to be "attentive and faithful to follow the way led by Divine Providence."[32] He had high hopes for this gentle leading:

> Leaving the care of our education to our parents … [God's providence] inspires and often moves them to act without their awareness, in order to give a happy success to his designs for us. And as we advance in age and our reason comes, his light leads us with a marvelous sweetness, and his grace strengthens us against the attractions of the World … so that we see some who are disposed from their childhood to the ecclesiastical state, or to religious life, having no more solid mark of their vocation than the sequence of means by which they have been led by divine providence. Others enter by the same way into offices, into commerce, and also into marriage.[33]

Yet even with his hopeful outlook about God's part in the process, he conceded that very few were in fact attentive to providence, and so they failed to hear God's call.[34]

Even when reformers did not explicitly discuss holiness in childhood and youth, deeply ingrained habits of devotion were implicitly demanded by the discernment methods they urged. A young person was ideally to have a pre-existing relationship of spiritual direction before deliberating about God's call.[35] Furthermore, exhortations about prayer during the time of discernment presupposed a lifestyle of deep and abiding devotion. Bourdaloue imagined frequent, intense dialogue: "So as to engage him more effectively to communicate to you his lights and to declare himself, you have no means more efficacious or more assured than prayer. Go therefore, as often as you can, to prostrate yourself before him and to speak to him like Samuel: Speak, Lord, and make known to me yourself what design you have formed for my person; for I am ready to hear you, to obey you, and to execute all your will."[36] Hence, if all young men and women were obliged to engage in vocational discernment, then all were obliged first to be *dévots* and *dévotes*.

Attention to these prerequisites reminds us again that vocational reform, in the mind of its rigoristic promoters, was integral to all church reform. Right discernment by all presupposed excellent religious formation for all, not just for pious elites and not just for future celibates. In other words, holiness during childhood and youth were for everybody. Notwithstanding the tensions over lay vocation highlighted in chapter 3, a pious young person – even one who developed a strong interior spiritual life – was not predestined for the habit or the collar. Rather, that youth was ready to seek out God's will by engaging in an active discernment process, the outcome of which was still to be determined in a concrete choice of state.

THE DISCERNMENT PROCESS

As in other aspects of their reform, seventeenth-century vocational rigorists inherited and reshaped many elements of their practical discernment methods. Many seventeenth-century reformers explained vocational discernment as a three-legged stool of prayer, wise counsel, and introspective deliberation. This triad had been used in the past without rigorist connotations, as is evident from the example of the "brief method" of vocational discernment given by François de Sales. In his eyes, these were three parts of a simple process: "After having asked the light of the Holy Spirit and applied our consideration to the search of his good pleasure, we take counsel with our spiritual director and, if the occasion arrives, with two or three other spiritual persons."[37] These three means would help his reader avoid a protracted discernment process, which he believed was among the greatest dangers when making any major decisions. The decision was to be made quickly and resolutely, without long deliberations or too many counsellors. Later reformers developed this threefold framework into elaborate, systematic methods, with special attention to the interior deliberation to be performed by the young discerner. In seeking to make vocational discernment a universal experience rather than the privilege of religious and social elites, reformers attempted to lay out a foolproof process. The result of that attempt was a convoluted set of expectations that might intimidate the most devout.

Explicit use of this threefold structure was strong in some Jesuit and Jesuit-friendly sources. The Jesuit preacher Louis Bourdaloue summed it up thus: "You wish presently to know what you should do to know God's plans for you, and what your vocation is … I understand it in three articles, which will serve you as rules, and which I pray you to observe with a complete fidelity. The first is to have recourse to God; the second, to address yourself then to the ministers of God; and the third, to consult yourself. Everything that is more reliable in connection to the choice of your state – to a good choice, I say, a choice wise and Christian – is found contained in these three duties."[38] He took the rhetoric of "consulting" three parties – God, one's spiritual director, and oneself – from earlier Jesuits, especially the Dutch theologian Lenaert Leys (1554–1623). The Carmelite Emanuel de la Croix directly cited Leys and the earlier Jesuit theologian Girolamo Piatti (1545–1591) as the sources of his dictum that "you should consult God, yourself, and your director."[39] Even in texts where this "three consultations" trope is absent, the three elements – prayer, spiritual direction, and introspection – are often easily found. Authors varied as to the order in which they discussed these three elements, which are better imagined as simultaneous and interdependent than as following one after another stepwise.

Prayer, or "consulting God," was held to have a certain primacy among the three parts of the discernment process. Since the goal was to do God's will, it was essential to ask him to reveal it. Jesuit writer Bernard Dangles promised God's generous response to prayer about one's vocation: "Pray to God often and for a long time with the greatest devotion and ardor you can muster, and you will see, in brief, that he will fill your soul with a clear knowledge of the state which you should take up and your will with a strong inclination to follow it."[40] Gobinet exhorted the young discerner to consult God "above all others" and to "humbly ask his holy inspirations, and grace to know his will."[41] Bourdaloue advised intent listening and earnest supplication: "As God does not explain himself immediately to us except by interior inspirations, you should above all listen in the bottom of your heart and give attention to that secret voice by which he has accustomed himself to speak to his elect. But, so as to engage him more effectively to communicate to you his lights and to declare himself, you have no means more efficacious or more assured than prayer … Join to it some particular devotions and some good works, above all the use of communion, and also some practices of Christian penitence."[42] As noted above, such a prayerful approach was scarcely possible to one not already possessed of devout habits. Hence Emanuel de la Croix stressed the importance of prayer at every point in the discernment process, even suggesting that his own book was to be read slowly and prayerfully.[43] Prayer – especially specific daily prayers for the good choice of a state – would be "more frequent and more fervent than usual" during the time of intense discernment.[44] Like Bourdaloue, Emanuel advised that prayer would be still more effective when combined with good works, penitential acts, and frequent reception of the sacraments.[45] To "consult God" was a unifying concept in the process of right discernment. But God's voice was to be heard not only – or even primarily – during moments of prayer, since a full discernment process demanded both the wise counsel of one's spiritual director and extensive interior deliberation.

Of the three elements of discernment, interior deliberation – "consulting oneself" – was the element that rigorist reformers expanded and systematized more than any other. They gave various answers as to what young people were meant to think about, and even within individual texts, tensions could abound. As we have seen, some writers gave a place, though a subordinate one, to temporal motivations, while others discounted them. Even more difficult to parse is the role in discernment of one's own inclinations and abilities. Was a particular interior desire of divine origin, or was it from the world or the devil? How should natural strengths and weaknesses fit into this calculus? Would God's grace overcome a perceived weakness in chastity for one who was called to a celibate life, or was the weakness itself a sign that one was not called to celibacy? Ultimately, one was to read one's own characteristics in light of their fitness for every aspect of the states of life under consideration. In the rigoristic world of seventeenth-century France, this often meant pondering the *dangers* of the various states. The difficulty of putting all these considerations together coherently should not be underestimated. Seeing this, reformers tried to offer means to avoid unending discernment, even while some of their advice perhaps contributed to the confusion.

Reformers' instructions to young people sometimes implied confidence in human faculties of discernment, at least when entrusted to God's purpose. Louis Bourdaloue's self-consciously Ignatian instruction of the choice of a state of life stated that "discernment and reason" were gifts from God that could penetrate the question of vocation: "Examine therefore, without flattering yourself, what is, of all the states of life, that in which you can most glorify God, that in which you can make most easily your salvation, that which you have considered most proper to the qualities of your spirit and of your heart."[46] Immediately a danger – "flattering oneself" – is apparent. Yet that was no excuse to withdraw from the intellectual labour of deliberating. Bourdaloue went on to specify the kinds of meditations that would best facilitate the process, and he specifically enjoined two of Ignatius's vocation mediations (to imagine what one would advise another person in one's place and to imagine what choice one would have wished to make at the moment of death) as fruitful starting points for one's prayerful musings.[47] From Bourdaloue's exhortation emerges a picture of a process that is difficult, but not impossible.

Some reformers weighed down the hope of deliberating successfully with the sheer volume of their advice on what need be considered. Gobinet guided the young person's deliberations quite carefully, because he believed that most would make disastrous wrong turns if left to their own devices. In keeping with the overriding fears inherent in vocational rigorism, the chief things he offered for consideration were the dangers and temptations inherent in each state of life. Knowledge of these temptations enabled one not only to choose a state well now but also to live that state well later. Forewarned is forearmed, and this was the case for every state of life.

Hence, according to Gobinet, the exaltedness of the ecclesiastical state "should not give glory to ecclesiastics, but much fear and trembling," on account of its great obligations and grave dangers.[48] Clerics often neglected the holiness necessary for that state, he wrote, especially through the corrupting influence of other clerics. They embraced ease and idleness, they failed to care for their flocks, and they sought wealth and luxury through pluralism of benefices or selfish use of ecclesiastical funds.[49] Deliberation over this state required particular self-examination for the marks of a true ecclesiastical vocation, which consisted in one's right motives combined with one's spiritual and moral fitness for it.[50] Any trace of evil motivations, such as seeking to live easily or to gain wealth, was a sign that one lacked a vocation.[51] Even with a good intention of seeking one's own sanctification and the salvation of souls, one was unfit if one incorrigibly possessed "rudeness or stupidity, coarseness, superficiality, ignorance, and other similar traits," or if one had a strong tendency toward some vice, such as "impurity, drunkenness, swearing, vengeance, avarice, ambition, and other similar vices."[52] And even a true vocation demanded a long preparation of holy life and diligent study before it could bear fruit in ordination.[53] Gobinet was no eager recruiter for the priesthood. Discernment was to be long and careful, a process of extended deliberation with constant attention to dangers without and imperfect motivations within.

Gobinet followed this discussion of the clerical state with similar long discussions of the religious life and the lay state, both of which likewise included extensive discussion of dangers and temptations. The three chief dangers in professed religious life were pride, returning to the world in effect or in desire, and negligence in the exercises of the life and rule.[54] An inclination towards religion had to be especially examined and tested to see if it were really from God, and Gobinet advised waiting to see whether it lasted for six months or a year.[55] Here Gobinet strongly countered the old Thomistic idea that an inclination toward religion need not be too much scrutinized before being followed.[56] This would have been unsurprising coming from a secular cleric, even in centuries past, but Gobinet's skepticism here is consistent with his equal-opportunity vocational rigorism. Entering *any* state, even the traditional "state of (acquiring) perfection," demanded a calling. A remark he added in a later edition of the text made the question of religious vocation still more complicated. In the first edition, he wrote that when a desire to enter religion did not endure beyond six months or a year, it was "only a human feeling," but, in his later revision, he suggested that it was just as likely "a good thought that God has given you to carry you toward virtue in the condition which you will embrace."[57] While this amendment further emphasized the potential for Christian virtue in every state of life, it also subtly undermined the reliability of one's deliberations. It nearly implied that God himself might temporarily mislead a young person with a false sense of religious vocation.

Because Gobinet rightly surmised that most of his readers would become married laymen, he gave them fodder for considering a variety of secular positions and professions. Most vocational reformers left their advice at the level of the three main states of life (clerical, religious, or married), but Gobinet was moved to cover many of the temptations inherent in specific lay roles. The "great" of the world had to be particularly vigilant, especially at court, where "common virtues are so easily corrupted, and the most solid virtues strongly shaken."[58] The chief remedies for these dangers included cultivation of humility, earnest prayer, and diligence in surpassing ordinary levels of virtue.[59] The military profession was the most dangerous and needed to be avoided except in cases of "inevitable necessity."[60] A lawyer had to avoid taking frivolous cases or neglecting poor clients, while a servant was not to take a position in a debauched house that would lead him to vice.[61] Gobinet, aware that many of his readers would be little empowered to avoid these spiritually dangerous professions, wished to give them every chance to prepare for the new temptations that would come to them as full-fledged adults.

All of these specific details on the states of life were to be fodder for Gobinet's idealized vision of a systematic process of deliberation. Concerned as he was about hasty decisions made on the basis of wrong motivations, he wrote that choosing a state required setting aside, around age eighteen or twenty, "five or six months, or more, according to the difficulty you feel in determining yourself on a state."[62] During this period – which would be full of intense prayer, the sacraments of confession and communion, good works, and the other means of sanctification – the young person was to devote time to discernment every day: "Apply some hour of the day to thinking seriously about the state which you should choose and to deliberating about it within yourself."[63] One began by deliberating between "the two general states," marriage and continence.[64] Whether one was indifferent or already inclined to one of the two, self-examination was to be rigorous and extensive. Awareness of one's own motives and of the dangers of each of the two general states was to be central in one's reflections.[65] If, after reflection, one was inclined to marriage, then one would further deliberate about professions in the world. Similarly, a young man inclined to continence would further discern between religion and the clerical life. In all cases, careful, lengthy deliberation was a must. Gobinet repeatedly used phrases such as "think seriously," "examine attentively," "take care not to follow your inclination right away," "examine it … for a long time," and "resolve on nothing except after having for a long time asked God … after having considered for a long time."[66]

Gobinet's exhortations to hesitation are among the best examples of how seventeenth-century rigorists had transformed the discernment methods inherited from earlier reformers. Although Ignatius of Loyola had cautioned against haste and advised carefully weighing one's inclinations toward one state or another, the letter and spirit of the *Spiritual Exercises* could hardly be stretched to support the idea of a minimally five-month-long period, with a daily hour of deliberating over the choice of a state of life. Still more clearly did Gobinet depart from the discernment process envisioned by François de Sales, despite his being an admirer of the latter's works.[67] De Sales had taught that bad motivations sometimes led to excellent vocations, whereas Gobinet advised minute scrutiny for any trace of imperfect intentions. And while de Sales had warned above all against long deliberation and attempts to learn God's will "through force of examination and subtlety of discourse," Gobinet insisted that discernment must be long and subtle.[68] Lengthy and convoluted self-examination was, in de Sales's view, a spiritually dangerous deviation from trust in God's loving care and prompt acceptance of his will. Gobinet's advice, by contrast, was a step-by-step guide to making sure the discernment process would take a long time and consist of constant cross-examination.

Gobinet was not the only reformer to make the process convoluted and demanding, as is evident in Emanuel de la Croix's *Le bon chois*. Taking cues straight from Ignatius and later Jesuits, Emanuel taught that a prerequisite to right discernment was "a perfect indifference for the world or for religious life, such that you are equally ready to follow one or the other state."[69] One who failed to achieve this indifference would "follow his own inclinations" and "easily take his own will for the will of God."[70] The waters became muddier when, a few pages later, Emanuel detailed the subject matter of a young discerner's meditations: "To deliberate well, it is necessary 1. to recognize your qualities of spirit and of body, your make-up, your temperament, *and your inclinations*. 2. It is necessary to know, at least vaguely, the different professions, and the different states to which you may be suited. 3. It is necessary to compare these states among themselves, and with your qualities of body and of spirit, to know, not the one that most agrees with your corrupt nature, but to know well the one in which you will make your salvation most easily and assuredly, and with the most honour and glory for God."[71] In Emanuel's view, this latter advice could jibe with "perfect indifference," since self-knowledge might help one overcome one's own inclinations, especially those stemming from "corrupt nature." Yet the process described here required extensive meditation on the self, with a goal of finding a good fit. One's own desires were to be suspected, but not always rejected.

It is in this respect that right discernment was perhaps most difficult, for how could one safely follow an interior desire that could either be a temptation or a sign of God's will? Although the problem was not new, what changed in the seventeenth century was the attempt to place the burden of high-stakes discernment onto a larger swath of the Catholic population. As Emanuel noted, young people were to choose not merely a "good means of saving yourself, but … the *best* … where you will have the least danger of doing evil and more opportunity to do good for yourself and your neighbor."[72] Like Bourdaloue, Emanuel suggested that a way to evaluate one's interior desires was through specific imaginative meditations from the *Spiritual Exercises* (what state one would wish one had chosen at the moments of death and of judgment; what would one advise another person in one's place).[73] But it would be difficult to come away from his text thinking that a one-shot meditation would resolve any uncertainties. Ruminating on oneself "without flattering oneself" (a phrase Bourdaloue also used) would never be easy.[74] Despite their attempt to make discernment clearer and easier, writers like Gobinet, Bourdaloue, and Emanuel de la Croix offered recipes for continual second-guessing. And much like rigorism in the administration of the sacraments, this advice demanded a well-perfected interior disposition of "perfect indifference" to the world and openness to God's will. Without this disposition, the whole process could be tainted and lead to ultimate damnation.

In the ideal, however, help was available. If "consulting oneself" lent itself to greater bewilderment, then wise counsel from others, primarily one's spiritual director, was needed as the third element of good discernment. Following principles of spiritual direction developed during the sixteenth century, seventeenth-century writers advised having one main spiritual director, who would have come to know the young discerner over a long period of time.[75] Gobinet taught that there was "nobody who could see more clearly in this matter" than the one who already had "knowledge of your conscience."[76] Emanuel – citing unpublished advice from François de Sales – likewise urged "that your director know you."[77] Bourdaloue offered similar advice concerning the relationship formed during ongoing spiritual direction: "Have a wise director, a man of God, in whom you will take confidence, and to whom you will expose with simplicity and with candor all your perceptions, all your thoughts, all the good and bad dispositions of your soul."[78] When it came time to choose a state of life, a good director would help the young person navigate the confusion of thoughts, inclinations, emotions, motivations, and inspirations, so as to reach at last the safe harbour of a good choice. Some reformers, such as Gobinet, imagined frequent conversation with one's director throughout the period of intense discernment: "During the whole time of your deliberation, communicate often with your confessor: declare to him all that you notice in yourself: the inclinations and repugnances that you feel toward the different states of life; the difficulties that you find there; the motives that carry you more to one state than to another."[79] In theory, then, a good director would have the learning and experience to sort through the chaotic fruits of introspection that Gobinet acknowledged were likely.

Some vocational reformers especially demanded that a director be "disinterested." This echoed sixteenth-century traditions on spiritual direction, as well as Ignatius of Loyola's insistence that the retreat master of the *Exercises* not sway the retreatant toward one or another state of life. In theory, directors would instead help identify what movements within the soul came from God. A spiritual director was, ideally, not to be a recruiter. Gobinet, fearing that secular priests and religious priests would draw their directees toward their own respective states, wrote that the director must be "entirely detached" and not have "any interest"; he must "strip himself of every inclination that he might have to carry someone to one state or to another."[80] According to Emanuel, a good director was "prudent, virtuous, spiritual, learned, and disinterested," with this last meaning that "he will seek purely your salvation and your greatest good, not his own advantage or that of someone other than you."[81] Charles Gonsin, an Oratorian, and bishop Claude Joly, in the diocesan catechisms they respectively compiled, both pressed for the "counsel of a wise and disinterested director" for anyone seeking holy orders.[82] Gonsin's catechism reads similarly regarding marriage, for which one must "ask advice from virtuous, prudent, and disinterested persons … those whom he has given us to direct our consciences," because "the vocation of God is necessary for every state."[83] In all of these cases, the director was to be detached from the outcome. His job was to help the young person seek God's will, not to fill the ranks of clergy and religious. Moreover, because vocational rigorism had made the right choice of a state so urgent, the director's abilities and good will were far more important than they might otherwise have been. A bad director would not simply hinder one's progress in seeking Christian perfection; he could lead a soul into peril of damnation, by making an error in judgment about God's calling.

Although much discernment advice on wise counsel focused on one's spiritual director, taking counsel from others was also encouraged. Generally, spiritual writers of this period did not manifestly disagree with François de Sales's advice, that, rather than getting "an examination by ten or twelve doctors" of theology, one might consult with one's director and at most "two or three other spiritual persons."[84] Given the assumption of a good principal director with extensive knowledge of the directee, multiplying counsellors would cause more trouble. Any chosen counsellors, such as other clergy and religious, would ideally be spiritually inclined, wise, virtuous, learned, and disinterested, just as a good director would be.[85] Some persons might also have a role in discernment *ex officio*. Joly, for example, wrote in his catechism that a youth seeking holy orders should take counsel "principally from his bishop."[86]

A matter of great contention, to be discussed in detail in the next chapter, was the role of one's parents in vocational discernment and choice. Some writers stressed parental authority as much as possible within the framework of vocational rigorism. Bourdaloue placed parents next to spiritual directors as "ministers of God," who were always to be listened to and who were to be obeyed whenever it did not endanger one's salvation.[87] Writing even more strongly with respect to the married vocation, Claude Joly and Jan Lindeborn (c. 1630–1696; a Dutch secular priest published during his lifetime in French translation) taught that to marry without parental consent was a great sin.[88] Other writers, however, emphasized great distrust of parents. Among the strongest words are those of Emanuel de la Croix, who discouraged consulting one's relatives at all unless they were "of eminent and well-known virtue."[89] Family members were "our enemies and against our salvation," because they were automatically "interested" parties, "blinded by natural and unruly affection."[90] Rigorism intensified either emphasis, whether on parental authority or on children's liberty. If taking counsel from parents was important and ignoring their advice was gravely sinful, then the fraught discernment process became even more muddled, especially when parental desires conflicted with one's interior inclinations or the counsel of one's director. Adding another factor to juggle might simply increase the likelihood of choosing wrongly. On the other hand, ignoring parental counsel would be crucial if parents urged a vocational choice that would lead to temporal failure and eternal disaster. From this rigorist perspective, following a parent's worldly, "interested" counsels or commands could lead to damnation.

CONCLUSION

The vocational rigorists of seventeenth-century France exemplify the simultaneous optimism and pessimism of their reforming era. Ecclesiastical and temporal modern authorities of all stripes saw before them a world of disorder, variously defined, but they held out hope for the remaking of societies and individuals. At the heart of many reforming efforts in such "disciplinary societies" were systematic plans, rules, and processes.[91] Vocational reformers insisted that very few were "getting it right" on the matter of choosing a state of life. Indeed, God's will was ignored in so many other areas precisely *because* Christians failed to follow his will in this pivotal choice. Yet, these clerics believed there was a way out; otherwise they would not have bothered to try to promote their methods of discernment among young French Catholics. In the transformed world they envisioned, vocational discernment was a normal Catholic practice. They tried to make that world real by arming the next generation with the right principles and methods by which to implement those principles.

These reformers' rigoristic worldview, however, shaped the tone and content of their advice, undermining their reforming intent. Pitfalls abounded in the very process which was meant to lead to the safe harbour of accepting God's call. A core element of deliberation was analyzing one's interior movements, but none of those movements were trustworthy. In contrast to François de Sales, they espoused lengthy, exacting "force of examination." Confusion, doubt, and incoherence would ideally be alleviated by the help of a good spiritual director. But if so many clergy were corrupt, how abundant were wise, learned, disinterested directors; how many had in fact chosen their own state because of worldly motives, and without being called there by God? Even the typically hopeful de Sales had written that only "one in ten thousand" would make a good spiritual director.[92] Living out a new culture of vocation would not be easy for the individual, and building a new culture of vocation would not be easy for reformers.

Any reform effort raises questions of feasibility in concrete circumstances. How could these idealized vocational discernment processes fit with the social and political realities of seventeenth-century France? Fundamentally, how much vocational choice could a young person have? Despite claiming that vocational discernment was for all, most of these reformers aimed their message primarily at social and economic elites. A few writers pushed vocational reform to peasants and lower-status artisans through catechisms, and certainly some parish priests would have adapted for their flocks the discernment principles found in model sermons, devotional manuals, and the experience of seminary formation. Nevertheless, the main thrust of discernment advice assumes a young reader will possess luxuries like education, regular spiritual direction, and the financial resources necessary to choose religious life or priestly formation. Moreover, even for a young person with all those advantages, not to mention the prerequisite pious upbringing, habits of prayer, and good motivations, the path to a vocational choice still needed to be made in the context of parental, societal, and state authority. The next chapter will explore just how vocational reformers attempted to help young people navigate the patriarchal realities surrounding the choice of a state of life.

5

Liberty: Parental Involvement without Parental Coercion

The great Jesuit preacher Louis Bourdaloue, cited so often in this book, had himself faced obstacles on his way to religious vows. An early biography recounts him stealing away from home to join the Jesuit novitiate at Paris. His father immediately set out to bring the headstrong youth back to Bourges. Nevertheless, the elder Bourdaloue soon became convinced that his son's rash actions were rooted in an authentic vocation, and he promptly relinquished him to the Jesuits.[1] Whether or not this account approximates the actual course of events, it reflects the preacher Bourdaloue's own subtle position on parental involvement in vocational choices.

This chapter will examine seventeenth-century reformers' complex approaches to the proper role of parents in vocational choice. An ecclesiastical drive for free consent to vocations was a medieval inheritance that had been enhanced at the Council of Trent. With the addition of a rigorist sense of urgency about right vocational choices – choices made from spiritual motives, in response to God's call – liberty from familial coercion became more important than ever. That is, when young people were not free to accept the state of life to which God had called them, they would lack the graces needed to live well. Consequently, their tendency to succumb to temptations would lead to suffering in this world and the next. Reformers thus brought a new motive for opposing coercion of entry into marriage, religion, or the clergy. But how could a push for liberty jibe with the social, cultural, and legal conditions of *ancien régime* France? The laws of France and the cultural habits of patriarchal elites favoured parental control and did not envision giving young men and women the liberty to engage in a discernment process and choose a state of life without hindrance. Analyzing reformers' efforts to combine freedom with parental involvement reveals the ways in which reality brought nuance to their ideals. This nuanced practicality helped make vocational reform more than a set of idealized prescriptions. By engaging with the demands of social realities, reformers made it plausible for Catholics to integrate vocational discernment into their social imaginary.

PARENTAL AUTHORITY IN EARLY MODERN LAW AND EXPERIENCE

Throughout Christian Europe in the early modern era, parental authority was on the agenda of temporal and ecclesiastical leaders, who looked to the family as both an object and a means of reform. Most immediately, the family was a locus for the formation of future generations of Christians and subjects. Furthermore, it was believed that right order in the family would help spark right order in society at large. Hierarchy was lived out in the habitual enactment of reciprocal rights and duties. Right subordination to an earthly father ideally reinforced right subordination to kings, clerics, and God himself. These various paternal figures were often in accord with one another, and reformers often sought to reinforce all of them. Yet conflicts of jurisdiction arose when the interests of these various father figures were at odds. These tensions reveal the divergent purposes that led to contrary programs of reform, and vocational choices were among the most important flash points for such conflicts.

This was certainly the case in France, where the king and judicial authorities (especially the Parlement of Paris) issued a series of edicts and decisions between 1556 and 1697 that dramatically increased the legal enforceability of parental choices for their adult children. A foundational 1556 edict required parental consent for marriage up to age thirty for men and twenty-five for women. Later legislation expanded the scope of this edict. For example, a 1629 ordinance required church courts to help enforce these laws, a 1639 edict removed age limits on the requirement for parental consent, and a 1697 edict enacted new punishments (including possible banishment) for priests who abetted marriages without parental consent. Throughout the same era, court decisions on particular cases routinely supported parents who sought to prevent their children from entering religious houses, often to the point of removing children who already had become novices. The judiciary justified its wide interpretation of parental authority by extending the meaning of *rapt*, the crime of coercing a marriage. Rapt was expanded to include the mere act of accepting marital or religious vows (or any entry into religion) made without parental consent; hence, attempts by adult children to commit to a state of life could be easily nullified in court. This legal shift was accompanied by high-profile printed propaganda, much of which depicted parents as victims of crafty (usually Jesuit) clerics who tricked impressionable children with their serpentine rhetoric, in violation of the honour of father and mother.[2] In law and in much of elite culture of seventeenth-century France, parental authority was stronger than ever.

These secular norms were directly at odds with Catholic doctrine and canon law, which had long opposed parental control over the vocations of marriage, religion, and holy orders. As discussed in chapter 1, the Council of Trent had strengthened medieval canons on vocational liberty, imposing anathema on those who forced a woman into a monastery, prevented a woman from entering a monastery without good reason, or, similarly, violated free consent to marriage. Further, the council anathematized the view that parental consent was necessary for a marriage to be valid. The French crown had especially lobbied to require parental consent for marriage and thus was especially displeased with some of the council's decisions.[3]

It would be simplistic to imagine two clear alliances of parents and state, on one side, against their children and the church, on the other, especially since many Catholic clergy believed in the general thrust of secular marriage law. Among the French at Trent, the Jesuits had been virtually alone in opposing the requirement of parental consent for marriage. Nevertheless, the French bishops were not mere hirelings of the crown in supporting the requirement. Many Catholic reformers since the late Middle Ages had favoured such a move, which, incidentally, most Protestant authorities integrated into their own reformation of marriage.[4] Over time, French Catholic clergy imposed their own restrictions that served the mutual interests of parents, the church, and the state in curbing the liberty of the young.[5] Notwithstanding jurisdictional squabbles, the disobedience of refractory clergy, and the complex relationship between law and practice, lay and ecclesiastical courts increasingly worked together over the course of the seventeenth century to bolster familial authority.[6]

It would likewise be simplistic to imagine that parents and children were necessarily at odds over vocational choices. Adult children, especially in elite families, normally had no objections to the Old Regime's patriarchal mentalities. Although parents sometimes "conditioned" or coerced vocational choices, many children were willing participants in family social and economic strategies. Moreover, committing to a state of life always involved social and economic considerations, even when a young person's ultimate motives were genuinely unworldly. Hence, entering into marriage, donning the habit, or taking orders might involve a wide array of family members and others in one's social sphere. When parents did oppose a child's vocational choice, their motives cannot always be reduced to strategies about property and inheritance. Clearly some parents who forbade a child's choice were moved by affection, for example, and feared to lose the child's presence. Scholars in recent decades have therefore shifted away from positing a strong binary opposition between parents and children and toward more nuanced explorations of tensions and shared values.[7]

Even a nuanced interpretation makes it apparent that this legal and cultural context was increasingly problematic for wholesale vocational reform. If the free choice of a state of life really did belong to each individual Catholic, who conformed to God's vocational will, then the legal powers given to parents by the French state were unacceptable. But a direct legal fight was neither desirable nor winnable. More plausible was a persuasive effort, aimed at altering old cultural habits. As it was, most parents and children shared a culture that prioritized worldly motivations in the choice of a state, and so vocational reformers needed to reach both parents and children with an alternative spiritualized vision. These reformers themselves generally accepted France's patriarchal values, and so they sought to integrate those values with Catholic theology and church law. Familial will necessarily affected and even determined young people's choices, and so the bulk of new preaching, writing, and guidance on vocation maintained that individual freedom could jibe with rightly understood parental involvement.

WOMEN RELIGIOUS AND VOCATIONAL LIBERTY

Many reformers closely associated parental control with the worldly motives that effected wrong vocational choices, asserting that greed was the chief vice moving parents to determine their children's futures. They particularly decried the forced monachization of women as a result of parental avarice. In an extended simile, Jean Cordier described the forced religious vocations of women as ritual human sacrifices: "How many Christians are there who esteem themselves happy after having sacrificed their children to the Devil of interest?"[8] Bourdaloue offered a similar vignette of a "victim ... carried into the temple, bound hand and foot, that is to say, in the disposition of a constrained will, her mouth silenced by fear and respect for a father whom she has always honoured."[9] This was done in "a spirit either ambitious or interested," because "the establishment of this daughter would be costly."[10] Cordier, Bourdaloue, and many of their contemporaries argued that young women needed to be no less free than young men to choose religion or marriage – or not. Although the options these reformers presented to women did not include secular professions, much less the clerical state, they generally held the same vocational discernment principles and methods to be applicable to men and women alike. Moreover, they were often more protective of women than of men, with respect to vocational liberty. The Council of Trent, as discussed earlier, had hurled anathemas at those who forced women particularly into religious vows, even though reformers were under no illusion that men were never coerced. In France, conflict over male children's vocations may have indeed come more frequently than female cases before secular judicial bodies and before the notice of the elite public.[11] Evidence from church courts, such as Rome's Sacred Congregation of the Council, show that men and women alike sought release from vows as redress for forced vocations, and many of both sexes were granted their petitions.[12] Nevertheless, the situation of women religious, both as beneficiaries of reform and as reformers themselves, deserves special consideration because it was so prominent in discussions of liberty.

Among the four major concerns of vocational reformers that structure this book – urgency, inclusiveness, method, and liberty – this last one received perhaps the most extensive commentary from women religious themselves. Women were less likely than the secular and regular male clergy to publish model sermons, devotional treatises, and catechisms. Their spiritual writing was sometimes, especially in contemplative orders, directed more to their own membership than to outside readers, or their teachings appeared in unpublished letters occasioned by concrete individual situations. Therefore, although this issue of genre made women less likely to write about all four aspects of the new culture of vocation, they were by no means passive spectators in reform. Their own experience – and that of girls in their educational charge – made them important participants in the early modern push for freedom from coercion in religious profession. Exploring examples of this advocacy by women religious can help us better understand how both male and female reformers shaped their approach to vocational liberty in the patriarchal context of the Old Regime.

Among the most striking examples comes from the famous convent of Port-Royal. Angélique Arnauld (1591–1661), Port-Royal's reforming abbess, concretely implemented much that the Tridentine council fathers and subsequent reformers had desired regarding liberty of religious profession. Although Mère Angélique and Port-Royal are best known for their later connection with the Jansenist movement and the figure of Saint-Cyran, the abbey's initial transformation was rooted in the Council of Trent, the Cistercian-Benedictine tradition, and Angélique's own conversion experience.[13] Her path to becoming a nun and an abbess exemplified the disorders of the age, for she was selected – through her grandfather's not-wholly-honest patronage – as successor to the abbacy at age eight, and she was formally elected at age ten in 1602. In 1608, on the occasion of a sermon by a travelling Capuchin preacher, she began to experience a deep conversion and soon set out to bring the abbey into strict monastic observance.[14]

Liberty of profession was a central plank of her reform agenda. Her own non-consensual entry into the convent had been transformed upon hearing the Capuchin's sermon: "God touched me so that, from that moment, I found myself more happy to be a religious, than I had thought myself unhappy to be one."[15] On a personal level, she resolved to renew publicly her religious vows, which she believed had thus far been invalid for having been coerced.[16] Still more significant was her rejection of the ordinary means of entry into the convent, that is, with acceptance of dowries from elite families. She came to believe that this common practice of "haggling over girls" and "demanding money for the reception of religious daughters" was the sin of "simony," and thus she began to judge candidates for entry on the basis of their fitness and desire for religious life, rather than the size of their dowries.[17] She especially followed these principles when she was commissioned to reform the abbey of Maubuisson, where she rejected many candidates from wealthy and elite families and hand-picked many undowered girls whom she found fit for monastic life.[18] In eliminating the requirement of dowry, Angèlique Arnauld went farther than many vocational reformers thought possible, facilitating real freedom to enter the monastic life unhindered by property questions.

Port-Royal continued and elaborated on this tradition of vocational liberty in later decades. The *Constitutions* of the abbey, formally issued under the authority of Angélique's sister and successor Agnès Arnauld (1593–1671), included the following provision: "We will not at all admit a girl to become a religious who is not truly called by God and who does not show by her life and actions a true and sincere will of serving God and of consecrating herself wholly to him. Without this, we must not ever receive them for other reasons, whatever spirit, nobility, or riches they might have."[19] This text only formalized what had already long been the convent's practice under both Arnauld sisters. Jacqueline Pascal (1625–1661), sister of Blaise Pascal, benefitted from this practice when she made her monastic profession at Port-Royal in 1653, after years of opposition first from her father and then from her brother. After having reluctantly delayed monastic entry several years until her father's death, Jacqueline found herself in a protracted property dispute with Blaise and their sister Gilberte, over her inheritance and convent dowry. Mère Angélique Arnauld, however, convinced of Jacqueline's true vocation, advised the long-frustrated candidate to enter without her dowry and to leave to the consciences of her wealthy siblings (soon to be even wealthier after Jacqueline renounced her possessions) the possibility of later making an equivalent donation to the convent. Arnauld thus showed her consistency in placing vocational liberty above the abbey's financial interest and above the desires of the candidate's family. Jacqueline's courage in entering – despite opposition and in a state of "poverty" – ultimately paid off. Blaise did eventually reconcile with her and donate to the abbey the equivalent of a large dowry. Moreover, his stronger association with Port-Royal and with Jacqueline soon helped occasion his deeper conversion. Jacqueline herself wrote extensively of her fight to enter freely and of the Arnauld sisters' teaching on the need to eliminate the obligation of monastic dowries.[20]

The Port-Royal nuns also emphasized vocational liberty in the education of girls. Angélique refused to admit any girl to the convent school if her parents had already determined her either for marriage or for religion. The abbey's strongly monastic education – marked by silence and asceticism – was intended not as recruitment or conditioning for monastic profession, but as the best foundation for the free choice of a state of life.[21] As discussed in the previous chapter, many vocational reformers had suggested that piety in childhood and youth was necessary as a remote preparation for right vocational discernment.[22] Convent education was to be a means of making that preparation. Other female congregations also insisted that they educated each girl for, as one Visitandine put it in a text mentioned in chapter 3, "whatever state to which God might destine her."[23] The Ursulines especially stressed that they were preparing almost all of their charges for virtuous Christian motherhood, and their pedagogical approach was notably less monastic than that of Port-Royal. Virtuous mothers, Ursulines believed, would be the means by which the whole of society might be reformed.[24] When nuns maintained the principle of liberty in the education of girls, they thus might also thereby promote vocational inclusiveness and right methods of discernment.

A passage from Jacqueline Pascal's *Rule for Children* again suggests the partial overlap between vocational reform in Port-Royal's stricter Jansenist context and the principles of the less rigorous of vocational rigorists. Written in the 1650s and first printed in 1665, this work explains the pedagogical philosophy and practice of Port-Royal after Pascal was charged with reopening the convent school.[25] In general spiritual conferences with the girls, she enjoined the nuns to speak of religious life joyfully but without excess, if the students themselves raised the subject.[26] But such conferences were not to be used to recruit for religious life, keeping in mind that "God does not give this grace of religious life to all, not even to all those who desire it."[27] Furthermore, Pascal encouraged reticence about the nuns' highly rigorist doctrines of salvation: "We should not … lay before them all that we believe about the small number of persons who will be saved in the world."[28] This last point is telling about the limits of vocational inclusiveness in a Jansenist context. Other reformers, even if vocational rigorists, might take pains to affirm how remaining in the world (and entering marriage in particular) was a path to salvation for those called there. Pascal and her sisters, however, held to a strict version of the Augustinian *massa damnata* theory that the number of the elect was small. Nevertheless, in Pascal's view, it did not follow either that vocational liberty could be violated or that religion was open to all comers. Excessive recruitment rhetoric and full-fledged avowals of the dangers of life in the world would be a sort of moral coercion toward religion, an attempt to lead girls to the convent who were not called by God. It was, as Ignatius of Loyola had suggested long before, better if God directly drew a young person to religion than if some human religious tipped the scales with a recruiting pitch. Even though Jacqueline Pascal was not hopeful about the mass of humanity, she offered a different kind of hope to her girls. She gave them a monastic-style formation that might just help them refuse to be "of the world" even should they, lacking a call to religion, remain "in the world."

Because of such approaches, teaching monasteries – especially those like Port-Royal wherein the girls participated in a strongly monastic way of life – had to contend with suspicions like those expressed by François Fénelon (1651–1715), who critiqued convent education as failing to prepare girls for devout adulthood in the world. Fénelon, eventually consecrated archbishop of Cambrai in 1695, wrote prolifically – and often controversially, as in the debates about Quietist spirituality – in a variety of genres over a long career. He was a strong advocate of vocational liberty in his *Education of Girls*, published in 1687: "Above all never let [your daughters] suspect that you wish to inspire in them the design of becoming nuns. For this thought will take away their confidence in their parents, persuade them that they are unloved, disturb their spirits, and make them play a forced part for many years."[29] When a girl, however, would "determine herself to become a religious without being pushed there by her parents," then those parents were by all means to help and encourage her in preparing for and accepting her vocation.[30] Fénelon later wrote more explicitly, in a posthumously published letter on educating girls, of his concerns about the inadequacies of convent schools. While he feared education in "a worldly convent still more than the world itself," he feared that education in a well-regulated convent often gave girls "a profound ignorance of the world" that endangered their ultimate formation.[31] In other words, the fact that most girls would remain in the world led Fénelon to take a very different practical approach than that of the Arnauld sisters and Jacqueline Pascal. For Pascal, monastic-style convent education was the best preparation for spiritual warfare in the world. For Fénelon, such an education was destined to leave a girl unready for the real spiritual challenges she would face.

These varied responses reveal a vibrant interest in women's vocational liberty among reformers of many different backgrounds – male and female, secular and regular, Jansenist and Jesuit. The perception that women especially needed defense from vocational coercion was widespread in early modern France. In some houses, such as Port-Royal, women in leadership positions accrued enough capital – financial and moral – to uphold vocational liberty not only in theory but also in practice. In so doing, they contributed to the propaganda fight against business as usual. The direction of inspiration among reformers was not simply a one-way, trickle-down phenomenon. To be sure, a Mère Angélique learned of Tridentine decrees against coercion through clerical contacts. But clerical reformers also learned from the experience of convents and of women for whom vocational coercion was a possibility. The extensive thought and energy they put into the question of women's liberty bore fruit in their approaches to vocational liberty for men, as well. But while a house like Port-Royal might establish practices that facilitated free profession of vows, that would not be enough. Law and culture remained serious obstacles to pure vocational freedom, and so clerics needed to pursue more subtle, less institutional means of reform on behalf of young men and young women.

DEFENDING VOCATIONAL LIBERTY

The reformers acknowledged that their persuasive effort was an uphill battle and that parental authority over vocations was virtually unquestioned. Bourdaloue may have been hinting at the overwhelming legal power of parents, when he described forcing vocations as "a custom in every family … a species of law … dictated by the spirit of the world."[32] This was a "law universally recognized in the world, and which it is scarcely permitted to the ministers of the church and to preachers to oppose," and it was "even commonly tolerated … by the most seemingly reformed and rigid" spiritual directors, and by theologians and philosophers who either were or seemed to be "the most severe in their moral doctrines."[33] Aside from his possible allusion to the legal framework of familial authority, his main point was that a culture of forced vocations, especially of girls, was more deeply ingrained than ever. Even among the clergy, few were willing and able to present an alternative.

Since patriarchal culture was so pervasive and, what is more, had strong biblical foundations (above all in the commandment to honour father and mother), a major task for the reformers was to make vocational liberty theologically respectable. It was not self-evident that young people should have any choice of a state, given the myriad affairs in which they were otherwise to submit to parents, even as adults. What then, were the limits of parental (especially paternal) authority? Bourdaloue based his argument in the theology of vocational grace discussed in chapter 2.[34] Although earthly fathers could rightly determine a child's temporal affairs, only God's "sovereign paternity" gave him authority "over the spirits and wills of men": "If all states of life are vocations from God; if there is a grace attached to each of these states, in order to attract us there according to God's ordering; if it is extremely dangerous for our salvation to take up a state without this grace, it therefore does not belong to a father to lead his children to a state, much less to engage them in it … For, in the last resort, a father in his family is not the distributor of vocations. This grace is not at all in his hands, to distribute to whom he wishes, nor as he wishes … Because every vocation is a grace, only God can give it."[35] Vocational liberty was not thus an absolute good, but rather would serve as a means for young men and women to respond to God's call. If the right choice of a state of life was a moral imperative, then one must "hate father and mother" (Luke 14:26) and "obey God rather than men" (Acts 5:29).

Similar arguments were premised on the choice of a state of life being an adult decision, upon which future adult responsibility hinged. Secular priest Jean Le Jau (1570–1631), in one of the earliest French-language treatises specifically on choosing a state of life, made puberty (fourteen for boys and twelve for girls) a turning point in children's liberty. Parents could nullify a prepubescent child's vows, but puberty marked the "age of discretion" at which young people became personally responsible for conforming to the divine will in all things, including the choice of a state.[36] The Jesuit writer Jean Cordier argued that, by age fourteen or fifteen, young persons were ready to choose, because the remainder of their lives would be their own spiritual responsibility, not that of their parents.[37]

Another tack was to demonstrate the antiquity of vocational liberty, by citing authorities from the church's long tradition. Jesuit writer Thomas Le Blanc (1599–1669) highlighted the examples of patristic and medieval saints who disobeyed their parents in entering religious life.[38] Saintly disobedience to parents was a reliable trope at least as old as the third-century account of Perpetua's martyrdom.

As further witnesses, Le Jau brought in church councils (such as the tenth synod of Toledo, a local Spanish synod that took place in 656), patristic writers (such as Ambrose, Chrysostom, and Augustine), scholastics (such as Aquinas and Antoninus of Florence), and even Roman civil law.[39] And even though the authority of the Council of Trent remained a point of contention in France throughout the early modern era, some works highlighted the excommunication imposed by Trent in cases of vocational coercion.[40] A father's right to determine his child's future seemed as old as humanity, and so an attempt to undermine that right needed demonstrable support from both ancient and recent authorities.

The motive for coercion most often cited was greed, as discussed above with respect to the forced monachization of women, and another major target of reform was the avaricious manner in which parents sought clerical benefices for their sons. Reform of the clergy was the chief disciplinary concern of the post-Tridentine era, and church leaders sought to link the reception of tonsure more clearly with real intentions of and fitness for priestly ordination. These efforts took effect unevenly throughout France over a long period of time, however, and parents continued to use the church as a source of income, without regard to their son having any sense of vocation or fitness for clerical life. A potential moral difficulty was that certification of reliable income, ideally from a benefice, was a prerequisite for priestly ordination, since clerical poverty was apt to lead to disorders and scandals.[41] This requirement of "clerical title" meant that even well-intentioned potential clerics and their parents needed to hunt for benefices via every legitimate avenue, such as the favour of a high-ranking clerical relative. Threading the moral needle demanded they seek the benefice only as a means and never as an end in itself.[42]

The reforming message about the discernment of rightly motivated clerical vocations was spread more widely than that concerning the other two vocations, as is evident in the diocesan catechisms used even in rural villages.[43] Although some examples from this genre of text explicitly discussed the need to be called before entering religion or marriage, appeals to vocational discernment principles in relation to the clerical state were more frequent. At the heart of this message to parents was, again, the danger of choosing a state out of worldly motivations. The catechism for Luçon and La Rochelle stated that to put a child in orders "under the hope of some benefice" and "to serve one's avarice and ambition" was "a very great sin that attracted the curse of God on parents and children."[44] In the catechism for Agen, Bishop Joly excoriated parents who "force their children into the Church, even though they be unworthy of it, or only to have more wealth, or to keep some benefice in the family": "They are the cause of the damnation of their children, and of the sins that they commit in that state, and they are damned with them ... They will answer before God concerning the scandal that their children have given to the whole Church."[45] The Meaux catechism produced under renowned pulpit orator Bishop Jacques-Bénigne Bossuet said that the chief condition for receiving tonsure was "to be called by God," explicitly opposing parental benefice-seeking to authentic vocational discernment.[46]

Yet love of money was not the only cause of coercion, as some parents were said to prioritize natural human affection over God's call. Rather than dismissing emotional rhetoric as a mask for financial strategy, vocational reformers acknowledged real affective motives for parental pressure.[47] Many preachers decried parental favouring of one child over others.[48] Others noted parents' excessive attachment to their children's presence, which led especially to fear of a child's strict cloister or faraway missions. Jean le Jau responded to this fear with a quotation from the early monastic father John Climacus: "It is better to sadden one's parents than to sadden our Lord Jesus."[49] Cordier suggested that parents who saw religious vows as a sorrowful separation should consider how they might respond to a child's accepting a faraway position at the royal court.[50] Quoting the church father Jerome, Thomas Le Blanc advised children faced with their parents' "pleadings" and "tears" that "cruelty, in this case, is the only true piety."[51] If parents' authentic natural affection might undermine their children's supernatural good, true parental and filial love demanded putting divine love first.

Despite these principles of freedom from parental control, very few writers advocated excluding parents altogether. Emanuel de la Croix took the latter extreme approach:

> In this affair [parents] are our enemies and against our salvation, just as the Savior taught when he said that he had come to separate the son from the father, and the daughter from the mother ... It is not necessary to consult one's parents ... because they are interested, and they seek their own satisfaction and advantage ... Parents are blinded by natural affection ... For this

> reason, St Bernard not only does not find that one lacks respect for a father or a mother, when one does not consult them on this occasion, but he strongly affirms that it is an act of great piety to despise their counsel, in order to follow that of Jesus Christ.[52]

Emanuel's position is one possible logical conclusion of the principles of liberty highlighted above. And yet, on the question of parental influence, his view is not characteristic of vocational reformers.

PARENTAL COOPERATION IN VOCATIONAL CHOICE

Most advice rather sought to preserve parental involvement, asking parents and children to share responsibility for vocational choices. Above all, children were to listen, even if they need not always obey. Gobinet thought that parents' wishes could help spark the discernment process: "If your parents wish that you be an ecclesiastic or a religious, examine first whether God calls you to one of these states."[53] A young person who discerned no such calling could decline and "make this resistance with all the respect that you owe to them, by remonstrating modestly with them, showing your inability to do what they desire, the reasons you have, and above all the repugnance you have toward the state to which they are carrying you."[54] Gobinet applied the same principle when a young person followed a religious or clerical calling against parental wishes. By contrast, once a young person chose to remain in the lay state, he wrote that parental wishes should normally be obeyed in choosing among lay professions and conditions.[55] All vocational choices were to be made with consideration of parental counsel and with the utmost filial respect, even if disobedience became necessary.

Bourdaloue's position was similar. Despite having vehemently denied parental authority over vocations, he commanded young persons to consult their parents:

> It would be a damnable independence, rather than an evangelical liberty, to wish, in the choice one makes of a state, to remove oneself absolutely from paternal authority … One is not always obliged to conform oneself to the desires of a father and a mother too preoccupied with the spirit of the world … but at least it is necessary to listen to them, to weigh their reasons, even to defer to them when one has no stronger reasons to oppose to

> them; in the last resort, whether one accedes to their will, or, for the interest of his salvation, one deviates from it, it is necessary always to give them all the testimonies of a filial submission and of the respect that one acknowledges is due to them.[56]

This might leave young men and women struggling to discern whether their parents were in fact too worldly to be obeyed and whether their own reasoning should trump that of their parents. Bourdaloue's exhortation to parents was similarly ambivalent: "It does not belong to you to dispose of your children, in that which regards their vocation and the choice that they have to make of a state. And I add however that you are responsible to God for the choice your children make, and for the state that they embrace. It seems at first that these two propositions contradict each other, but ... they accord perfectly with one another."[57] Good Christian parents were to "intervene in this choice, to participate in it, to have in it a right of direction and of supervision."[58] Whether coercive parents forced a bad choice or indifferent parents neglected to prevent a bad choice, the temporal and spiritual consequences would be dire. Bourdaloue thus laid a heavy moral burden on both parents and children, and he was not confident that many bore their burdens well.

Jean Cordier's advice was similar but markedly more hopeful. Without denying children's liberty, he advocated the combined efforts of parents and children, because young persons tended to be driven by inclination and parents tended to be driven by reason: "If fathers wish to have no faults, they will relax much in order to follow the inclination of their children. If children wish to make a good choice, they will take account of their fathers' counsel. Reason will find itself weak, if it is not seconded by inclination; inclination will be rash, if it is not guided by reason ... To make a good choice, it is necessary that the reason of the father and the inclination of the son reach an agreement about it."[59] If parents and children in seventeenth-century France typically cooperated in pursuing worldly ends in their choices of state, Cordier asked that they cooperate in pursuing God's purposes instead. Cordier, Bourdaloue, Gobinet, and other reformers thus envisioned devout families together seeking spiritual goods.

Such parental cooperation in children's vocational choices was not merely a vain hope; it was a practical necessity. Few young persons, even if they wished, could slip away to marry or to enter religion, much less successfully defy parental wishes in the long term. Without parental support, there were formidable legal and financial obstacles to committing to any state of life – married, religious, or clerical. For this reason, these clerics still insisted on parents' responsibility to provide for their children's placement. According to Cordier, this provision should occur *after* the child had discerned God's plan for a right choice of state: "If anyone asks them, 'To what do you destine your son? What will your daughter become?' let them answer only this: 'God is their master; he will dispose of them as he wishes. When he will have made known to them what he desires, we will do our best to furnish them the means of putting it into action.'"[60] This principle demanded that the age of engaging in a profession match the age of vocational discernment, and so Cordier proposed an education that would delay apprenticeships and other professional endeavours until age twelve to fifteen. After a boy made a choice of state and even of a worldly profession, parents would facilitate the finances and logistics.[61] By such a reform of education, Cordier hoped to preserve a space for vocational discernment, while acknowledging the need for parents to provide for their children's future.

Diocesan catechisms likewise often emphasized parents' duty to establish children professionally, but here we see less effort to reconcile that duty with children's vocational liberty. Joly's catechism for Agen and the Besançon catechism both attended to vocational questions, and both left unclear how parents' and children's roles fit together. Parents were to have their children take up a fitting trade or profession, and, surprisingly, that meant parents were to engage in vocational discernment on their children's behalf: "Q. What should fathers and mothers do before engaging their children in a profession in life? A. They should pray and consult God, to know whether their children are called there and make known to them the obligations of their state."[62] The advice on vocational matters that Joly gave in other texts to young people themselves was here simply redirected to their parents. His catechism was similarly ambiguous on discerning a clerical calling. He first mandated that the candidate himself deliberate and consult with his confessor to see whether he is "called to the ecclesiastical state."[63] Then, on the next page, he instructed parents:

> Q. What should fathers and mothers do before placing their children in the Church? A. They should: 1. Examine whether the inclinations of their children are fit for the ecclesiastical state.

> 2. Make prayers and do other good works in order to obtain from God the grace of knowing their vocation. 3. Consult their confessors. 4. Not engage them at all by constraint, nor before the proper time, nor for the present chance of some benefice. 5. Make them to understand in advance what the functions and obligations of this state are, and know from them whether they are resolved to satisfy them … 7. Present them to the Bishop, and follow his counsels.[64]

Although some of the children's liberties are here preserved, *parents* were to be the main actors who placed, examined, prayed, consulted confessors, engaged, and presented to the bishop.

There is a subtle persuasive method in leaving unresolved this tension between vocational liberty and parental involvement. Parents' arrangement of financial and logistical matters for a vocation – whether marriage, religion, or ordination – remained necessary in early modern France. A marriage contract, establishing a series of property exchanges among the groom, the bride, and their respective families, was normally drawn up during a large gathering at the bride's family home and signed by a dozen witnesses, including extended kin and a local priest.[65] In 1693, Louis XIV set a cap on convent dowries – still necessary for the maintenance of most women's houses – of 8,000 *livres* in Paris and 6,000 elsewhere.[66] The priestly ordination of a secular cleric almost always required parents either to arrange the granting of a benefice by a well-connected clerical relative or, more commonly, to set aside family property to provide a sufficient regular income for the priest.[67] If parents thus always dealt with the financial questions concerning entry into a state of life, Joly and others hoped that parents would simultaneously consider the spiritual questions of vocation, applying principles of right discernment together with their children. This was an attempt to integrate long-standing practice with more recently developed principles of free discernment and choice.

CONCLUSION

Vocational reformers' approach to liberty reveals the inevitable distance between ideals and realities, and a conscious effort to bridge that gap. The ideals of liberty, enshrined in canon law and in theology, were traditional in ecclesiastical thinking well before the early modern period. As they did with other aspects of vocational teaching, rigorists expanded the significance of this liberty, making it a prerequisite to rightly choosing the state to which one was called by God, and hence a prerequisite to receiving the graces needed to fulfil one's duties. The Council of Trent had reiterated and strengthened existing principles of vocational liberty, but seventeenth-century rigorists absorbed those principles and made them part of a bigger picture. Vocational liberty then existed in the context of a wholesale effort to build a culture of vocational discernment. Liberty in the choice of a state of life, as a modifier of patriarchal authority over both male and female children, thus did not stand alone, but it became integral to Catholic vocational modernity.

Moreover, far from expressing disembodied ideals, pastoral literature on parental coercion developed in response to the concrete conditions of seventeenth-century France. In certain respects, and despite the internal reform of institutions like Port-Royal, the legal and cultural forces arrayed against children's liberty pushed opponents of coercion towards a more vociferous opposition, not so much in law as in a battle of pastoral words. And yet these writers were men of their own place and time who expected and typically valued parents' involvement in their children's vocational choices. So, while insisting on individuals' free vocational choice, many reformers also sought to bring parents into the process of right vocational discernment. Parents would be a help, rather than a hindrance, if they cooperated in following right principles. It was for these reasons that vocation advice by Gobinet, Bourdaloue, Joly, and Cordier addressed parents directly, rather than only addressing the young people themselves. And these texts were no dead letter. They were read by *dévot* elites at home, heard in many pulpits as model sermons were imitated, learned in catechism classes, and used as the basis of spiritual direction and confessional practice.[68]

Even so, many parents would remain hostile or indifferent to this holistic vocational worldview. Consequently, Cordier, who was so keen on parent-child cooperation, could also advise this: "If the parents are neither of a humor nor of a degree of virtue to enjoy God's designs; if one knows that they will employ all their power to impede it, one can … refrain from giving them notice until after the thing is done. Such has been the practice of the saints."[69]

Conclusion

As we have seen, seventeenth-century French Catholic vocational reform was characterized by four concerns – urgency, inclusiveness, method, and liberty. Vocational rigorists sought to convince French Catholics of the dire spiritual and temporal repercussions of ignoring or rejecting God's call to a state of life. Those consequences would apply to every Catholic who failed to discern rightly, since a vocation was necessary even for remaining in the world and entering marriage. A matter of such urgent and universal concern demanded a solution, which reformers offered by way of systematic discernment methods for each young man and woman to follow. Still, these decisions needed to be made in the context of the social and legal realities of Old Regime patriarchy. So rather than espousing some kind of hyperindividualism – which was neither desirable nor imaginable – the reformers sought to persuade parents to cooperate in a systematic discernment process, rather than to hinder it with their worldly motives. But what does all of this mean for the world beyond early modern France?

FRENCH VOCATIONAL REFORM AND GLOBAL CATHOLIC MODERNITY

The core features of seventeenth-century vocational reform became enduring features within the variegated landscape of Catholic modernity. This is not to say that no other approaches to vocation were possible, or that there has been no further development in Catholic vocational culture. It is clear, however, that seventeenth-century reformers established commonplaces that have informed the beliefs and practices of many Catholics for centuries.

In many cases, such as that of Charles Gobinet's *Instruction for Youth in Christian Piety*, seventeenth-century vocational texts were widely reprinted and translated. Gobinet's treatise was continually republished in several languages through the nineteenth century. The first translation appears to have been a 1687 English edition, printed in London during the reign of James II (a Catholic), and the work came into Dutch by 1693, Italian by 1708, German by 1714, Spanish by 1731, Polish by 1768, and Arabic by 1879. Its translators included a Spanish infantry captain, a canon of the Lateran Basilica in Rome, a Polish priest of the Piarist teaching congregation, and a Bavarian civil servant who was taking refuge at a Franciscan house during his Prince-Elector's temporary exile. During the nineteenth century, Gobinet's *Instruction* was promoted at French parish missions, recommended by the bishops of Philadelphia and Boston, used by an English Catholic schoolmaster in Bristol, and published by Franciscans in Jerusalem.[1] For over two centuries, seculars, professed religious of various congregations, and laymen alike all looked to this book as a tool for forming young Catholics, even if it is largely forgotten today.

The circuitous publication history of Emanuel de la Croix's *The Good Choice* similarly reveals enduring interest in the works of seventeenth-century vocational reformers. As noted previously, this author is best identified as a Discalced Carmelite who was the brother of the controversial Jesuit writer Louis Cellot.[2] Interest in the text spread beyond Jesuits and Carmelites; in fact, an Italian translation by a Barnabite priest was published in 1718.[3] In 1844, a priest named Amédée Vignolo, heavily involved in youth ministry in the diocese of Marseille, sought the original French text from numerous libraries without success. Vignolo thereupon personally retranslated the text, which had been a guidebook for his own youthful discernment, back into French from the Italian. He believed that many other discernment guides were plagued by "vague considerations," whereas this one was "superior to all of them" in its clarity and concision, its completeness and order, and its firm grounding in scripture and Catholic tradition. Although Vignolo took a few liberties with his translation for the benefit of his nineteenth-century readers, he believed that Emanuel de la Croix's guidebook was still the best tool for teaching right vocational choice to young Catholics.[4]

As Vignolo intimated, many other works on vocational discernment were available in the middle of the nineteenth century, including newly written books manifesting the principles of seventeenth-century reformers. In 1860, for example, Jean-Baptiste Malou, the bishop of Bruges, published in French a vocational discernment treatise, which was soon translated into German and English.[5] The continuity between this text and its early modern predecessors is exemplified by Bishop Herbert Alfred Vaughan's summary of right discernment in his preface to the English edition: "Three things are needful, in order to ascertain our vocation when in doubt about it: prayer, reflection, and wise counsel."[6] The early modern triad endured. Furthermore, just as Vignolo had altered passages in *The Good Choice* text for the needs of his particular flock, Vaughan used his lengthy preface as an opportunity to reflect on vocational choice in the peculiar circumstances of English Catholics. And so, seventeenth-century vocational reformers had indeed made their principles into commonplaces, and future generations adopted their concepts and methods. Hence, vocational teaching is an example of how global Catholicism in recent centuries is marked by an increasingly shared "repertoire of ideas and practices."[7] While varying approaches to vocational choice have coexisted in modern Catholicism, the seventeenth-century French rigorist strand remained one of the strongest influences on pastoral care of the young into the twentieth century, well beyond the confines of the francophone world.

THE DECLINE OF HELL, THE TRIUMPH OF THE THERAPEUTIC, AND THE REMNANTS OF RIGORISM

The twentieth century was a dynamic era of Catholic vocational reform, and dissecting the shifts that came before and after Vatican II – especially with respect to the vocation of the laity – would be beyond the scope of this book. Instead, I will identify some significant twentieth-century challenges to seventeenth-century vocational discernment methods and principles. These challenges transformed this long tradition but did not altogether destroy it, and, in less rigorist forms, it still serves as the core of vocational discernment advice given to many young Catholics.

One of the first major setbacks for seventeenth-century French vocational paradigms came in the form of the "Lahitton Affair," a dispute over seminary formation and the priestly call. Briefly summarized, a theologian named Joseph Lahitton lambasted the approach to vocational discernment that prevailed in many seminaries as overly introspective and theologically groundless. He particularly set his sights on the long-dominant Sulpician theory of a supernatural, interior "attraction" (*attrait*) as the chief manifestation of a priestly vocation. Lahitton argued that a priestly vocation was not an interior call, attraction, or inclination to be discerned, but was primarily an exterior act of calling, through the church in the person of the bishop. Strident debate ensued, until his position was vindicated as orthodox by the judgment of a papally appointed commission of cardinals. While this dispute concerned the ecclesiastical state most directly, Lahitton suggested that similar principles would apply to other callings.[8] A Dominican theologian named Richard Butler several decades later made a complementary critique regarding the call to religious vows. Modern theology and pastoral care, he wrote, had made this call into "an unnecessary mystery" and had led young men and women to treat discernment as a "scavenger hunt for a divine communication" in "one's 'heart of hearts,'" or the identification of "a strong attraction" inside oneself.[9] Lahitton and Butler were ultimately pushing back against the "inward turn," a centuries-long trend of interiorization in Catholicism and in Western civilization generally.[10] Vocational discernment, in their view, was among the spiritual practices that had become dysfunctionally introspective, because early modern reformers had reified vocation and advocated continual self-examination and re-examination as the method of discovering it.

Introspective methods of vocational discernment nevertheless continued to flourish at the highest levels of the church. Although Lahitton's position was vindicated as an orthodox option, many Catholic theologians and prelates wished to preserve the interiority that was a mainstay of post-Reformation spirituality. Pope John Paul II spoke frequently on the topic of vocation, calling it, for example, "a mysterious inner voice of Christ" to be found "in the hidden recesses of the human heart."[11] More "unnecessary mystery," Butler might have said. Pope Benedict XVI wrote that "inner attentiveness" to the voice of Jesus, "heard deep within us," was integral to discerning God's call, at least to the priesthood or consecrated life.[12] These popes did not reduce vocation entirely to the interior or exclude a role for the church community and hierarchy, but neither had the majority of seventeenth-century vocational reformers done so. Nevertheless, Lahitton and Butler had not been simply knocking down straw men. If their objections pointed out certain introspective excesses, interior discernment – with the vagueness that often attended it – remained intact.

The rigorist character of vocational discernment tropes has most evolved with respect to urgency and the consequences of wrong choices. As shown in chapter 2, those who failed to choose the state to which God had called them were said to be subject to suffering both in this world and in the next. Manifesting the long-term "decline of Hell," present-day discernment advice rarely bears warnings about damnation for those who choose wrongly.[13] Nevertheless, many twentieth- and twenty-first-century writers have partially echoed the seventeenth-century rigorists, by labelling as a sin the neglect or rejection of God's call. In fact, theologians explicitly debated the level of moral obligation that God's call entailed.[14] Some denied the fundamental premise behind rigorist vocational reform, "that God has designated a particular state for each individual human being."[15] Such debates were needed because early modern vocational reformers had successfully embedded in Catholic culture the idea of a universal obligation to discern and accept God's call. In contrast to their early modern forbears, however, very few of the most rigorous twentieth-century writers would doubt the possibility of repentance from a wrong choice of state.

More often, we encounter in recent times a rhetoric of warning about happiness, wherein right vocational choice remains a prerequisite of personal fulfillment. Popes John Paul II, Benedict XVI, and Francis all have invoked the sadness of the Gospel's "rich young man" (Matt. 19:22; Mark 10:22; Luke 18:23) as the archetypical result of, in John Paul II's words, "life choices which distance us from him," including the rejection of "the personal call to love: in matrimony, in the consecrated life, in the ordained ministry, in the mission *ad gentes*."[16] The everyday literature of vocation advice is still more concrete. A representative "Frequently Asked Questions" page on the website of the Diocese of Harrisburg, Pennsylvania allows some happiness for those who have chosen wrongly but warns that "they will not be as happy or blessed as they might have been had they followed their proper vocation."[17] A US bishop warned in a 2008 pamphlet that those who were "careless or haphazard in discerning their vocation" or who rejected God's call to a state, provided they also ultimately sought to live a holy life, would not be punished with "eternal unhappiness" but would experience "less joy, contentment, and fulfillment."[18] More drastically, a recent discernment manual proclaims that following God's call (whether to marriage, religion, or the priesthood) yields "peace, joy, love, and holiness," but that failure to do so brings more hardship to life, partly by making one's journey to heaven more arduous. This would be the case whether one consciously sinned by "knowingly" rejecting a call from God or one simply was blissfully unaware of the idea of vocation. The text highlights the example of a disastrous marriage, ending in separation, as the unhappy manifestation of inadequate vocational discernment.[19] In short, when early modern rigorists discussed the temporal and eternal dangers of wrong vocational choices, they emphasized the eternal, whereas recent commentators have stressed the temporal, normally eschewing altogether any talk of damnation.

In this shift, we find that Catholic vocational culture and secular vocational culture have grown increasingly similar, with both exhibiting a sort of temporal rigorism that enshrines earthly contentment as the reward of good choices. In an absolute sense, right vocational choice becomes less urgent, since dissatisfaction on earth is inherently less troublesome than an eternity in hell. From another perspective, however, this shift reflects a broad shift in values across the west. Contentment in this life has become increasingly more prized since the early modern era, and arguably the twentieth-century witnessed "the triumph of the therapeutic," wherein "a sense of well-being has become the end, rather than a by-product of striving after some superior communal end."[20] One need not assert, however, a stark reversal of ends and by-products to see a rhetorical shift, wherein individual fulfillment is treated as the main motivator of contemporary audiences. Catholic spiritual guides might still talk of higher ends, such as God's will and holiness, and secular gurus might speak of one's calling as involving "a contribution … to our human community."[21] But both types trade on fears that a missed vocation will bring about suffering in this life, including a gnawing dissatisfaction, a sense of being "out of place."

What might the state of present-day interest in vocation tell us about the success of the rigoristic vocational reformers of seventeenth-century France? By their own high standards, as with all early modern reformers, they failed. They did not transform French society; not all young Catholics were inspired to follow a well-ordered discernment process culminating in the acceptance of God's call. Yet, even in an age that has become disdainful of religious rigorism and that allows individual flourishing to trump transcendent considerations, the influence of seventeenth-century vocational reform endures. Urgency, inclusiveness, method, and liberty still characterize western Catholic vocational cultures. Even as fears of damnation have gone by the wayside, lay and clerical leaders continue to treat vocational discernment as an essential part of the pastoral care of youth. The inclusiveness of vocational culture has only grown, with strong Vatican-II-era emphases on marriage as a vocation, and now with expanded notions of the single life as a vocation. Methods of discernment, with ordered step-by-step processes, frequently asked questions, and even fill-in-the-blank workbooks to aid introspection are offered online and in print. And liberty – the oldest and most officially mandated aspect of early modern vocational reform – remains integral to Catholic law and theology. It is mentioned less frequently in sermons than in times past, on account of a widespread (and generally accurate) perception that less enforcement is now needed, at least in the developed world, where social and familial pressures have weakened.

One of the latest fruits of early modern Catholic vocational reform was the 2018 General Assembly of the Synod of Bishops, for which Pope Francis chose the theme "Young People, the Faith, and Vocational Discernment." Renewed attention to clerical sexual abuse overshadowed the meeting and drained some of the energy from its focus on vocational themes. Even so, in the proceedings of the synod and in the documents it produced, bishops treated vocational discernment as a topic worthy of deliberation at the highest levels of the hierarchy, because it was believed to be of urgent concern for every Catholic young person.[22] The bishops rightly noted that "different spiritualities have addressed the topic of discernment with different emphases, and in relation to different charismatic sensitivities and historical epochs."[23] What many of them may not have realized is how deeply their conversation was rooted in the reforming efforts of seventeenth-century French vocational rigorists, who should be considered key players in the formation of Catholic modernity.

VOCATIONAL REFORM AND MODERNITY: TRANSCENDING THE ANCIEN RÉGIME

This brief narrative of the afterlife of early modern Catholic vocational reform shows that its central elements were not dependent on the social structures of seventeenth-century France. In some respects, reformers worked to undermine existing social imaginaries. Indeed, the attempt to transform vocational culture and to inculcate a new "vocational social imaginary" was part of a modernizing process that left the Old Regime behind. As suggested in this book's introduction, the trajectory of vocational reform reveals one way that Catholics participated in and contributed to the tensions within modernity. Like many other modern efforts to transform humanity, Catholic vocational reform emphasized individuality and liberty without losing a strong communal ethos, and it enjoined highly introspective meditation on one's own identity while remaining oriented toward external action and subject to external authorities.

But, however the concept is defined, "modernity" is not some undifferentiated mass of concepts or tendencies. Moreover, if we allow for "multiple modernities," then we implicitly ask what distinguishes one manifestation of the modern from another. Whereas some modern aspirations, especially those explicitly called "enlightened" or "revolutionary," have aimed at throwing off past ideas and structures, participants in Catholic modernity have often intentionally favoured tradition and aspired to a universality – that is, catholicity – not bound by the concerns of only one era. Even when engaging in innovation and seeking progress, Catholic reformers in every age have often framed their efforts as returns to a better past, as critiques of the present in the light of the past. Seventeenth-century Catholic vocational reformers were no different, and, although the circumstances of their era shaped their vision in ways they could not themselves fathom, they aimed to transcend what they saw as the parochial, worldly concerns of the age.

Viewed another way, early modern Catholic vocational reform has contributed to the changing shape of modernity, as becomes apparent when we analyze it according to three "ideal types" employed by philosopher Charles Taylor: ancien régime, mobilization, and authenticity.[24] These three categories are "defined in terms of two aspects: the social matrix within which religious life was carried on, and the forms of spirituality which this life consisted in."[25] Although the three ideal types roughly correspond to three "ages" in which they respectively have dominated, Taylor emphasizes that multiple forms have coexisted in different eras. Analyzing Catholic vocational culture through these lenses allows us to think more clearly about the highly variegated expressions of modernity.

Early modern vocational reform conformed in many ways to the principles of ancien régime religion while simultaneously exemplifying religious mobilization. It will be helpful to quote at length from Taylor's comparative summary of these first two ideal types:

> (ii) AR [ancien régime] forms pre-exist the actual human beings which belong to them, and define their status and role; they are already there "since time out of mind"; whereas M [mobilization] offers a model which we are called upon to realize; human agency puts this design into effect in secular time ... Instead of being enjoined to remain in (or, after an unfortunate revolutionary hiatus) to return to their pre-existing places, people have to be induced, or forced, or organized to take their parts in the new structure; they have to be recruited into the creation of the new structures.
>
> (iii) AR forms are "organic," in the sense that society is articulated into constituent "orders" (nobility, clergy, bourgeoisie, peasants), and institutions (Assembly of clergy, Parliaments, estates), and smaller societies (parishes, communes, provinces), such that one only belongs to the whole through belonging to one of these constituent parts; whereas M societies are "direct-access"; the individual is a citizen "immediately"; without reference to these different groupings, which can be made and un-made at will.[26]

The spiritual hierarchy of "constituent 'orders'" or states of life (laity, clergy, religious) was a given "since time out of mind," a set of pre-existing forms of life that defined one's "status and role." But this spiritual set of états did not correspond to the états and orders that chiefly organized the body politic of ancien régime France. Rather, France's social and political matrix was constituted primarily, using Taylor's examples, by divisions among "nobility, clergy, bourgeoisie, peasants" and bodies such as "Assembly of clergy, Parliaments, estates ... parishes, communes, provinces." Despite sharing the patriarchal values of their contemporaries, vocational reformers tried to enshrine a spiritual hierarchical scheme that would take priority over the temporal ones that held sway. Hence, for example, the edicts of kings and parlements in favour of parental authority were to be circumvented when necessary. Moreover, for the individual, one's proper state of life was not "given" or "organic" in the temporal frame. A vocation was "given" by God but not by accident of birth;

embracing a state demanded conscious decision, action, movement. Once a state was entered, certainly, one would "remain in" that role and participate in ancien régime hierarchies through that role, but one did not simply get there by nature.

This seeming discrepancy confirms what Taylor notes about the distinction between the fact of mobilization in general and the "Age of Mobilization" (roughly 1800–1960). He specifically highlights the seventeenth-century French Catholic Reformation as an effort of mobilization, and, as this book has aimed to demonstrate, vocational reform was an integral part of that larger reform movement. In his view, the term "mobilization" can be applied generally to any major reform movement that seeks that people "adopt new structures" and "alter their social imaginaries, and sense of legitimacy, as well as their sense of what is crucially important in their lives or society."[27] Yet the Catholic Reformation in France, though it exemplified mobilization in one sense, would not constitute an "age of mobilization" because "the wider social context, that of Kingdom and Church … were not themselves seen as the products of mobilization, but on the contrary as already there, the unchanging and unchangeable backdrop of all legitimacy."[28] The post-revolutionary era of the nineteenth century, by contrast, demanded that religious movements, including the Catholic revival in France and elsewhere, mobilize men and women without the "backdrop."

This helps explain the place of seventeenth-century vocational reform in the "second confessional age" that began around 1800.[29] With ever-increasing literacy, the growth of mass printing, and a renewed spirit of internal mission, nineteenth-century Catholic movements brought seventeenth-century spiritual texts and commonplaces well beyond the audience of devout elites. In this age of mobilization, older attempts at mobilization took on new life. The severe weakening of ancien régime social structures (the old "backdrop") made religious mobilization not only more urgent but also more feasible. Much less was "given" and religion in general required voluntary adherence more than ever before. In such a context, many young people were less constrained by social and familial expectations, and so they could more readily accept a mobilizing message about right vocational discernment. Modernity had already made choice more possible in many arenas, and so more people might be persuaded to conform their choice of a future life to what they held to be divine imperatives.

The age of mobilization was not, however, the apotheosis of subjective individualism, whose time would yet come. Taylor stresses that mobilization, while appealing to individuals, has always been oriented to communal life. As noted above, in the age of mobilization, individuals had "to be recruited into the creation of the new structures" – youth groups, sports clubs, schools, sodalities, confraternities, and often the ghetto in which these communal structures were contained.[30] Early modern models of vocational reform, since they already expressed both individual and communal values, could be well adapted to the needs of this era. For some, the renewed and expanded promotion of a vocational social imaginary was thus an integral part of the nineteenth century mobilizing modernity, rather than a reactionary throwback.

Vocational discernment culture's endurance to the present day has been enabled by its adaptability to the next step in the journey of modernity, Taylor's third ideal type, which he calls "authenticity" or "expressive individualism."[31] In his view, hints of the expressive individualist ethos can be found in the nineteenth century, especially among participants in the culture of Romanticism, but the mass acceptance of expressive individualism began in the 1960s, a "hinge moment" in which we can see a "precipitate fall" of those "new structures" established in the age of mobilization.[32] By the end of the 1960s, the communal values and structures inherent in previous mobilization had been greatly undermined, and new forms of individualism came to dominate Western culture. But it has remained possible within that frame to convince men and women to accept elements of traditional religion, sometimes by appealing therapeutically to the desire for individual fulfillment. And the idea of being individually called by God fits with a culture that has come to care deeply about a sense of identity and about "narrative, a more intense telling of our stories."[33] Moreover, the eclipse of older communal forms of life has led many contemporary moderns to yearn for a sense of meaning.[34] That yearning has been fulfilled for many by the belief that they are called, that they are needed to fill a particular purpose, that they have a place in the world bigger than their own immediate consumerist desires.

While some base their sense of calling in secular values or in non-dogmatic forms of spirituality, others have looked explicitly to the long tradition of Christian vocational cultures. The very language of "vocation" or "being called" is, of course, biblical, and interpretations of this language have shifted repeatedly since the days of St Paul. Both Protestant and Catholic reformers in the early modern era took the early traditions that had developed from scriptural language and turned them into complete vocational social imaginaries, complete visions of how God's act of calling ought to determine the individual and communal lives of Christians. The core of those early modern visions of vocation remains an integral part of our hyperpluralist present. Many moderns find that versions of those faith-based visions yield much-needed answers to what Brad Gregory has called "the Life Questions," essentially boiling down to "What kind of person should I be?" and "What is meaningful in life, and what should I do in order to lead a fulfilling life?"[35] But these traditions have not only formed a narrow class of orthodox believers. Without the moves made by early modern Christian reformers, we would not see today's frequent employment of vocational concepts in secular contexts. Christian reformers made vocation a permanent part of the modern repertoire of self-understanding. Claims about calling, even without a divine caller, are answers to the Life Questions. The language of vocation, imbued with a wealth of new implications by early modern Christians, enables many today to narrate their journey and feel certain that they are not "dislocated bones" in the body of humanity.[36]

Notes

INTRODUCTION

1 "Si on recherche la cause des desordres que nous voyons en chacun des estats, Ecclesiastiques, Religieux, & laïques, dans lesquels plusieurs s'acquitent tres mal de leur devoir, on trouvera qu'une grande partie du mal vient de cette source: à sçavoir de l'entrée qui a esté mauvaise; Et de ce que la pluspart entrent dans les conditions legerement, sans examiner s'ils y sont propres, & appellez de Dieu." Gobinet, *Instruction de la jeunesse*, 522. Except as otherwise noted, all citations of this work come from the 1655 first French edition.

2 Gobinet, *Instruction de la jeunesse*, 517–703.

3 "Ce choix est de telle consequence que de luy depend tout le bien d'un homme, & pour cette vie, & pour le salut eternel." Ibid., 520.

4 "Est-ce que les états du monde relévent moins du souverain domaine de Dieu, & de sa Providence, que ceux de l'Eglise? Est-ce qu'il ne faut pas une grace de vocation pour l'état du Mariage, aussi bien que pour celui de la Religion; Est-ce que les conditions du siecle n'ont pas autant de liaison que les autres, avec le salut?" Bourdaloue, *Sermons*, 24–5. Bourdaloue was known as "the king of preachers and the preacher of kings," on account of his eloquence and his frequent court preaching. He died in 1704, and his collected sermons were published posthumously in multiple volumes by fellow Jesuit preacher François de Paule Bretonneau. The authenticity and dating of his sermon texts were the subject of extensive nineteenth and early twentieth century debate; for one of the culminating contributions on these authorship questions, see Griselle, *Bourdaloue: histoire critique*. For more on his life and preaching, see Castets, *Bourdaloue*.

5 Buechner, *Wishful Thinking*, 95.

6 Stedman, "Do Only Religious People Have a 'Calling'?"
7 Bauman, *Liquid Modernity*, 139.
8 Davis, *Dedicated*, 21.
9 Weber, *Protestant Ethic*. For more on subsequent debate over the Weber thesis, see Lehmann and Roth, *Weber's Protestant Ethic*; Swatos and Kaelber, *The Protestant Ethic Turns 100*.
10 O'Connor, *Layman's Call*, 2.
11 Congar, *Lay People in the Church*, xxvii; original text Congar, *Jalons pour une théologie du laïcat*, 8.
12 The following examples are a small fraction of twentieth-century Catholic writing on the laity: Hesburgh, *Theology of Catholic Action*; Balthasar, *Der Laie und der Ordenstand*; Phillips, *Le rôle du laïcat*; Rahner, "Uber das Laienapostolat"; Schillebeeckx, *Layman in the Church*; Thorman, *Emerging Layman*; O'Gara, *Layman in the Church*; Gerken, *Toward a Theology of the Layman*; Brungs, *A Priestly People*; Suenens, *Coresponsibility in the Church*; Kelly, *Lay Spirituality*; Doohan, *Lay-Centered Church*; Doohan, *The Laity: A Bibliography*; Green, *Come Down, Zacchaeus*; Aumann, *On the Front Lines*; Lakeland, *Liberation of the Laity*; Fox and Bechtle, *Called and Chosen*; John Paul II, *Christifideles laici*.
13 Pillorget, "Vocation religieuse et état"; Viguerie, "La vocation sacerdotale et religieuse"; Hanley, "Family and state"; Hanley, "Engendering the state"; Rapley, "Women and the religious vocation"; Diefendorf, "Give Us Back Our Children"; Schutte, *By Force and Fear*.
14 Dinet, "Les entrées en religion."
15 McGoldrick, "'Everything in Marriage Is Holy'"; Hahnenberg, *Awakening Vocation*, 28–34.
16 Delumeau, *Sin and Fear*, 439–41; Walch, *La spiritualité conjugale*, 65, 93, 112, 185–6, 259, 298–9.
17 Among the most explicit analyses is Parsons, "Vocation in Seventeenth-Century France."
18 For a summary of how scholars integrated Catholicism into their accounts of the rise of modernity, see Bireley, *Refashioning of Catholicism*, 2–8.
19 See Smith and Vaidyanathan, "Multiple Modernities"; Taylor, "Catholic Modernity."
20 Smith and Vaidyanathan, "Multiple Modernities," 259.
21 John Bossy classically argued for an early modern Christian shift in emphasis from a "body of people" to a "body of beliefs," defined by central authorities; Bossy, *Christianity in the West*, 171. Brad Gregory more recently argued for secularization and individual autonomy as

consequences of moves made by Reformation-era reformers, quite contrary to those reformers' intentions; Gregory, *Unintended Reformation.*

22 Charles Taylor has explored modern selfhood (including its relationship with religion) in numerous works, including Taylor, *Sources of the Self*; and Taylor, *A Secular Age*.

23 Sluhovsky, *Becoming a New Self*, 4. Sluhovsky does not extensively explore vocational discernment as such, nor did he concentrate his narrative on the seventeenth century, but some the practices he analyzes were building blocks of seventeenth-century vocational reform. Parsons has more strongly suggested the "communitarian" ends of Catholic vocational reform in Parsons, "Vocation," 340.

24 See above, 120n21.

25 Sluhovsky, *Becoming a New Self*, 4.

26 Diefendorf, *Planting the Cross*, 1–2.

27 Numerous examples of this dynamic are found in this classic source collection: Olin, *Catholic Reformation*.

28 Taylor, *Secular Age*, 146.

29 Ibid., 171–2.

30 For various accounts of the chronology and definition of rigorism, see Quantin, *Le rigorisme chrétien*; Bergin, *Church, Society and Religious Change*, 394–423; Wright, *Divisions of French Catholicism*; Parish, *Catholic Particularity*, 140–61; Gay, *Morales en conflit*, 35–6; Bergin, *Politics of Religion*, 181–205; Quantin, "Catholic moral theology."

31 Bergin, *Church, Society and Religious Change*, 429–31.

32 On the choice of a state of life in a handful of early modern Italian Jesuit sources, see Turrini, "La vita scelta?"

33 Sluhovsky, *Becoming a New Self*, 3.

34 Fraine, *Bible on Vocation*, 4–8.

35 Ibid., 32–40.

36 Ibid., 44.

37 Holl, "The Word Vocation," 127–8; Frey, "Luther, Weber, Agamben."

38 Price, "Early Monastic Tradition."

39 Holl, "The Word Vocation," 132.

40 Lawrence, *Medieval Monasticism*, 32–3, 165; Van Engen, "Professing Religion," 324; De Jong, *In Samuel's Image*, 1.

41 Leclercq, "Lettres de vocation."

42 Holl, "The Word Vocation," 126–7.

43 Constable, *Three Studies*, 252, 255.

44 Aquinas, *Summa Theologiae*, II-II.183.1.co. See also a discussion of this section of the *Summa*, in Bonino, "Charisms, Forms, and States."

45 Constable, *Three Studies*, 263.
46 Ibid., 252. This system is analyzed extensively in Freedman, *Images of the Medieval Peasant.*
47 Constable, *Three Studies*, 252.
48 Brundage, *Law, Sex, and Christian Society*, 34, 87–8, 175, 334–5, 414; Van Engen, "Professing Religion," 324, 331–6.

CHAPTER ONE

1 "Tyrannis ista detestabilis clericorum in laicos"; "aequaliter sacerdotes." Luther, *De captivitate*, 563–4.
2 "Et sacerdotium nihil est, qua ministerium." Ibid., 564.
3 "Esto itaque certus, & sese agnoscat quicunque se Christianum esse cognoverit, omnes nos aequaliter esse sacerdotes, hoc est, eandem in verbo & sacramento quocunque habere potestatem, verum, non licere quenquam hac ipsa uti nisi consensu communitatis, aut vocatione maioris." Ibid., 566.
4 Wingren, *Luther on Vocation*, ix, 2–3, 31–3; Luther, *De votis monasticis*.
5 "Augsburg Confession," 27.2–3, 27.49–60.
6 Brown, *Pastor and Laity*, 46–8, 76–8; Van Engen, *Sisters and Brothers*, 212–18.
7 "Augsburg Confession," 27.60.
8 "Confutatio Confessionis Augustanae," 176.
9 Melanchthon, "Apology," 27.5 (my translation and emphasis), 27.36–9.
10 Calvin, *Institution*, 4.13.1–3.
11 Ibid., 4.13.11.
12 Ibid.
13 E.g., Ibid., 4.13.1–3.
14 Two contrasting classic studies of the Protestant reformation of marriage are Ozment, *When Fathers Ruled,* and Roper, *The Holy Household.* For succinct accounts of Lutheran and Calvinist marital reforms, respectively, see chapters 5 and 6 of Witte, *From Sacrament to Contract*.
15 Luther, "Estate of Marriage," 36–7. See discussion of this work in Ozment, *When Fathers Ruled*, 3.
16 Ozment, *When Fathers Ruled*, 1–2; Witte, *From Sacrament to Contract*, 139–45.
17 For example, the Strasbourg reformer Martin Bucer; Bucer, "De coelibatu sacerdotum," 117. See also Selderhuis, *Marriage and Divorce*, 181, 236–7, 328–9, 348.

18 Council of Trent, Session 24 "Canons on the sacrament of marriage," no. 9, in Tanner, *Decrees*, 755.

19 Council of Trent, Session 7, "First decree [on the sacraments]: Canons on the sacraments in general," nos. 1, 9, 10, in Tanner, *Decrees*, 684–5; Council of Trent, Session 23, "Canons on the sacrament of order," nos. 3, 4, 7, in Tanner, *Decrees*, 743–4.

20 Council of Trent, Session 7, "First decree [On the sacraments]: Canons on the sacraments in general," no. 1, in Tanner, *Decrees*, 684; Council of Trent, Session 24 "Canons on the sacrament of marriage," no. 1, in Tanner, *Decrees*, 754.

21 Council of Trent, Session 25, "Decree on regulars and nuns," in Tanner, *Decrees*, 776–84; see also Schutte, *By Force and Fear*, 4–6.

22 Council of Trent, Session 25, "Decree on regulars and nuns," chap. 15, in Tanner, *Decrees*, 781.

23 Ibid., chap. 16, in Tanner, *Decrees*, 781.

24 Ibid., chap. 17, in Tanner, *Decrees*, 781.

25 Ibid., chap. 18, in Tanner, *Decrees*, 781–2; see Schutte, *By Force and Fear*, 4–7.

26 Although men and women alike were forced into religious vows, cultural attention over the centuries has focused largely on the coercion of women. Analyzing the literary and scholarly assumption that involuntary monachization was chiefly or exclusively a women's problem, Anne Jacobson Schutte noted that "the social and legal subordination of women over a very *longue durée*" made women "much more plausible victims than men" in fiction and thus "excellent tragic heroines"; Schutte, *By Force and Fear*, 50.

27 Council of Trent, Session 25, "Decree on regulars and nuns," chap. 19, in Tanner, *Decrees*, 782; see Schutte, *By Force and Fear*, 4–7.

28 Council of Trent, Session 24 "Canons on the reform of marriage," chaps. 1, 9, in Tanner, *Decrees*, 755, 759. On the debate at the council over parental consent to marriage, see Christensen-Nugues, "Parental Authority."

29 Lanza, *From Wives to Widows*, 28; Christensen-Nuges, "Parental Authority," 56, 58.

30 The spread of the *Exercises* was intimately entwined with the success of the early Jesuits. The *Exercises* formed them, and they promoted the *Exercises*. The substance of the text iself began to take shape in the winter of 1522–23. I will refer both to the original Spanish "autograph" text (a manuscript copied by an unidentified secretary, with corrections in Ignatius's hand) and to the Latin first printed edition of 1548; Ignatius of Loyola, *Texte autographe*; Ignatius of Loyola, *Exercitia Spiritualia*.

Translations into English are my own, though I have consulted and benefitted from Louis J. Puhl's translation, published in 1951. The 1548 Latin was unpaginated, and further notes will refer to the text by its English title, using the marginal reference numbers employed in many modern editions, including those of Puhl and Gueydan. For the complex early manuscript and printing history of the *Exercises*, see de Dalmases, "Histoire de la redaction."

31 For the sake of brevity, I use the terms "retreat," "retreatant," and "director," traditional shorthand terms, in place of Ignatius's own usage. Ignatius simply calls the retreat "the exercises" (*los exercicios*; *exercitia*) throughout the text. The retreatant can be more precisely termed "the exercitant," "the one receiving the exercises," or "the one exercising" (*el que se exercita*; *el que rescibe los exercicios*; *exercendus*; *exercitia accepturus*). The "director," emphasizing that he is a mediator rather than a source, is most often called "the one who gives the exercises" (*el que da los exercicios*; *tradens exercitia*; *exercitia traditurus*). See O'Malley, *First Jesuits*, 131.

32 Sluhovsky, *Becoming a New Self*, 69, 71–3.

33 Ignatius of Loyola, *Spiritual Exercises*, nos. 169–89.

34 The length of time of each week was adaptable to the needs of the person, and the meditations could be made without fully leaving one's duties in the world. Ignatius of Loyola, *Spiritual Exercises*, nos. 4, 18–20.

35 Harman, "Vocation and the *Spiritual Exercises*," 112, 114–15.

36 Javier Melloni notes, "*The Ignatian name for union with God is 'election.'* Such union comes about in the act and art of choosing in each moment in terms of God's will ... the act and art of 'allowing' oneself to be chosen. This ultimately is what discernment is about: allowing oneself to be taken by God, allowing Him to act through oneself in every event of history. Thus for Ignatius union is always a quest and a tendency, never a definitive state" (emphasis original); Melloni, *The Exercises of St Ignatius Loyola in the Western Tradition*, 50.

37 Ignatius of Loyola, *Spiritual Exercises*, nos. 169, 171, 172, 177. Where the Spanish reads "una vida o estado" ("a life or state"), the Latin reads "vitae genus" ("kind of life"), often equivalent in the Middle Ages to "status"; see page 14, above. Melanchthon, for example, had also used *vitae genus* to refer to state of life; Melanchthon, "Apology," 27.38.

38 Ignatius of Loyola, *Spiritual Exercises*, nos. 171, 189.

39 Harman, "Vocation and the *Spiritual Exercises*," 112.

40 "En toda buena election en quanto es de nuestra parte, el ojo de nuestra intention deve ser simple, solamente mirando para lo que soy criado, es

asaber para alabanza de dios nuestro señor y saluacion de my anima, y asi qualquier cosa que yo eligiere deve ser a que me ayude para al fin para que soy criado, no ordenando ny trayendo el fin al medio mas el medio al fin." "Ad bene quippiam eligendum, nostrae sunt partes: ut oculo puro ac simplice spectemus, quorsum fuerimus creati, nimirum ad laudem Dei et salutem nostram: quapropter eligenda sunt ea tantum, quae conducunt ad dictum finem, cum ubique, fini medium, non medio finis habeat subordinari." Ignatius of Loyola, *Spiritual Exercises*, no. 169.

41 Ibid.

42 "Por que toda vocacion divina es siempre pura y limpia sin mixtion de carne ny de otra affection alguna dessordenada." "Cum haec [divina vocatio] semper pura et clara sit, non carnali ullo affectu, vel studio perverso mixta." Ibid., no. 172.

43 "Demanera que el que los da no se decante ny se incline ala una parte ny ala otra, mas estando en medio como un peso, dexe inmediate obrar al criador, con la criatura y ala criatura con su criador y señor." "Quapropter dictanti exercitia standum est in quodam aequilibrio, sinendumque, ut citra medium, Creator ipse, cum creatura, & haec vicissim cum illo rem transigat." Ibid., no. 15.

44 Ibid., no. 14.

45 Ibid., nos. 175–8.

46 Ibid., no. 175.

47 "El segundo quand se toma hasaz claridad y cognoscimiento por experientia de consolationes y desolationes y por experientia de discretion de varios espiritus." "Secundum est, quoties satis clarum compertumque sit beneplacitum divinum, docente id aliquo consolationum, desolationum, vel diversorum spirituum praevio experimento." Ibid., no. 176.

48 Ibid., nos 313–36; see especially the rules designed for the second week, nos. 328–36.

49 "Dixe tiempo tranquillo, quando el anima no es agitada de varios spiritus y usa de sus potencias naturales libera y tranquilamente." "Porrò tranquillitas ea tunc noscitur adesse, quotiescunque anima nullis agitata variis spiritibus, vires naturales suas liberè exercet." Ibid., no. 177.

50 Ibid., nos. 178–83.

51 Ibid., nos. 184–8.

52 "Desseando yo toda su perfection." "Cui nihil non perfectionis inesse cupiam." Ibid., no. 185.

53 See, for example, Stopp, "St Francis De Sales at Clermont College."

54 Although de Sales was born and resided as priest and bishop in what was then the Duchy of Savoy, rather than the Kingdom of France, he and his

works easily and frequently passed between France and Savoy. Culturally and linguistically, he is properly a figure of French Catholic spirituality, despite the technicalities of political boundaries. On Salesian *douceur*, see Donlan, *The Reform of Zeal*, 10–11.

55 "Les moyens de parvenir a la perfection sont divers selon la diversité des vocations; car les Religieux, les vefves et mariés doivent tous rechercher cette perfection, mais non pas par mesme moyen." François de Sales, Lettre CCXVII à la Présidente Brulart (1), in *Oeuvres*, 12:268.

56 "Un chacun selon sa qualité et vocation. La devotion doibt estre differemment exercee par le Gentil-homme, par l'artisan … par la vefve, par la mariee." François de Sales, *Introduction à la vie devote*, édition princeps, in *Oeuvres*, 3:17*. A few other examples of his inclusive usage are François de Sales, *Introduction à la vie devote*, édition princeps, in *Oeuvres*, 3:36*, 3:51*, 3:92*, 3:139*, 3:178*.

57 "Des trois grandes vertus propres pour acquerir la perfection." Ibid., 3:90*.

58 François de Sales, Ibid., 3:91*.

59 For details on the book's publication history, see Mellinghoff-Bourgerie, "Four Centuries of Editions." The *Introduction* was especially important, for example, to Vincent de Paul and the institutions he established; see Forrestal, *Vincent de Paul*, 48, 59, 99.

60 François de Sales, *Introduction à la vie devote*, édition princeps, in *Oeuvres*, 3:41*–3*.

61 "Signifiee par ses commandemens conseils et inspirations." François de Sales, *Traitté de l'Amour de Dieu*, in *Oeuvres*, 5:59.

62 "Le commandment nous oblige sous peyne de peché, et le conseil nous invite sans peyne de peché." Ibid., 5:83.

63 Ibid., 5:77, 87–8.

64 Ibid., 5:75, 84.

65 "Elle fait des Martyrs plus vermeilz que la rose, des Vierges plus blanches que le lys; aux uns elle donne le fin violet de la mortification, aux autres le jaune des soucis du mariage, employant diversement les conseilz pour la perfection des ames qui sont si heureuses que de vivre sous sa conduite." Ibid., 5:77.

66 Ibid., 5:76.

67 "La perseverance en la vocation." "La paix et douceur de coeur." Ibid., 5:93–104.

68 "Briefve methode pour connoistre la volonté de Dieu." Ibid., 5:105–7.

69 Ibid., 5:105–6.

70 "Le choix de la vocation … et telles semblables choses meritent qu'on pense serieusement ce qui est plus selon la volonté divine." Ibid., 5:106.

71 "Es choses mesme de consequence il faut estre bien humble, et ne point penser de treuver la volonté de Dieu a force d'examen et de subtilité de discours." Ibid., 5:107.

72 Ibid.

73 "Bien appellees de Dieu." "La bonne vocation n'est autre chose qu'une volonté ferme et constante qu'a la personne appellee de vouloir servier Dieu en la manière et au lieu auquel sa divine Majesté l'appelle." François de Sales, *Les Vrays Entretiens spirituels*, XVII, in *Oeuvres*, 6:310, 312.

74 "Une bonne volonté de s'amender, de se sousmettre, et se servier des medicamens propres à leur guerison." Ibid., 6:313, 326.

75 "Mal nourries et mal civilisées, qui auront la nature rude et grossiere." "Ces filles-là, apres beaucoup de travail, font de grands fruicts en la Religion, deviennent des grandes servantes de Dieu et acquierent une virtu forte et solide, car la grace de Dieu supplée au defaut." Ibid., 6:326–7.

76 "Dieu a plusieurs moyens d'appeller ses serviteurs et servatnes à son service." Ibid., 6:315.

77 "Des ennuis, desastres et afflictions." Ibid., 6:315–16.

78 "Mais Dieu bien souvent en cecy fait voir la grandeur de sa clemence et misericorde, employant ces intentions, qui d'elles-mesmes ne sont aucunement bonnes, pour faire de ces personnes-là des grands serviteurs de sa divine Majesté." Ibid., 6:318–19.

79 "Voire, sa liberalité est si grande, qu'il donne ces moyens à ceux auxquels il ne les a pas promis et auxquels il ne s'est pas obligé pour ne les avoir pas appellés." Ibid., 6:321–2.

80 "Il ne faut pas attendre qu'il nous parle sensiblement, ou qu'il nous envoye quelque Ange du Ciel pour signifier sa volonté … Il ne faut non plus un examen de dix ou douze docteurs pour voir si l'inspiration est bonne ou mauvaise, s'il la faut suivre ou non." Ibid., 6:313–14.

81 Worcester, "St Francis de Sales and Jesuit Rhetorical Education," 110.

82 "Principes & fondements de ceste perfection." "Selon sa vacation [sic] & profession." Binet, "Abregé de la perfection chrestienne," 850. The French word "vacation" can be rendered as "state" and often has the sense of employment or trade ["métier"]. I avoid translating it as "vocation," because it lacks a strong connection with an act of "calling."

83 "Une entiere & parfaicte indifference à toutes les choses creées." Ibid., 855.

84 "À faire bon choix d'une vacation [sic] qui soit conforme à la volonté de Dieu." Ibid.

85 "Toujours agir avec charité." Chantal, "Entretien LVIII," 420–1.

86 Ibid., 419–20.

87 "Ma chère Soeur, Notre-Seigneur ne vous manquera pas de sa grâce si vous ne lui manquez pas de fidélité, et vous aurez sujet de ne rien craindre; il faut se confier en lui, il ne délaisse jamais ceux qui espèrent en sa bonté." Ibid., 424.

88 "Car, si elle ne fait pas grand bien à la maison, elle n'y fera pas grand mal." Ibid., 421.

89 On Camus's basic biography and on this particular work, see Worcester, *Seventeenth-Century Cultural Discourse*, 26–33, 218–20. On Camus's relationship with Salesian principles, see Pocetto, "Jean-Pierre Camus."

90 "La vocation à quelque vacation [sic] ou condition." "Puisqu'en toutes on se peut sauver & en toutes se perdre." Camus, *L'Esprit du B. François de Sales*, 322–3.

91 "Il y en a, disoit-il, qui se rompent la teste & s'alabicquent le cerveau à force de mediter & de consulter quel genre de vie ils doivent embrasser, ou le celibat, ou le mariage, ou le cloistre, ou telle vacation dans le si siecle." Ibid., 323–5.

92 "Couronné de misericorde." Ibid., 322.

93 Ibid., 328.

CHAPTER TWO

1 "Il n'y a rien dont le salut dépende davantage que de bien choisir l'état où l'on doit vivre, parce qu'il est certain que presque tous les péchés des hommes viennent de l'engagement de leur état … Car que feroit-ce, si vous veniez à vous y tromper, et à prendre une autre voie, que celle où Dieu vous a préparé des graces pour faire votre salut?" Bourdaloue, *Exhortations et instructions*, 435–6.

2 I have found only one other passing use of the term "vocational rigorism" ("le rigorisme vocationnel") by another author; see Gilbert, *"Le grand secret de la vocation"*, 451.

3 For scholarship on the chronology and definition of rigorism, see 121n30.

4 "Parmi ces pratiques pastorales, il y a au premier chef le délai et le refus d'absolution, en particulier aux habitudinaires et aux occasionnaires, la pratique de pénitences rigoureuses et éventuellement publiques, ainsi qu'une pratique inquisitive non seulement de la confession elle-même, mais encore de ses motivations spirituelles par la poursuite d'un discernement effectif du degré d'attrition du pénitent." Gay, *Morales en conflit*, 35.

5 Wright, *Divisions of French Catholicism*, 191. For more on Borromeo's approach to confession, see Boer, *Conquest of the Soul.*

6 Wright, *Divisions of French Catholicism*, 33–4, 127.

7 Ibid., 162–3.
8 Bergin, *Church, Society and Religious Change*, 400; Arnauld, *De la frequente communion*. Formal approbations from numerous French bishops and theologians fill several pages of this "bestseller."
9 Jansen, *Augustinus*. The difficulty of resolving these questions points back to Augustine of Hippo and the Pelagians. Both modern scholars and seventeenth-century parties to the dispute, such as Blaise Pascal, have seen it as a perennial debate inherent in Christianity; see Parish, *Catholic Particularity*, 141–3.
10 Bergin, *Church, Society and Religious Change*, 396–7.
11 Doyle, *Jansenism*, 11.
12 Parish, *Catholic Particularity*, 147–8. On the importance of this sort of rhetorical use of moderation and mean in theological disputes (and more broadly), see Shagan, *The Rule of Moderation*. Although Shagan makes a particular argument about England, he more broadly discusses "the intrinsically aggressive character of moderation" in general (7).
13 Delumeau, *Sin and Fear*, 4 (originally published as *Le péché et la peur*). Other works highlighting anxiety, especially surrounding the penitential cycle of sin and confession, are Delumeau, *L'aveu et le pardon*; Ozment, *Reformation in the Cities*, 22–32; Ozment, *Age of Reform*, 216–22; and, in a more nuanced manner, Thayer, *Penitence, Preaching*. For critiques of this narrative, see Tentler, *Sin and Confession*; Cameron, *The European Reformation*, 310–12; Taylor, *Soldiers of Christ*. Thomas Worcester notes that Delumeau himself purposely balanced *Sin and Fear* with other works, especially *Rassurer et protéger*. Worcester moreover critiques an overly binary approach in both Delumeau and Taylor that views complex early modern beliefs through the lenses of fear-reassurance and pessimism-optimism; Worcester, *Seventeenth-Century Cultural Discourse*, 2.
14 This focus on sin expressed a long-term tendency in western (that is, Latin as distinct from Greek) theology, beginning especially with St Augustine, to treat God's grace primarily as a "medicinal" remedy for sin. The Greek tradition, by contrast, more strongly developed the ideas that grace wrought "deification" and a "filial relation to the Father in Christ." See Sweeney, *Abiding the Long Defeat*, 37–8, 42; Dupré, *Passage to Modernity*, 33, 172.
15 "Racine." Saint-Cyran, *Lettres chrestiennes*, 2:79.
16 Some might suggest that it is more precise to speak of "moralism" rather than "rigorism" in the case of vocational reform. Agnès Walch refers to "moralism" as a tendency to offer as strict moral rules what was seen by others as negotiable spiritual counsel. Another definition of "moralism" is

a tendency to subordinate religion to morality. In the Catholic context, it consists in emphasizing conformity to minimal standards of avoiding mortal sin as the foundation for participation in the life of faith. See Walch, *La spiritualité conjugale*, 317–18; Taylor, *A Secular Age*, 497–8. While the phenomena investigated in the present study includes elements of these moralisms, the term "rigorism" still best expresses the fact that these seventeenth-century reformers overtly and frequently linked their vocational reforms to questions of grace and of salvation.

17 "L'importance de bien choisir un estat de vie, & les moyens de le faire comme il faut, qui est un sujet peu connu aux Ieunes gens, & encore moins pratiqué." Gobinet, *Instruction de la jeunesse*, unpaginated preface. The *Instruction* saw numerous editions in several languages well into the nineteenth century, including a first English translation in 1687 (during the reign of James II) and an 1879 Arabic translation (printed by Franciscans in Jerusalem). In 1847 the missionary priest Adrien Nampon still strongly recommended the work: Martin, *Une Religion des livres*, 461–2.

18 Gobinet, *Instruction de la jeunnesse*, unpaginated preface. Gobinet was the first principal of the collège after a reform in which the Collège du Plessis, of medieval origin, was incorporated into the Sorbonne.

19 Gres-Gayer, *Jansénisme en Sorbonne*, 317. The *Introduction to the Devout Life* was high on Gobinet's suggested reading list for young men. Helms, "Introduction," 10; Goré, *L'itinéraire de Fénelon*, 51. In homage to de Sales, Gobinet called his young reader "Theotime" ("the one who honours God"); de Sales had used the same addressee in his *Treatise on the Love of God*. Gobinet's attempt to balance rigor and gentleness is evident in a new part of the *Instruction de la jeunesse*, added in 1668, entitled *Instruction sur la Penitence, et sur la sainte Communion*. There he both affirmed that attrition (imperfect contrition) with confession was sufficient for forgiveness of sins and warned against the many ways a confession could be invalidated by incompleteness. He also simultaneously advised frequent communion and warned against ways of receiving communion unworthily. Gobinet, *Instruction sur la Penitence, et sur la sainte communion*, 36–50, 131–57, unpaginated "avant-propos" to *Instruction sur la sainte communion*.

20 "Et certainement, si on recherche la cause des desordres que nous voyons en chacun des estats, Ecclesiastiques, Religieux, Laïques, dans lesquels plusieurs s'acquittent très-mal de leur devoir, on trouvera qu'une grande partie du mal vient de cette source: à sçavoir de l'entrée qui a esté mauvaise; Et de ce que la pluspart entrent dans les conditions legerement, sans

examiner s'ils y sont propres, & appellez de Dieu." Gobinet, *Instruction de la jeunesse*, 522.

21 "Ce choix est de telle consequence que de luy depend tout le bien d'un homme, & pour cette vie, & pour le salut eternel." Ibid., 520.

22 "De ce choix dépend pour la plus part, la bonne ou mauvaise vie, l'heureuse ou malheureuse mort, & le salut eternel ou la damnation eternelle d'un chacun." Dangles, *Particuliere conduite*, 44–5.

23 "Il n'y a pas de condition plus miserable. Le deplaisir de se voir engagé contre son inclination, joint aux difficultez qu'il souffre à s'acquitter de son devoir, le jette dans le chagrin, & dans une melancholie qui le ronge incessamement: le rend insupportable aux autres, & à soy mesme." Gobinet, *Instruction de la jeunesse*, 521.

24 "C'est qu'il estoit entré dans cet état, dans cet emploi sans consulter Dieu, sans vocation. Un os qui est hors de sa place, soufre beaucoup, & fait souffrir tout le corps." Nepveu, *Pensées*, 360.

25 "Avec quelles peines peut-il faire son salut dans un estat, auquel il n'a ny habilleté, ny vocation de Dieu? Le manquement de ces deux choses sont causes qu'il commetra un nombre innombrable de pechez qu'il n'auroit point faits dans un autre estat. Le defaut de capacité luy fait trouver des difficultez continuelles à satisfaire au devoir & aux obligations particulieres de son estat. Le defaut de vocation est cause qu'il manque de beaucoup de graces qu'il auroit receuës: dans un autre estat." Gobinet, *Instruction de la jeunesse*, 521–2.

26 "Voie ... où Dieu vous a préparé des graces pour faire votre salut." Bourdaloue, *Exhortations et instructions*, 435–6.

27 "La grace de vocation est une grace importante, une grace critique, une grace universelle, qui en renferme une infinité d'autres. Manquez à la vocation, toutes ces graces vous manqueront." Nepveu, *Pensées*, 360–1.

28 "Apres la grace du Baptesme, qui commence nôtre salut, & la grace de bien mourir qui l'acheve; la grace de bien choisir une profession est la plus importante, & la plus necessaire pour tout le cours de la vie; parce qu'elle est comme le milieu & le lien qui joint la grace du Baptesme à la grace finale." In the context of the passage, he is using "profession" in the same way as "état"; hence my non-literal translation. Emanuel de la Croix, *Le bon chois*, 15. Although my identification of this author – named in the book only as "Emanuel de la Croix, prêtre [priest]" – is based on circumstantial evidence and subject to revision, I will proceed with reasonable confidence in this conclusion. The Emmanuel de la Croix who was surnamed Cellot in the world professed Discalced Carmelite vows in 1629 in the Paris province. He became vicar of the Carmelites at Mount Carmel in

Palestine in 1648. In 1662, he returned to France, making him well placed to publish a book in 1667, a few years before his death in 1671. This Emmanuel had been quite welcoming to Jesuit visitors in the Holy Land, both because of his brother and also due to the extensive involvement of Jesuits in sixteenth-century Discalced Carmelite reforms. Villiers de Saint-Etienne, *Bibliotheca carmelitana*, 444; Ambrosius a S. Teresia, *Nomenclator missionariorum*, 133; Giordano, *Le Carmel en Terre Sainte*, 105; Besson, *La Syrie Sainte*, 44–5. The author of *The Good Choice* may have omitted further information on himself in order simultaneously to maintain monastic humility and to avoid repelling anti-Jesuit readers for whom the name Cellot was already odious. The text itself drew explicitly on the *Spiritual Exercises* and later Jesuit theologians, but Emanuel's muted references to them do not lend themselves to the conclusion that he was a Jesuit himself. He tended to avoid naming Jesuits in the body of the text when citing them in marginal notes; for example, he called Ignatius of Loyola simply "a great saint" ("un grand Saint") and the Jesuits Leys and Piatti "two learned and devout theologians" ("deux sçavans & devots Theologiens") (30, 34, 52, 131). Finally, the author's glowing language about religious vows indicates that he was more likely to be a regular priest than a secular (86–95). Henceforth I will maintain the spelling "Emanuel," as in *The Good Choice*, and treat "de la Croix" as the religious name meaning "of the Cross," rather than as the surname "La Croix." On Emanuel's controversial brother Louis Cellot, see Wright, *Divisions of French Catholicism*, 137–8, 141, 148, 161–5, 181.

29 "Toutes sortes de graces peuvent-elles nous ... faire acquiter de ces devoirs? non sans doute: autres sont les graces des Ecclesiastiques, autres celles de Religieux, autres celles des Vierges, autres celles des mariez. Il en faut d'immediates, de speciales, de propres à ce dernier état, & elles dépendent d'une premiere qui est la grace de la vocation, grace par laquelle Dieu nous appelle & nous l'appellons, grace par laquelle nous sommes dans la voie que nous lui avons demandé de nous montrer, grace enfin qui a comme une influence generale sur toutes les autres." [Richard], *Discours moraux*, 226.

30 "La chose est impossible aux hommes, mais elle ne l'est pas à Dieu. Elle est impossible à ceux qui s'ingèrent d'eux-mêmes & sans la grace de la vocation dans le mariage, ou qui l'ayant cette grace, n'en font pas l'usage qu'ils doivent. Mais à ceux qui y sont fideles, tout devient possible." Bourdaloue, *Sermons*, 106.

31 "Des moiens de se sanctifier dans son etat." "Quoique Dieu donne des graces ordinaires, communes & suffisantes à ceux qui se sont choisis un

etat de vie sans sa participation, il est a craindre qu'il ne leur refuse les graces extraordinaires & choisies ausquelles leur salut est attaché. Tu t'es appellé toi-meme, ou bien tu as fait la sourde oreille quand Dieu t'appeloit; tu auras des graces communes & suffisantes, mais pour des extraordinaires ne t'y fie pas; tu n'a pas repondu à la grace de ta vocation, peutetre [sic] Dieu t'en donnera-t'il encore une autre, mais s'il ne t'en donne pas comment te sauveras-tu?" Joly, *Prones*, 303–4. Coming from a strong Sulpician background, Joly was "rigorist, anti-regular, and friend of Port-Royal," and he famously suspended all priests' right to hear confession in his diocese, with an eye toward reforming confessional practice along rigorist lines; Bergin, *Crown, Church and Episcopate*, 427.

32 "Dieu, par sa providence particuliere, ayant resolu dans ses decrets eternels, d'appeller & de sauver dans le temps, les uns par un estat particulier, & les autres par un autre; il a aussi attaché ses graces singulieres à cét état particulier, & non pas à l'autre. De sorte que celuy qui suivra l'état auquel Dieu l'appelle, y recevra une grande abondance de graces extraordinaires qui luy rendront aisé tout ce qu'il y pourroit trouver de difficile à faire, & de rude à soûfrir, qui l'aideront à triompher sans beaucoup de peine des tentations les plus fortes, & à convertir en couronnes les attaques les plus pressantes; qui le garantiront des dangers & des occasions les plus à craindre; en un mot qui luy faciliteront merveilleusement la pratique des vertus les plus relevées, & la victoire des vices les plus engageans. Que si par sa mauvaise volonté ou par des respects humains, il s'engage à un autre estat qu'à celuy auquel Dieu l'appelle, & à auquel Dieu a attaché ce grand nombre de graces non communes; il aura bien des graces ordinaires, avec lesquelles il pourra faire son salut; mais il n'aura ny cette abondance de graces, ni ces graces victorieuses & triomphantes que Dieu luy auroit données en l'autre estat où il l'appelloit. Et en suite manquant de ces graces abondantes & extraordinaires, il succombera aux moindres tentations; tous les dangers seront presque pour luy des dangers mortels; tout le bien qu'il faudra faire, luy paroîtra comme impossible, & tout ce qu'il faudra souffrir, luy sera insupportable." Emanuel de la Croix, *Le bon chois*, 12–13.

33 See 131n28.

34 Ignatius of Loyola, *Spiritual Exercises*, nos. 172, 189.

35 François de Sales, *Les Vrays Entretiens spirituels*, XVII, in *Oeuvres*, 6:321–2. See 127n79.

36 "Cette Instruction regard une jeune personne de qualité." Bourdaloue, *Exhortations et instructions*, 435.

37 "Mais si ce n'est pas par cette vocation divine que je l'ai embrassé, n'y a-t-il plus de ressource pour moi, et que ferai-je? Vous ferez ce que fait le pécheur pénitent. En se convertissant à Dieu, il répare, par la grace de la pénitence, ce qu'il a perdu en se dépouillant de la grace d'innocence. De même vous réparerez après le mariage, le mal que vous avez commis en vous engageant dans le mariage; & puisque vous n'avez pas eu les premières graces de cet état, vous aurez recours à Dieu pour obtenir les secondes; car Dieu a de secondes graces pour suppléer au défaut des premieres, et c'est dans ces secondes graces que vous devez mettre votre confiance." Bourdaloue, *Sermons*, 107.

38 "Rien n'est plus à craindre que de ne pas repondre à la vocation de Dieu, qui n'appelle pas toujours plusieurs fois." Joly, *Prones*, 304–5.

39 "Dans tout notre Evangile je ne vois pas que le pere de famille ait appellé deux fois les memes personnes." Ibid., 304.

40 "Dieu peut faire en votre faveur un miracle, comme il en fit un aux Noces de Cana, et vous pouvez reparer cette faute, en y menant une vie sainte." Ibid., 165.

41 Clugny was said to have a preference for directing "simple persons … of low birth" ("des gens simples, & de basse naissance") over the rich and powerful, the former being more docile to God's work and the latter often being more attached to worldly things. *Abrege de la vie du Pere François de Clugny*, 5, 65–6, 156.

42 "Mais celle [la vocation] qui nous appelle à une condition, ou genre de vie, n'est pas d'une obligation si étroite … Elle ne nous engage pas absolument, nous étant plutôt proposée comme un conseil, que comme un commandement." Clugny, *Catechisme de la dévotion*, 12.

43 See François de Sales, *Traitté de l'Amour de Dieu*, in *Oeuvres*, 5:83–4.

44 "Tout le secret pour tirer profit de ces genres de vie, où l'on se trouve attaché avec des noeuds qui ne se peuvent rompre, c'est d'y être tels que Dieu veut que nous y soyons, par l'exercice d'une veritable dévotion." Clugny, *Catechisme de la dévotion*, 17.

45 Gobinet, *Instruction de la jeunesse*, 522.

46 "La diversité des états & la varieté des genres de vie, font subsister l'Eglise, & la mettent dans sa beauté. Si un corps n'avoit que des yeux, ou des pieds il seroit monstrueux: Nous sommes tous membres d'un même Corps, dont Jesus-Christ est le Chef." Clugny, *Catechisme de la dévotion*, 10.

47 "D. Les peres & les meres qui forcent leurs enfans d'estre d'Eglise, bien qu'ils en soient indignes, ou seulement pour avoir plus de bien, ou conserver quelque Benefice en leur famille offensent-ils Dieu? R. Ouy, ils pechent mortellement. 2. Ils sont cause de la damnation de leurs enfans, &

des pechez qu'ils commettent en cet estat, & se damnent avec eux. 3. Ils répondront devant Dieu du scandale que leurs enfans donnent à toute l'Eglise." Joly, *Les devoirs du chrestien*, 243–4.

CHAPTER THREE

1 Emphasis added. "La Providence de Dieu a estably le Mariage non seulement pour l'interest general de l'Univers, mais pour le bien particulier de ceux qu'il appelle à cét estat … Ce fut un de ces Mariages qui sont conclus dans le Ciel avant qu'ils se fassent sur la terre, puis qu'il a servy d'occasion, & de moyen pour la sanctification de l'un & de l'autre." Biroat, *Oraison funèbre de feue très-haute et très-puissante princesse Madame Éléonor de Bergh*, 16–17. See Dusch, "Eléonore de Bergh"; on Biroat, see Bell, *A Saint in the Sun*, 73.

2 Emphasis added. "Ainsi, MESSIEURS, vous tous que la naissance *& même la vocation du Ciel appelle* à cette glorieuse profession, qui est la défense des Autels de Dieu, de l'autorité de votre Prince, & de la sûreté de votre Patrie, ne la regardez point comme un obstacle formel à votre salut & à votre gloire chrétienne." This oration was preached in 1675. Mascaron, "Oraison funebre de trés-haut et trés-puissant prince Henry de la Tour-d'Auvergne," 329. On Mascaron, see Bergin, *Crown, Church, and Episcopate*, 451.

3 Emphasis added. "Sa mere … ne laissoit pas … de ne leur point inspirer le choix d'un état étant bien persuadée que c'est l'affaire du St Esprit." "Tout ce qu'une fille doit sçavoir pour vivre chrétiennement dans quelque état que Dieu la destinât." "Abregé de la vie et des vertus de nostre trés chere Soeur Françoise Agnés Descomps," 13–14. For more on the historiography of death notices and especially on their value as sources for the culture of vocational discernment, see Lane, "Gentle Holiness." The biographer's defense of the *pensionnat* speaks to critiques of convent education such as those made by François Fénelon. Orders varied in the extent to which they sought recruits among girls in their charge. Visitandine boarders were more likely than, for instance, Ursuline boarders to become nuns. Rapley, "Fénelon Revisited," 300, 311.

4 Placher, *Callings*, 331–2.

5 O'Connor, *The Layman's Call*, 2.

6 Bériou and d'Avray, "Henry of Provins"; Peregrinus de Opole, "Dominica secunda post epiphaniam Domini," in *Sermones*, 48–9.

7 For a comparison between medieval and early modern French sermons on marriage, see d'Avray, "The Gospel of the Marriage Feast."

8 See this interpretation in Parsons, "Vocation in Seventeenth-Century France."

9 Thomas Aquinas, *Summa Theologiae*, II-II.189.10.ad3. See Bolin, "The will to enter religious life."

10 "Selon les vues et selon les desseins de sa providence." Bourdaloue, *Exhortations et instructions*, 436.

11 "Encore que tous les estats soient bons, tous neantmoins ne sont pas bons à tous." "Dieu qui a estably par sa providence la diversité des estats & des employs de la vie des hommes, les distribuë aussi par sa sagesse differemment, destinant les uns à un employ, & les autres à un autre ... C'est pour cela qu'il donne aux hommes des inclinations differentes: des habilletez naturelles diverses tant du corps que de l'esprit: & qu'il leur distribue aussi diversement ses graces, selon les diverses necessitez des estats differens ausquels il les appelle." Gobinet, *Instruction de la jeunesse*, 518–19.

12 "Dieu, par sa providence particuliere, ayant resolu dans ses decrets eternels, d'appeller & de sauver dans le temps, les uns par un estat particulier, & les autres par un autre." Emanuel de la Croix, *Le bon chois*, 12.

13 "C'est que ce qui contribue davantage à notre salut, ce n'est point précisément la sainteté de l'état, mais la convenance de l'état avec les desseins & les vues de Dieu, qui nous l'a marqué, & qui nous y a fait entrer." Bourdaloue, *Sermons*, 16.

14 "La diversité des états & la varieté des genres de vie, font subsister l'Eglise, & la mettent dans sa beauté. Si un corps n'avoit que des yeux, ou des pieds il seroit monstrueux: Nous sommes tous membres d'un même Corps, dont Jesus-Christ est le Chef. Il faut donc qu'il y ait entre nous de la diversité, & de l'inegalité." Clugny, *Catechisme de la dévotion*, 10.

15 "La perfection qui s'acquiert par la dévotion, ne dépend pas de l'état, ny de la condition, où l'on est : mais de la fidelité à pratiquer les vertus, qui luy sont convenables ... La perfection d'un voyageur, ne dépend pas du Chemin ... Les vertus ... se peuvent trouver également parfaites dans deux personnes, qui seront en deux états de vie inégaux en excélence." Ibid., 7–8.

16 "La sanctification de vôtre ame: & le salut du prochain." "De vivre plus à vôtre aise dans l'estat Ecclesiastique; d'y trouver le repos, l'oisiveté, les delices; d'y amasser des richesses; d'y estre honnoré & estimé des hommes." Gobinet, *Instruction de la jeunesse*, 568–9.

17 "L'intention qu'il faut avoir en ce dessein est de se retirer du monde pour faire penitance, & pour se sanctifier interieurement par la pratique des vertus Chrestiennes ... Car si autre motif vous porte à cet estat, vôtre dessein n'est pas de Dieu." Ibid., 593.

18 "Mais la principale disposition est d'y estre appellé de Dieu. *Ceux-là offensent-ils Dieu qui ne se font tonsurer, ou ne font tonsurer leurs enfans que pour posséder des Bénéfices?* Ouï: ils offensent Dieu griévement; car cette vocation doit venir de Dieu, & non pas d'eux." *Catechisme du diocese de Meaux*, 173.

19 "Il en est comme des Religieux, on y persevere, on y goûte de continuelles délices, quand on y est appelé de Dieu." La Colombière, *Reflexions chrêtiennes*, 63.

20 These aspects of seventeenth-century vocational reform have been highlighted by Delumeau, *Sin and Fear*, 439–41; Parsons, "Vocation in Seventeenth-Century France."

21 "Il faut avoir beaucoup plus de signes que Dieu vous appelle à l'estat seculier, pour le suivre, que non pas à l'estat Religieux, parce que Nostre Seigneur a souvent conseillé de suivre le Religieux, & jamais le seculier, voire nous a declaré qu'au seculier y avoit toute sorte de dangers pour le salut eternel; & au contraire que l'estat Religieux est un chemin asseuré du Paradis." Dangles, *Particuliere conduite*, 48.

22 "Il n'y a rien dont le salut dépende davantage que de bien choisir l'état où l'on doit vivre, parce qu'il est certain que presque tous les péchés des homes viennent de l'engagement de leur état ... Car que feroit-ce, si vous veniez à vous y tromper, et à prendre une autre voie, que celle où Dieu vous a préparé des grâces pour faire votre salut?" "Je ne vous en dis pas davantage. C'est au Seigneur à s'expliquer, & vous serez toujours bien partout où vous serez sous sa conduite & par sa vocation." Bourdaloue, *Exhortations et instructions*, 435–6, 449.

23 "C'est le chemin le plus seur, le plus facile & le plus court pour arriver au Ciel." Emanuel de la Croix, *Le bon chois*, 61–2, 86.

24 Ibid., 61–9.

25 "Ce que je viens de dire ne doit pourtant pas vous empêcher de demeurer dans le monde, si vous estes certain que Dieu vous y appelle; seulement devez-vous prendre bien vos mesures & chercher vos asseurances pour y vivre en crainte, & y faire vôtre salut avec tremblement. Premunissez-vous fortement contre tant d'ennemies, dont les attaques perpetuelles vous y rendront vôtre salut bien difficile. Que si vous ne sentez pas que Dieu vous appelle au monder, benissez-le mille fois de ce qu'il veut vous tirer de ce lieu si glissant & si plein de precipices pour vous mettre en une condition plus asseurée." Ibid., 68–9.

26 "Les infinis avantages de la Religion." Ibid., 94. These advantages of religious life he summarized under three points: "1. It consecrates to God as perfectly as is possible our bodies, our souls, and our goods. 2. It delivers

us as far as is possible from all impediments to our salvation. 3. It gives us the most excellent means to win heaven and to acquire a very high degree of holiness." "Je reduis les avantages de la Religion à trois: 1. Elle consacre à Dieu le plus parfaitement qu'il se peut nos Corps, nos ames, & nos biens. 2. elle nous delivre autant qu'il est possible de tous les Empeschemens de nôtre salut. 3. Elle nous donne les moyens les plus excellens pour gagner le Ciel & pour acquerir une tres-haute sainteté." Ibid., 87–8.

27 Emphasis added. "La Religion nous delivre de tous les empeschemens de nôtre salut, qui sont les richesses, les voluptez, l'orgueil, les mauvaises compagnies, la volonté propre, le propre iugement & generalement toutes les occasions d'offenser Dieu." Ibid., 91.

28 "Une marque de predestination si asseurée que sans une revelation particuliere, il n'est pas possible d'en avoir un témoignage plus certain." Ibid., 95.

29 See page 55, above.

30 Ignatius of Loyola, *Spiritual Exercises*, no. 15.

31 See pages 33–4, above, for his sanguine view of entering religion for imperfect reasons, even contrary to God's original call.

32 Saint-Cyran, *Lettres chrestiennes*, 2:78–85.

33 "Le joug si rude du mariage." Ibid., 1:180.

34 "Mais puisque Dieu vous trouve libre & desgagé du mariage (qui est un des grands empeschmens de la bonne vie pour les penitens) vous estes obligé de vous humilier davantage pour obtenir la grace de bien vivre, & pour passer à la pratique de plusieurs moyens de vostre salut qui sont interdits aux personnes mariées, ausquelles pour cette raison le salut est plus difficille." Ibid., 2:423.

35 See page 27, above.

36 Bergin, *Church, Society and Religious Change*, 183–207.

37 Kaufman, "John Colet's *Opus de Sacramentis*."

38 Gilbert, "*Le grand secret de la vocation*", 445–55.

39 [La Chétardie], *Catechismes ou abregés de la doctrine chrétienne*, 297, 299, 301, 308–10.

40 "Mais la principale disposition est d'y estre appellé de Dieu. *Ceux-là offensent-ils Dieu qui ne se font tonsurer, ou ne font tonsurer leurs enfans que pour posséder des Bénéfices?* Ouï: ils offensent Dieu griévement; car cette vocation doit venir de Dieu, & non pas d'eux." *Catechisme du diocese de Meaux*, 173.

41 "A ceux que sa vocation / Engage à cette function." d'Heauville, *Catechisme en vers*, 81.

42 "C'est parce que la vocation de Dieu est necessaire à tout état … Et comme Dieu ne nous fait connoître ordinairement sa volonté, que par l'entremise de ceux qu'il nous a donnez pour diriger nos consciences." Gonsin, *Catechisme dogmatique et historique*, 259. Batterel, *Memoires domestiques*, 451–2.

43 "Avoir consulté Dieu pour sçavoir si on y est appellé." Joly, *Les devoirs du chrestien*, 247.

44 "D. Que doivent faire les Peres & Meres avant que d'engager leurs Enfans dans une profession de vie? R. Ils doivent prier & consulter Dieu, pour sçavoir si leurs Enfans y sont appellez, & leur faire connoistre les obligations de leur estat." Ibid., 93. See also *Catechisme nouveau*, 44.

45 "Un estat proprement de penitence." "Un estat de perfection." Beuvelet, *Meditations*, 15. On Beuvelet, see Grandet, *Les saints prêtres français*, 254–6.

46 Beuvelet, *Meditations*, 32–3.

47 "*Est-ce assez d'estre appellé à l'estat du Mariage en general?* / Non, il faut de plus que cette vocation s'étende à telle ou telle personne en particulier avec qui l'on doit contracter." Beuvelet, *La Vraye et solide devotion*, 430.

48 La Font, *Prosnes*, 1:278–87, 3:194–5. See also a model sermon – especially intended for use by parish priests – by Père Loriot, an Oratorian; Loriot, *Sermons*, 273–7. Jean Delumeau mentions La Font, Loriot, and several other clerics whose "almost interchangeable" marital vocation doctrine was "widely diffused, in both town and country." Delumeau, *Sin and Fear*, 440.

49 See Lane, "Gentle Holiness."

CHAPTER FOUR

1 Her father, Robert Myron (or Miron) was the king's ambassador to Switzerland from 1617 to 1627, and Madelene was seven years old upon her family's return to France. She entered religion at age fifteen. Pommereuse, *Chroniques*, 78–80. See also Miron de l'Espinay, *Robert Miron*, 171. Her biographer Pommereuse (also Pommereu, or Marie-Augustine de Sainte-Paule) served as archivist at the Ursuline mother house in Paris, and the individual biographies in her *Chroniques de l'ordre Des Ursulines* are intended to advance a coherent heroic account of her congregation and its mission. See Keller-Lapp, "Devenir des Jésuitesses"; Suire, *La sainteté française*, 51.

2 "S'éloignant d'elle-mesme des choses legeres & pueriles, pour se porter aux serieuses & solides." Pommereuse, *Chroniques*, 79.

3 "Elle conceut les premiers desirs d'estre Religieuse, qui crurent toûjours depuis." Ibid.
4 "Son humeur estoit aisée, douce, & égale, & sa conversation agreeable & obligeante." Ibid.
5 "Enfin elle avoit toutes les qualitez propres pour composer une parfait Ursuline." Ibid.
6 "Avec meure deliberation." Ibid.
7 See Emanuel de la Croix, *Le bon chois*, 39; Drillat, "Visitandines françaises," 194–5.
8 "L'importance de bien choisir un estat de vie, & les moyens de le faire comme il faut, qui est un sujet peu connu aux Ieunes gens, & encore moins pratiqué." Charles Gobinet, *Instruction de la jeunesse*, unpaginated preface.
9 Ignatius of Loyola, *Spiritual Exercises*, no. 169.
10 "Les uns regardent dans l'estat qu'ils veulent embrasser, la douceur de la vie: les autres les richesses & l'agrandissement: les autres l'honneur & la reputation: & en un mot tous regardent les biens temporels, & la vie presente; mais peu se proposent la Vertu, & le salut eternal, qui es ce qu'il faut regarder icy premierement & avant toutes choses." Gobinet, *Instruction de la jeunesse*, 524–5.
11 "On n'y entre que par intérêt, que par ambition, que par passion, que pour y chercher des établissemens de fortune." Bourdaloue, *Exhortations et instructions*, 437.
12 "Les marques du bon & du mauvais chois." "Par des motifs ou mauvais, ou temporels & terrestres, ou inutiles au salut." Emanuel de la Croix, *Le bon chois*, 134, 137.
13 "Par exemple, choisir par caprice & par fantaisie, pour avoir ses plaisirs, ses commoditez, ses divertissemens, de l'honneur & des richesses; pour plaire à ses parens, & pour contenter leur inclination; pour faire fortune, agrandir sa maison, relever sa famille, vivre avec plus de liberté." Ibid., 137.
14 For early modern French inheritance law and familial strategies, see Giesey, "Rules of Inheritance."
15 "Se laissant emporter à leurs passions (à qui la plus grande partie des hommes obeïssent)." Clugny, *Catechisme de la dévotion*, 16.
16 "La seconde faute est la mauvaise intention de ceux qui entrent dans le Mariage, qui ne se proposent point d'autre fin dans cet état que la volupté, & la joüissance des plaisirs qu'ils esperent y trouver, & qu'ils s'imaginent tout autres qu'ils ne sont en effet." Gobinet added this section on marriage in a later revision, and it was present at least as early as this 1688 edition.

When cited specifically, the year of this edition will be noted in parentheses. Gobinet, *Instruction de la jeunesse* (1688), 608.

17 "On se marie par ambition, par avarice, par amour, et ainsi on fait dans la passion la chose du monde qui demanderoit le plus de sens froid, on la fait dis-je dans la passion, & par passion." La Colombière, *Reflexions chrêtiennes*, 64. On La Colombière's preaching and on his famous connection with Marguerite-Marie Alacoque (1647–1690), mystic of the Sacred Heart, see O'Brien, "Une 'manière' de prêcher"; O'Brien, "Claude La Colombière (1641–82)."

18 "Il en est comme des Religieux, on y persevere, on y goûte de continuelles délices, quand on y est appelé de Dieu." La Colombière, *Reflexions chrêtiennes*, 63.

19 "Il n'y a rien dans cette vie ... de plus facile, plus leger, & plus agreable aux hommes que la charge d'un Evesque, d'un Prêtre, & d'un Diacre, si on s'en acquitte par negligence & en se flattant: mais ... il n'y a rien plus miserable, plus triste & plus damnable devant Dieu. De plus ... il n'y a rien en cette vie ... plus difficile, plus penible, & plus dangereux, que la charge d'un Evesque, d'un Prêtre, & d'un Diacre, si on s'en acquitte comme il faut, & selon la volonté de nôtre Maistre: mais aussi ... il n'y a rien de plus heureux devant Dieu." St Augustine of Hippo, Epistle 184, as quoted in Gobinet, *Instruction de la jeunesse*, 583–4.

20 "L'intention qu'il faut avoir en ce dessein est de se retirer du monde pour faire penitance, & pour se sanctifier interieurement par la pratique des vertues Chrestiennes ... Car si autre motif vous porte à cet estat, vôtre dessein n'est pas de Dieu." Gobinet, *Instruction de la jeunesse*, 593.

21 See pages 33–4, above.

22 Emphasis added. "Il faut regarder icy premierement & avant toutes choses." "Les motifs temporels n'entrent point en cette deliberation qu'apres cette fin premiere & principalle." Gobinet, *Instruction de la jeunesse*, 524–5, 544.

23 "Ce n'est pas qu'il soit absolument mauvais d'avoir égard à tout cela. Il y a une prudence humaine qui n'est point contraire à la sagesse évangélique, pourvû qu'elle lui soit subordonnée. Mais l'abus est de n'écouter que cette prudence du siécle, de ne se conduire que par les principes du siécle, de ne regarder les choses que par rapport au siécle, & de ne s'y déterminer qu'autant que les considérations du siécle nous y portent." Bourdaloue, *Exhortations et instructions*, 438.

24 "Une égalité de naissance, de condition, d'humeur, d'aage, de corps & d'esprit, qui sont comme les principes de toute la bonne intelligence, & de tout le bon-heur qu'on peut esperer des Alliances." Cordier, *La famille*

sainte, 3:1056. Cordier served in a number of prominent teaching and leadership positions in the society over the course of his career. *La famille sainte* (originally published in 1643), was dedicated to Jean Bouchu, first president of the parlement of Dijon; the networks to which Bouchu belonged exemplify the ready audience of "notables urbains" for these kinds of *dévot* treatises; see Walch, *La spiritualité conjugale*, 161–2.

25 Gobinet, avoiding haste, suggested ages sixteen to twenty, and the Jesuit Jean-Joseph Surin (1600–1665) thought that normally God called young people to a state in that same age range. Jean Cordier gave the still earlier age of fourteen or fifteen. Emanuel de la Croix, citing the Council of Trent's ages of entry into religion (fifteen for boys and twelve for girls), argued against deferring the choice of a state, since further increase in age would merely increase temptations, making it more difficult to come to know God's will. Gobinet, *Instruction de la jeunesse*, 543; Surin, *Catechisme spirituel*, 475, 480; Cordier, *La famille sainte*, 1:396; Emanuel de la Croix, *Le bon chois*, 138. Surin, though most famous for his involvement in the Loudun possessions, was otherwise a prolific spiritual writer. For a partial bibliography, see Marin, "A Jesuit Mystic's Feminine Melancholia," 75–6.

26 "La cause plus ordinaire du mauvais choix que plusieurs font de leur condition est la vie dereglée & remplie de pechez, qu'ils menent durant qu'ils sont jeunes." Gobinet, *Instruction de la jeunesse*, 530.

27 "Ils ont donné leurs premieres années au diable." Ibid., 530–1, 536.

28 Even though later editions of the work added the *Instruction sur la Penitence et sur la sainte Communion* after the fifth section on the choice of a state of life, this new part was essentially a separate treatise that expanded on topics already present in earlier parts of the original work.

29 "Les tenebres dans l'entendement du pecheur, & la froideur dans sa volonté." Emanuel de la Croix, *Le bon chois*, 16–17.

30 "Les dispositions éloignées." Ibid., 23–9.

31 "La grace de bien choisir une profession est … comme le milieu & le lien qui joint la grace du Baptesme à la grace finale." Ibid., 15.

32 "Il se faut rendre attentif, & fidelle à suivre la conduite de la Divine Providence, qui commence à nous acheminer à l'estat, où Dieu nous desire dés le moment de nôtre naissance." Clugny, *Catechisme de la dévotion*, 14.

33 "Laissant le soin de nôtre éducation à nos parens, qu'elle inspire, & qui les fait agir souvent sans qu'ils y pensent, pour donner un heureux succés aux desseins qu'elle fait sur nous. Et à mesure que nous avançons en âge, & que la raison nous vient, sa lumiere nous conduit avec une merveilleuse douceur, & sa grace nous fortifie contre les attraits du Monde, qui en

jettent plusieurs dans l'égarement, ainsi nous en voyons qui dés leur Enfance, se disposent à l'estat Eclésiastique [sic], ou Religieux, n'ayant point d'autre marque plus solide de leur vocation, que l'enchaînement des moyens, par lesquels ils y sont conduits par la divine providence. Les autres entrent par la même voie dans les charges, dans le trafic, & même dans le mariage." Ibid., 14–15.

34 "*Il est vray, que ceux qui sont fidelles à suivre la voix de Dieu, & dociles au mouvement de son esprit, sont heureux, mais qu'ils sont rares*" (emphasis in original). Ibid., 16.

35 Gobinet, *Instruction de la jeunesse*, 551; Emanuel de la Croix, *Le bon chois*, 39.

36 "Mais afin de l'engager davantage à vous communiquer ses lumieres & à se déclarer, vous n'avez point de moyen plus efficace ni plus assuré que la prière. Allez donc aussi souvent que vous le pourrez, vous prosterner devant lui, & lui dire comme Samuël: Parlez, Seigneur, et découvrez-moi vous-même quel dessein vous avez formé sur ma personne; car me voilà prête à vous entrendre, à vous obéir, & à exécuter toutes vos volontés." Bourdaloue, *Exhortations et instructions*, 441–2.

37 "Mais apres avoir demandé la lumiere du Saint Esprit, appliqué nostre consideration a la recherche de son bon playsir, pris le conseil de nostre directeur et, s'il y escheoit, de deux ou trois autres personnes spirituelles." François de Sales, *Traitté de l'Amour de Dieu*, in *Oeuvres*, 5:107.

38 "Vous voulez présentement sçavoir ce que vous devez faire pour connoître les vûes de Dieu sur vous, & quelle est votre vocation. C'est ce que je vais vous expliquer, & ce que je comprends en trois articles, qui vous serviront de régles, & que je vous prie d'observer avec une entière fidélité. Le premier est d'avoir recours à Dieu; le second, de vous adresser ensuite aux ministres de Dieu; & le troisiéme, de vous consulter vous-même. Tout ce qu'il y a de plus solide par rapport au choix de votre état, je dis à un bon choix, à un choix sage et chrétien, se trouve renfermé dans ces trois devoirs, dont voici la pratique." Bourdaloue, *Exhortations et instructions*, 440–1.

39 "Je vous répons, avec deux sçavans & devots Theologiens, que vous devez consulter Dieu, vous-mesme, & vôtre Directeur." Emanuel de la Croix, *Le bon chois*, 34; Lessius, *Disputatio de statu vitae deligendo*, 51–6; Platus, *De bono status religiosi*, chap. 36. In Latin editions, Leys was published as Leonardus Lessius and Piatti as Hieronymus Platus. Leys had explicitly used the language of three consultations, while Piatti's arguments merely implied the three elements. For more on Leys's view of vocation, see Turrini, "La vita scelta?," 151–3.

40 "Priez Dieu souvent & long-temps avec le plus de devotion & d'ardeur que vous pourrez, & vous verrez en bref qu'il remplira vostre ame d'une claire connoissance de l'estat qu'avez à prendre, & la volonté d'une forte inclination à le suivre." Dangles, *Particuliere conduite*, 49.
41 "Celuy qui doit estre consulté par dessus tous les autres, à sçavoir Dieu mesme ... Luy demander humblement ses saintes inspirations, & la grace de connoître sa volonté." Gobinet, *Instruction de la jeunesse*, 527.
42 "Comme Dieu ne s'expliquer immédiatement à nous que par des inspirations intérieures, vous devez d'abord l'écouter dans le fond de votre coeur, & vous rendre attentive à cette voix secrete par laquelle il a coutume de parler à ses élûs. Mais afin de l'engager davantage à vous communiquer ses lumieres & à se déclarer, vous n'avez point de moyen plus efficace ni plus assuré que la prière ... Ce qui achevera enfin de l'intéresser en votre faveur & de le disposer à vous accorder votre demande, ce sera d'y joindre quelques dévotions particulieres et quelques bonnes oeuvres, sur-tout l'usage de la communion, & même quelques pratiques de la pénitence chrétienne." Bourdaloue, *Exhortations et instructions*, 441–2.
43 Emanuel de la Croix, *Le bon chois*, 6–7.
44 "Vous consulterez Dieu par des prieres plus frequentes & plus ferventes que de coûtume." Ibid., 34.
45 Ibid., 35.
46 "Car Dieu ne nous a donné le discernement et la raison, qu'afin que nous nous en servions dans toutes les affaires qui nous regardent, mais particuliérement en celles qui nous sont d'une aussi grande conséquence, que l'est le choix de notre état. Examinez donc sans vous flatter, quel est de tous les états de la vie, celui où vous pouvez plus glorifier Dieu, celui où vous pouvez faire le plus aisément votre salut, celui auquel vous êtes plus propre eû égard aux qualités de votre esprit de votre coeur." Bourdaloue, *Exhortations et instructions*, 445.
47 Ibid., 447–8.
48 "Cet estat si relevé ne doit pas donner de la gloire aux Ecclesiastiques, mais beaucoup de crainte & de tremblement." Gobinet, *Instruction de la jeunesse*, 561.
49 Ibid., 565–7.
50 Ibid., 568, 570.
51 Ibid., 568–9.
52 "Les defauts d'esprit sont la grossierté où stupidité, la rudesse, la legereté d'esprit, l'ignorance & autres semblables ... Il en faut dire autant des defauts qui se trouvent dans les moeurs. Tout homme qui a vescu dans le

peché, où qui est encore sujet à quelque vice notable, comme l'impureté, l'ivrognerie, le jurement, la vengeance, l'avarice, l'ambition, & autres semblables, ne doit pas croire estre propre, ny appellé de Dieu à l'estat Ecclesiastique." Ibid., 570–1.

53 Ibid., 572–7, 578–83.

54 Ibid., 589.

55 Ibid., 594.

56 See 136n9.

57 "Si cette inclination ne continuë pas, c'est un signe que ce n'estoit qu'un mouvement humain." "Si cette inclination ne continuë pas, c'est une marque que ce n'êtoit qu'un mouvement humain, ou une bonne pensée que Dieu vous a donnée pour vous porter à la vertu dans la condition que vous embrasserez." Gobinet, *Instruction de la jeunesse*, 594; Gobinet, *Instruction de la jeunesse* (1688), 561.

58 "Les vertus communes s'y corrompent facilement, les plus solides y sont fort ébranlés." Gobinet, *Instruction de la jeunesse*, 622.

59 Ibid., 623–6.

60 "Si quelque necessité inevitable vous destine à cet estat." Ibid., 627.

61 Ibid., 638–40.

62 "Proposez vous un temps suffisant pour vacquer entierement à cette importante deliberation; par exemple un temps de cinq ou six mois, ou davantage, selon la difficulté que vous sentirez à vous determiner à un estat." Ibid., 543–4.

63 "Appliquez vous quelque heure du jour à penser serieusement à l'estat que vou devez choisir, & à en deliberer en vous mesme." Ibid., 544–7.

64 "Le choix des deux estats generaux." Ibid., 547.

65 Ibid., 547–50.

66 "Penser serieusement"; "examiner meurement"; "prenez garde de ne point suivre tout d'abord vôtre inclination"; "examinez-la ... long-temps"; "n'en resoudre rien qu'apres avoir long-temps demandé à Dieu ... apres avoir consideré long-temps." Ibid., 546–50.

67 See 130n19.

68 See 127n71.

69 "Il faut mettre vôtre coeur en une parfaite indifference pour le monde, ou pour la Religion, en sorte que vous soyez également prest à suivre cét état, ou cét autre, selon que vous connoîtrez la volonté de Dieu." Emanuel de la Croix, *Le bon chois*, 30.

70 "Cette inclination ... le portera à chercher des raisons pour suivre son inclination, & ensuite de ces raisons, il prendra facilement sa volonté propre pour la volonté de Dieu." Ibid., 31.

71 Emphasis added. "Pour bien deliberer, il faut 1. reconnoître vos qualitez d'esprit & de corps, vôtre naturel, vôtre temperament & vos inclinations. 2. Il faut connoître, pour le moins confusément, les differentes professions, & les differens états ausquels vous pouvez estre propre. 3. Il faut comparer ces états entr'eux, & avec vos qualitez d'esprit & de corps, pour sçavoir, non pas lequel agrée le plus à vôtre nature corrompuë, mais pour bien reconnoître dans lequel vous ferez vôtre salut avec plus de facilité, & d'asseurance pour vous, & avec plus d'honneur & de gloire pour Dieu." Ibid., 33–4.

72 "Car il ne s'agît pas seulement de choisir un bon moyen de vous sauver, mais de choisir entre plusieurs bons moyens, celuy qui sera le *meilleur* ... où il y aura le moins de danger de faire le mal, & plus d'occasion de faire le bien pour vous, & pour le prochain" (emphasis added). Ibid., 37.

73 Ibid., 128–9.

74 "Sans se flater." Ibid., 36–8. See 144n46.

75 On spiritual direction in the sixteenth century, see Sluhovsky, *Becoming a New Self*, chap. 2.

76 "Il faut consulter in ce choix principalement celuy qui a connoissance de la conscience, n'y ayant personne qui puisse voir plus clair que luy dans cette affaire." Gobinet, *Instruction de la jeunesse*, 551.

77 "Il est nécessaire que vôtre Directeur vous connoisse." Emanuel de la Croix, *Le bon chois*, 39.

78 "Ayez un directeur sage, un homme de Dieu, en qui vous preniez confiance, & à qui vous exposiez avec simplicité & avec candeur toutes vos vûes, toutes vos pensées, toutes les bonnes & mauvaises dispositions de votre ame." Bourdaloue, *Exhortations et instructions*, 443.

79 "Durant tout le temps de vôtre deliberation communiquez souvent avec vôtre confesseur: declarez-luy tout ce que vous remarquerez en vous: les inclinations: & les repugnances que vous sentez à diverses conditions: les difficultez que vous y trouvez: les motifs qui vous portent à un estat plustot qu'à un autre." Gobinet, *Instruction de la jeunesse*, 550. For another advocate of such frequent conversation, see Dangles, *Particuliere conduite*, 49.

80 "Qu'il se dépoüille de toute inclination qu'il pourroit avoir de porter à un estat plûtot qu'à un autre ... Il faut estre entierement detaché en cette conduite, afin de ne prendre pas son inclination pour la volonté de Dieu. Beaucoup moins faut il avoir aucun interest; ce qui est un crime en cette occasion." Gobinet, *Instruction de la jeunesse*, 552.

81 "Consultez un bon Directeur ... Il doit estre prudent, vertueux, spirituel, sçavant, & desinteressé ... Desinteressé, afin qu'il cherche purement vôtre

salut, & vôtre plus grand bien, non pas son avantage, ou celuy de quelqu'autre que vous." Emanuel de la Croix, *Le bon chois*, 38–9.

82 They both use the exact same phrase, "un sage et desinteressé Directeur." Gonsin, *Catechisme dogmatique et historique*, 243–4; Joly, *Les devoirs du chrestien*, 390.

83 "Elles doivent ... demander avis à des personnes vertueuses, prudentes & desinteressées ... C'est parce que la vocation de Dieu est necessaire à tout état ... Et comme Dieu ne nous fait connoître ordinairement sa volonté, que par l'entremise de ceux qu'il nous a donnez pour diriger nos consciences." Gonsin, *Catechisme dogmatique*, 259.

84 "Un examen de dix ou douze docteurs." "Deux ou trois autres personnes spirituelles." François de Sales, *Les Vrays Entretiens spirituels*, XVII, in *Oeuvres*, 6:314; François de Sales, *Traitté de l'Amour de Dieu*, in *Oeuvres*, 5:107.

85 E.g., Gobinet, *Instruction de la jeunesse*, 550.

86 "Principalement de son Evesque." Joly, *Les devoirs du chrestien*, 390.

87 "Les ministres de Dieu." Bourdaloue, *Exhortations et instructions*, 444–5.

88 Joly, *Les devoirs du chrestien*, 246; Lindeborn, *Instructions chrestiennes*, 103. Lindeborn's work was translated into French by Nicholas Fontaine, an associate of the Jansenist hub of Port-Royal; see Walch, *La spiritualité conjugale*, 163.

89 "Il ne faut non plus consulter les parens, s'ils ne sont d'une vertu eminente, & bien reconnuë." Emanuel de la Croix, *Le bon chois*, 44.

90 "En cette affaire ils sont nos ennemis & contraires à nôtre salut ... Il ne faut pas consulter les parens, parce que comme dit S. Hierôme ils sont interessez ... Les parens sont aveuglez par l'affection naturelle & dereglée qu'ils ont pour leur proches." Ibid., 44–5.

91 See Taylor, *A Secular Age*, chap. 2.

92 "Et pour cela choisissez en un entre mille, dit [Jean d']Avila, et moy je dis entre dix mille." François de Sales, *Introduction à la vie devote*, édition princeps, in *Oeuvres*, 3:20*.

CHAPTER FIVE

1 Pringy, *La Vie du Pere Bourdaloue*, 4.

2 Hanley, "Engendering the state," 9–11; Lanza, *From Wives to Widows*, 27–8; Diefendorf, "Give Us Back Our Children," 285–6, 288–93.

3 See earlier discussion of Tridentine reforms on pages 24–5.

4 Christensen-Nugues, "Parental Authority," 53–6, 58.

5 Farr, *Authority and Sexuality*, 93.

6 Ibid., 73, 88–9, 95–7. On the relationship between law and practice, see Ibid., 122–3; Lanza, *From Wives to Widows*, 36–9, 44–50; Breen, "Law, society, and the state."

7 Pillorget, "Vocation religieuse et état"; Dinet, *Vocation et fidelité*, 36–47; Dompnier, "Vocations d'ancien régime"; Hardwick, *The Practice of Patriarchy*, 75; Lanza, *From Wives to Widows*, 21–50; Schutte, *By Force and Fear*; Roger, "Contester l'autorité parentale"; Hanley, "Family and State in Early Modern France"; Hanley, "Engendering the State"; Rapley, "Women and the Religious Vocation,"; Diefendorf, "Give Us Back Our Children." Poorer segments of the population were typically less interested in questions of parental authority over vocations: Tulchin, "Low Dowries, Absent Parents."

8 "Combien y a-t'il de Chrestiens, qui s'estiment heureux, apres avoir sacrifié leurs enfans au Diable d'interest?" Cordier, *La famille sainte*, 1:289–90.

9 "Cependant on conduit cette victime dans le Temple, les pieds et les mains liées, je veux dire, dans la disposition d'une volonté contrainte, la bouche muette par la crainte et le respect d'un pere qu'elle a toujours honoré." Bourdaloue, *Sermons*, 21.

10 "Un esprit ou ambitieux, ou intéresseé." "L'établissement de cette fille coûteroit." Ibid., 19, 20.

11 Diefendorf, "Give Us Back Our Children."

12 Schutte, *By Force and Fear*, 8–13.

13 For a thorough exploration of these Arnauld's reforms in their Tridentine and Benedictine-Cistercian context, see Cutter, "Monastic Reform."

14 Cutter, "Monastic Reform," 426–8, 434–6; Conley, *Adoration and Annihilation*, 45–6.

15 "Dieu me toucha tellement que, dès ce moment, je me trouvai plus heureuse d'être Religieuse, que je ne m'étais estimée malheureuse de l'être." Arnauld, *Relation*, 40.

16 Conley, *Adoration and Annihilation*, 46.

17 "Marchander les filles." "C'était simonie que d'exiger de l'argent pour recevoir des filles Religieuses." Arnauld, *Relation*, 65–6. See Cutter, "Monastic reform," 432, 437–9.

18 Cutter, "Monastic reform," 438; Conley, *Adoration and Annihilation*, 47.

19 "Que l'on n'admette point de fille pour estre religieuse qui ne soit veritablement appellée de Dieu; & qui ne montre par sa vie & par ses actions une vraie & sincere volonté de servir Dieu, & de se consacrer toute entiere à luy; sans cela il n'en faut jamais recevoir pour quelques raisons que ce soit, quelque esprit, quelque noblesse, & quelques richesses qu'elle puisse avoir." *Les Constitutions du monastere*, 59. See Cutter, "Monastic Reform," 439; Conley, *Adoration and Annihilation*, 154.

20 Conley, *The Other Pascals*, 22–7, 52–8.
21 Conley, *Adoration and Annihilation*, 86–8.
22 See pages 74–6, above.
23 See 135n3.
24 Rapley, "Fénelon revisited," 311.
25 Conley, "A Rule for Children: Introduction," in Pascal, *A Rule for Children*, 69.
26 Pascal, "Reglement pour les enfans," in *Les Constitutions du monastere*, 494.
27 "Dieu ne fait pas cette grace de la Religion à tout le monde, ny même à tous ceux qui la desirent." Ibid., 495. Translations of this text are mine, but I have consulted John J. Conley's English translation of this passage in Pascal, *A Rule for Children*, 104.
28 "Nous ne devons pas … leur témoigner tout ce que nous croyons du peu de personnes qui se sauvent dans le monde." Pascal, "Reglement pour les enfans," in *Les Constitutions du monastere*, 494.
29 "Sur tout qu'on ne les laisse jamais soupçonner qu'on veut leur inspirer le dessein d'être Religieuse; car cette pensée leur ôte la confiance en leurs parents, leur persuade qu'elles n'en sont point aimées, leur agite l'esprit, & leur fait faire un personnage forcé pendant plusieurs années." Fénelon, *Education des filles*, 183–4.
30 "Si au contraire elle se détermine à se faire Religieuse sans y être poussée par ses parens." Ibid., 255.
31 "Ainsi je craindrois un Convent mondain encore plus que le monde même. Si au contraire un Convent est dans la ferveur & dans la regularité de son Institut, une jeune fille de condition y croît dans une profonde ignorance du siecle." Fénelon, "Avis de Monsieur de Fenelon," 274–5. See Rapley, "Fénelon Revisited," 300.
32 "C'est une coutume dans toutes les familles, c'est une espece de loi. Loi dictée par l'esprit du monde." Bourdaloue, *Sermons*, 19.
33 "Loi reconnue universellement dans le monde, & contre laquelle il est à peine permis aux Ministres de l'Eglise, & aux Prédicateurs de s'élever. Loi même communément tolérée … par les Directeurs des ames les plus réformés en apparence, & les plus rigides, par les Docteurs les plus sévéres dans leur morale, & qui affectent plus de l'être, ou de le paroître." Ibid., 19–20.
34 See pages 45–8, above.
35 "Paternité souveraine." "C'est à lui, & non point à d'autres, d'exercer sur les esprits & sur les volontés des hommes cette supériorité de conduite, ou plutôt d'empire, qui fait l'engagement de la vocation." "Si tous les états du monde sont des vocations du Ciel; s'il y a une grace attachée à tous ces

états, pour nous y attirer selon l'ordre de Dieu; s'il est d'un danger extrême pour le salut de prendre un état sans cette grace, ce n'est donc pas à un pere d'y porter ses enfans, beaucoup moins de les y engager … Car enfin, un pere dans la famille, n'est pas le distributeur des vocations. Cette grace n'est point entre ses mains, pour la donner à qui il veut, ni comme il veut … Parce que toute vocation étant une grace, il n'y a que Dieu qui la puisse communiquer." Bourdaloue, *Sermons*, 9–11, 14–15.

36 "Aage de discretion." Le Jau, *Chemin royal*, 775, 777. Le Jau's positions included vicar general of the diocese of Evreux and *doyen* of the diocesan cathedral, and he dedicated the book to one of the most influential *dévots*, Michel de Marillac, *garde des sceaux* of France.

37 Cordier, *La famille sainte*, 1:395–6. For a similar argument, see Gobinet, *Instruction de la jeunesse* (1688), 523.

38 Le Blanc, *Le bon escolier*, 310–14. Le Blanc served in numerous Jesuit leadership positions, especially in scholarship and education. Walch, *La spiritualité conjugale*, 140.

39 Le Jau, *Chemin royal*, 777–85.

40 Cordier, *La famille sainte*, 1:290; Lindeborn, *Instructions chrestiennes*, 66; Cheminais, *Sermons*, 342. Printed sermons of the Jesuit preacher Timoléon Cheminais (1652–1689) experienced enduring popularity; see Henryot, "Le prédicateur et ses livres," 53.

41 Bergin, *Church, Society and Religious Change*, 64–7, 75–6.

42 Ignatius of Loyola had noted the importance of choosing God's service first and a benefice as a means. See page 26–7.

43 On the vital role of catechisms in the early modern French church, see Carter, *Creating Catholics*.

44 "*Sous l'Esperance de quelque Benefice.*" "Servir … à son Avarice & à son Ambition." "On doit dire que c'est un tres-grand peché qui attire la Malediction de Dieu sur les Peres & sur les Enfans." *Catechisme ou doctrine chrétienne*, 320.

45 "D. Les peres & les meres qui forcent leurs enfans d'estre d'Eglise, bien qu'ils en soient indignes, ou seulement pour avoir plus de bien, ou conserver quelque Benefice en leur famille offensent-ils Dieu? … Ils sont cause de la damnation de leurs enfans, & des pechez qu'ils commettent en cet estat, & se damnent avec eux … Ils répondront devant Dieu du scandale que leurs enfans donnent à toute l'Eglise." Joly, *Les Devoirs du chrestien*, 243–4. See similar wording in the Besançon *Catechisme nouveau*, 104–5.

46 "D'y estre appellé de Dieu." *Catechisme du diocese de Meaux*, Paris 1687, 173. For further catechism examples, see [Pouget], *Instructions générales*, 3:254; *Le Vray thresor du chrestien*, 117.

47 This complements Barbara Diefendorf's argument about parents' integration of affection and authority; see Diefendorf, "Give Us Back Our Children," 271–4, 277.

48 For example, Joly, *Prones*, 178–9.

49 "Il vaut trop mieux contrister les parens, que nostre Seigneur Jesus." Le Jau, *Chemin royal*, 817.

50 Cordier, *La famille sainte*, 1:293.

51 "Prieres ... larmes." "La cruauté, dans cette occurance, est la seule veritable pieté." Le Blanc, *Le bon escolier*, 310, 314.

52 "En cette affaire ils sont nos ennemis & contraires à nôtre salut, ainsi que le Sauveur nous l'apprend quand il dit qu'il est venu separer le fils d'avec le Pere, & la fille d'avec la Mere ... Il ne faut pas consulter les parens, parce que ... ils sont interessez, & qu'ils cherchent leur satisfaction & leur avantage ... Les parens sont aveuglez par l'affection naturelle ... Et c'est la raison pour laquelle saint Bernard, non seulement ne trouve pas que l'on manque de respect envers un Pere ou une Mere, quand on ne les consulte pas en cette rencontre, mais il asseure hautement que c'est un acte de grande pieté, de mespriser leur conseil, pour suivre celuy de Jesus-Christ." Emanuel de la Croix, *Le bon chois*, 44–6.

53 "Si vos parens veulent que vous soiez Ecclesiastique ou Religieux, examinez premierement si Dieu vous appelle à l'un de ces êtats." Gobinet, *Instruction de la jeunesse* (1688), 518.

54 "Souvenez-vous pourtant de faire cette resistance avec tout le respect que vous leur devez, en leur remonstrant modestement que vous ne pouvez pas faire ce qu'ils desirent, les raisons que vous en avez, & sur tout la repugnance que vous avez à l'êtat auquel ils vous portent." Ibid., 518–19.

55 Ibid., 520.

56 "Ce seroit une indépendance condemnable, plutôt qu'une liberté évangelique, de vouloir, dans le choix qu'on fait d'un état, se soustraire absolument à l'autorité paternelle ... On n'est pas toujours obligé de se conformer aux désirs d'un pere & d'une mere, trop préoccupés de l'esprit du monde ... Mais au moins faut-il les écouter, peser leurs raisons, y déférer même lorsqu'on n'en a point de plus fortes à y opposer; enfin, soit que l'on condescende à leurs volontés, ou que pour l'intérêt de son salut, on s'en écarte, leur donne toujours tous les témoignages d'une soumission filiale & du respect qu'on reconnoît leur devoir." Bourdaloue, *Exhortations et instructions*, 444–5.

57 "Il ne vous appartient pas de disposer de vos enfans, en ce qui regarde leur vocation & le choix qu'ils ont à faire d'un état. Et j'ajoute toutefois que vous êtes responsables à Dieu du choix que font vos enfans, & de l'état

qu'ils embrassent. Il semble d'abord que ces deux propositions se contredisent, mais … elles s'accordent parfaitement entre elles." Bourdaloue, *Sermons*, 7–8.

58 "D'intervenir à ce choix, d'y participer, d'y avoir un droit de direction & de surveillance." Ibid., 39.

59 "Si les peres ne veulent point faire de fautes, qu'ils se relaschent de beaucoup pour suivre l'inclination de leurs enfans. Si les enfans veulent faire un bon choix, qu'ils fassent estat du conseil de leurs peres. La raison se trouvera foible, si elle n'est secondée de l'inclination: l'inclination sera temeraire, si elle n'est guidée de la raison … Pour faire un bon choix il faut que la raison du pere, & l'inclination du fils en tombent d'accord." Cordier, *La famille sainte*, 1:281. This particular passage concerned choosing among worldly professions, and he repeated the principle in reference to all kinds of vocational choices, such that of entering religion and that of entering marriage and selecting a particular spouse; see Cordier, *La famille sainte*, 1:292–3, 297–300, 396–7.

60 "Si on leur demande à quoy destinés vous vostre fils? que deviendra vostre fille? qu'ils ne répondent rien sinon, Dieu en est le maistre, il en dispoera à sa volonté. Quand il leur aura fait connoistre ce qu'il desire, nous nous efforcerons de leur fournir les moyens pour l'executer." Cordier, *La famille sainte*, 1:288.

61 Ibid., 1:283–4.

62 "D. Que doivent faire les Peres & Meres avant que d'engager leurs Enfans dans une profession de vie? R. Ils doivent prier & consulter Dieu, pour sçavoir si leurs Enfans y sont appellez, & leur faire connoistre les obligations de leur estat." Joly, *Les devoirs du chrestien*, 93; see *Catechisme nouveau*, 43–4.

63 "Il faut 1. S'examiner soy-mesme, & sçavoir de nostre Confesseur, si Dieu nous appelle à l'estat Ecclesiastique." Joly, *Les devoirs du chrestien*, 243.

64 "D. Comment est-ce que les Peres & Meres doivent faire avant que de mettre leurs enfans dans l'Eglise? R. Ils doivent. 1. Examiner si les inclinations de leurs enfans sont convenables à l'estat Ecclesiastique. 2. Faire des prieres & autres bonnes oeuvres pour obtenir de Dieu la grace de connoistre leur vocation. 3. Consulter leurs Confesseurs. 4. Ne les point engager par contrainte, ny avent le temps, ny par l'occasion presente de quelque Benefice. 5. Leur faire entendre auparavant quelles sont les fonctions & les obligations de cet estat, & sçavoir d'eux s'ils sont resolus d'y satisfaire … 7. Les presenter à l'Evesque, & suivre ses avis." Ibid., 244–5.

65 Hardwick, *Practice of Patriarchy*, 61.

66 Bergin, *Church, Society and Religious Change*, 149.

67 Ibid., 65–6.

68 There is evidence for the strong reception of most of these texts. Bourdaloue's lasting preeminence is well known, and his sermons were frequently reprinted. Gobinet's *Instruction de la jeunesse* saw numerous editions in several languages into the nineteenth century, including the first English translation in 1687 and an 1879 Arabic translation. In 1847, missionary priest Adrien Nampon still strongly recommended the work. Martin, *Une religion des livres*, 461–2. Joly's sermons were reprinted several times over the course the eighteenth century and appeared in Migne's nineteenth-century collection *Orateurs sacrés*. Hébrard, *Histoire de Messire Claude Joly*, 490–3. Cordier's treatise saw thirteen editions between 1643 and 1687, as well as at least one eighteenth-century edition and one nineteenth-century edition. Martin, *Religion des livres*, 351. Emanuel de la Croix's treatise – the least accommodating to parents – was reprinted in 1690, 1697, and 1699. Though more obscure, it had some audience, perhaps mediated by Carmelite priests. Diocesan catechisms, used both by *curés* and by lay schoolmasters, were at the heart of education in seventeenth- and eighteenth-century France, especially of rural Catholics. Joly's catechism was in its fourteenth edition by 1751; Bossuet's was reprinted at least six times by 1781; the La Rochelle-Luçon catechisme was reprinted numerous times and the bishop of Angers soon added his sponsorship. Carter, *Creating Catholics*, 4–8, 12–14, 272, 280–3. Although Le Blanc's *Bon escolier* appears to exist in only one edition, his approach to vocation undoutedly affected those under his spiritual care, especially students at Jesuit *collèges* and members of Marian congregations. Walch, *Spiritualité conjugale*, 140. Ecclesiastical court records show that confessors sometimes successfully convinced family members to relent in the coercion of vocations. Schutte, *By Force and Fear*, 60. Biographies of devout elites also sometimes implied acceptance of the principles of rigorist vocational reform. Forrestal, "A Spiritual Inheritance?," 39.

69 "Mais si les parens ne sont point ny d'humeur, ny de vertu à gouster les desseins de Dieu; si on sçait qu'ils employeront toute leur puissance pour les empescher, on peut & je crois, que c'est le meilleur de ne leur en point donner advis, qu'apres la chose faite. Les saints l'ont ainsi pratiqué." Cordier, *La famille sainte*, 1:397.

CONCLUSION

1 Gobinet, *The Instruction of Youth in Christian Piety* (1687); Gobinet, *Onderwijs der jeugd*; Gobinet, *Instruzione della gioventù*; Gobinet,

Underweisung der Jugend; Gobinet, *Instruccion de la juventud*; Gobinet, *Nauki o nabywaniu cnoty*; Ghūbīnīt, *Kitāb irshād al-aḥdāth mundhu al-ṣubūwah wa-al-shubūbīyah fī manhaj al-taqwá al-Masīḥīyah*; Eisenhart, "Heckenstaller, Urban"; Martin, *Une religion des livres*, 461–2; Gobinet, *The Instruction of Youth in Christian Piety* ([1850?]), 2; Hankins, "The Contention of Power," 170–1.

2 See 131n28.

3 Emmanuel de La Croix, *La buona elezione*. There may be a 1669 Italian edition.

4 "Il en existe plusieurs, nous l'avouons; mais celui-ci nous parait supérieur à tous: sans se livrer à de vagues considérations, son Auteur va droit au but." Emmanuel de la Croix, *La Vocation*, v–ix, xi–xvi.

5 Malou, *Règles pour le choix d'un état de vie*; Malou, *Regeln Für Die Wahl Eines Lebensstandes*; Malou, *On the Choice of a State of Life*.

6 Herbert [Alfred Vaughan], "Preface," in Malou, *On the Choice of a State of Life*, viii.

7 Harrison, *The Missionary's Curse*, 207.

8 Darricau, "Un débat sur la vocation," 65–77; Hahnenberg, *Awakening Vocation*, 47–8, 86–9.

9 Butler, *Religious Vocation*, 8, 10.

10 See Taylor, *Sources of the Self*; Sluhovsky, *Becoming a New Self*. For a summary of key points, see Taylor, *Secular Age*, 257–8.

11 John Paul II, "Homily at the Eucharistic Concelebration in the Grounds of the Papal Seminary" (Pune, India, 10 February 1986), no. 3, https://w2.vatican.va/content/john-paul-ii/en/homilies/1986/documents/hf_jp-ii_hom_19860210_pont-ateneo-pune.html.

12 Benedict XVI, "Message of the Holy Father for the 50th World Day of Prayer for Vocations, 21 April 2013."

13 "Even orthodox Christianity," as Charles Taylor (among others) has noted, experienced a "decline of Hell" that began in the seventeenth century and slowly came to fruition in subsequent centuries. Never has the Catholic hierarchy condoned a complete repudiation of Hell, but from the most solemn papal pronouncement to the typical Sunday sermon, the rhetorical motivating force of hellfire has come to be little used. Study of French sermons shows a trend of decline especially during the nineteenth century. Taylor, *Secular Age*, 13; Gibson, "Hellfire and Damnation"; Walker, *Decline of Hell*.

14 One relatively recent Catholic theologian who referred explicitly to such a sin is Grisez, *Living a Christian Life*, 125. For a summary of the theological debate as of the middle of the twentieth century, with a focus on the religious state, see Schleck, *Theology of Vocations*, 207–28.

15 Vermeersch, *Religious and Ecclesiastical Vocation*, 43.

16 John Paul II, "Message of His Holiness Pope John Paul II for the XXXII World Day of Prayer for Vocations," nos. 1–2; Benedict XVI, "Message of the Holy Father Benedict XVI on the Occasion of the Twenty-Fifth World Youth Day (March 28, 2010)," nos. 3–4; Francis, "Morning Meditation in the Chapel of the Domus Sanctae Marthae: Sisters and Priests Free from Idolatry."

17 "Vocations and Discernment FAQ."

18 Bruskewitz, *God's Plan for You*, 18.

19 Elliott, *Discernment Do's and Don'ts*, xviii–xix.

20 Rieff, *The Triumph of the Therapeutic*, 223.

21 Winfrey, "What Oprah Knows for Sure about Finding Your Calling." See also Pete Davis, who writes that "the stakes are high," both personally and societally; for "browsing forever can lead to great despair, while dedication can lead to great joy," and "there are so many big problems to solve" but "simply not enough people dedicated to tackling them." Davis, *Dedicated*, 17.

22 See "Final Document of the Synod"; Francis, "Christus Vivit."

23 "Final Document of the Synod," no. 104.

24 These categories are explored especially in Taylor, *A Secular Age*, chaps. 12–13.

25 Ibid., 437–8.

26 Ibid., 459–60.

27 Ibid., 445.

28 Ibid.

29 Ibid., 471.

30 Ibid., 460, 471–2.

31 See especially ibid., chap. 13.

32 Ibid., 472–3.

33 Ibid., 714.

34 Ibid., 726.

35 Gregory, *The Unintended Reformation*, 74. Gregory, it should be noted, critiques Taylor for overemphasizing the degree to which present-day people, both religious or antireligious, are either conflicted or ambivalent about their own truth claims. See Gregory, *The Unintended Reformation*, 10–12.

36 See 131n24.

Bibliography

Abregé de la vie du Pere François de Clugny, prêtre de l'Oratoire. Lyon: Antoine Briasson, 1698.

"Abregé de la vie et des vertus de nostre trés chere Soeur Françoise Agnés Descomps," n.d., 4-LD173-2 (2), Agen, 10 September 1714. Bibliothèque nationale de France, Collection of Visitation circular letters.

Ambrosius a S. Teresia. *Nomenclator missionariorum Ordinis Carmelitarum discalceatorum*. Roma: Curia Generalitia, 1944.

Aquinas, Thomas. *Summa Theologiae*. Vol. 47. 60 vols. London: Blackfriars, 1973.

Arnauld, Angélique. *Relation écrite par la Mère Angélique Arnauld sur Port-Royal*. Edited by Louis Cognet. Paris: Bernard Grasset, 1949.

Arnauld, Antoine. *De la frequente communion*. Paris: Antoine Vitré, 1643.

"Augsburg Confession." In *Concordia Triglotta: Libri Symbolici Ecclesiae Lutheranae, Germanice-Latine-Anglice*, edited by F. Bente, translated by F. Bente and W.H.T. Dau, 37–95. St Louis, MO: Concordia Publishing House, 1921.

Aumann, Jordan. *On the Front Lines: The Lay Person in the Church after Vatican II*. New York: Alba House, 1990.

Balthasar, Hans Urs von. *Der Laie Und Der Ordenstand*. Einsiedeln: Johannes, 1948.

– *The Laity in the Life of the Counsels: The Church's Mission in the World*. Translated by Brian McNeil and D.C. Schindler. San Francisco: Ignatius Press, 1993.

Batterel, Louis. *Memoires domestiques pour servir à l'histoire de l'Oratoire*. Vol. 3. Paris: Alphonse Picard et fils, 1904.

Bauman, Zygmunt. *Liquid Modernity*. Cambridge, UK: Polity Press, 2000.

Bell, David N. *A Saint in the Sun: Praising Saint Bernard in the France of Louis XIV*. Collegeville, MN: Cistercian Publications, 2017.

Benedict XVI. "Message of the Holy Father Benedict XVI on the Occasion of the Twenty-Fifth World Youth Day (March 28, 2010)." Vatican City, 22 February 2010. http://www.vatican.va/content/benedict-xvi/en/messages/youth/documents/hf_ben-xvi_mes_20100222_youth.html.

– "Message of the Holy Father for the 50th World Day of Prayer for Vocations, 21 April 2013." Vatican City, 6 October 2012. http://www.vatican.va/content/benedict-xvi/en/messages/vocations/documents/hf_ben-xvi_mes_20121006_l-vocations.html.

Bergin, Joseph. *Church, Society and Religious Change in France, 1580–1730*. New Haven, CT: Yale University Press, 2009.

– *Crown, Church and Episcopate Under Louis XIV*. New Haven, CT: Yale University Press, 2004.

– *The Politics of Religion in Early Modern France*. New Haven, CT: Yale University Press, 2014.

Bériou, Nicole, and David L. D'Avray. "Henry of Provins, O.P.'s Comparison of the Dominican and Franciscan Orders with the 'Order' of Matrimony." *Archivum Fratrum Praedicatorum* 49 (1979): 513–17.

Besson, Joseph. *La Syrie Sainte*. Vol. 2. Paris: Jean Henault, 1660.

Beuvelet, Mathieu. *La Vraye et solide devotion*. 3rd ed. Paris: Georges Iosse, 1661.

– *Meditations sur les principales veritez chrestiennes et ecclesiastiques*. Vol. 2. Paris: Georges Josse, 1655.

Binet, Estienne. "Abregé de la perfection chrestienne." In *Recueil des oeuvres spirituelles*, 2nd ed., 847–83. Rouen: Richard L'Allemant, 1627.

Bireley, Robert. *The Refashioning of Catholicism, 1450–1700: A Reassessment of the Counter Reformation*. Washington, DC: Catholic University of America Press, 1999.

Biroat, Jacques. *Oraison funèbre de feue très-haute et très-puissante princesse Madame Éléonor de Bergh, duchesse de Bouillon*. Paris: Edme Couterot, 1663.

Boer, Wietse de. *The Conquest of the Soul: Confession, Discipline, and Public Order in Counter-Reformation Milan*. Leiden: Brill, 2001.

Bolin, Joseph. "'The Will to Enter Religious Life Does Not Need to Be Tested to See Whether It Is from God' (ST II-II 189:10): Can Aquinas' Understanding of Vocation Still Work?" In *The Disciples' Call: Theologies of Vocation from Scripture to the Present Day*, edited by Christopher Jamison, 67–84. London: Bloomsbury, 2013.

Bonino, Serge-Thomas. "Charisms, Forms, and States of Life (IIa IIae, Qq. 171-189)." In *The Ethics of Aquinas*, edited by Stephen J. Pope, translated by Mary Thomas Noble, 340–52. Washington, DC: Georgetown University Press, 2002.

Bossy, John. *Christianity in the West, 1400–1700*. Oxford: Oxford University Press, 1985.

Bourdaloue, Louis. *Exhortations et instructions chrétiennes*. Vol. 2. Paris: Rigaud, 1723.

– *Sermons du père Bourdaloue, de la Compagnie de Jesus. Pour les dimanches*. Vol. 1. Paris: Rigaud, 1716.

Breen, Michael P. "Law, Society, and the State in Early Modern France." *Journal of Modern History* 83, no. 2 (2011): 346–86.

Brown, D. Catherine. *Pastor and Laity in the Theology of Jean Gerson*. Cambridge, UK: Cambridge University Press, 1987.

Brundage, James A. *Law, Sex, and Christian Society in Medieval Europe*. Chicago: University of Chicago Press, 1987.

Brungs, Robert A. *A Priestly People*. New York: Sheed and Ward, 1968.

Bruskewitz, Fabian. *God's Plan for You: Understanding Your Personal Vocation*. Irving, TX: Basilica Press, 2008.

Bucer, Martin. "De coelibatu sacerdotum." In *Scripta duo adversaria D. Bartholomaei Latomi* LL. *Doctoris, et Martini Buceri theologi*, 53–121. Strasbourg: Wendelinus Rihelius, 1544.

Buechner, Frederick. *Wishful Thinking: A Theological* ABC. New York: Harper & Row, 1973.

Butler, Richard. *Religious Vocation: An Unnecessary Mystery*. Chicago: H. Regnery Co., 1961.

Calvin, John. *Institution de La Religion Chrestienne*. Geneva: Jean Crespin, 1560.

Cameron, Euan. *The European Reformation*. 2nd ed. Oxford: Oxford University Press, 2012.

Camus, Jean-Pierre. *L'Esprit du B. François de Sales*. Vol. 5. Paris: Gervais Alliot, 1641.

Carter, Karen E. *Creating Catholics: Catechism and Primary Education in Early Modern France*. Notre Dame, IN: University of Notre Dame Press, 2011.

Castets, Ferdinand. *Bourdaloue, La Vie et La Prédication d'un Religieux au XVIIe Siècle*. Paris: Ch. Delagrave, 1901.

Catechisme du diocese de Meaux. Paris: Sebastien Mabre-Cramoisy, 1687.

Catechisme nouveau, Dressé en faveur de la Jeunesse du Diocese de Besançon, pour la faciliter à apprendre les verités du Christianisme. Besançon: Loüis Rigoine, 1687.

Catechisme Ou Doctrine Chrétienne. Imprime Par Ordre de Messeigneurs Les Evêques de La Rochelle & de Luçon, pour l'usage de Leurs Diocéses. La Rochelle: La Veuve Barthelemy Blanchet, 1676.

Chantal, Jeanne-Françoise Frémyot de. "Entretien LVIII, Sur la réception des sujets." In *Sainte Jeanne-Françoise Frémyot de Chantal: sa vie et ses oeuvres*, Vol. 2, 419–25. Paris: E. Plon, 1875.

Cheminais, Timoléon. *Sermons du pere Cheminais de la Compagnie de Jesus*. 3rd ed. Vol. 2. Paris: George & Loüis Josse, 1693.

Christensen-Nugues, Charlotte. "Parental Authority and Freedom of Choice: The Debate on Clandestinity and Parental Consent at the Council of Trent (1545–63)." *Sixteenth Century Journal* 45, no. 1 (2014): 51–72.

Clugny, François de. *Catechisme de la dévotion. Ou instruction familiére de tout ce qu'il faut savoir, & de tout ce qu'il faut faire, pour vivre d'une vie vraîment Dévote dans le siécle, en quelque condition que l'on soit, principalement pour les personnes simples*. Lyon: Jean Certe, 1681.

"Confutatio Confessionis Augustanae." In *Philippi Melanthonis Opera quae supersunt omnia*, edited by Karl Gottlieb Bretschneider and Heinrich Ernst Bindseil, 27: 81–184. Braunschweig: C.A. Schwetschke et Filium, 1859.

Congar, Yves M.-J. *Jalons pour une théologie du laïcat*. Paris: Éditions du Cerf, 1953.

– *Lay People in the Church: A Study for a Theology of the Laity*. Translated by Donald Attwater. Westminster, MD: Newman Press, 1959.

Conley, John J. *Adoration and Annihilation: The Convent Philosophy of Port-Royal*. Notre Dame, IN: University of Notre Dame Press, 2009.

– *The Other Pascals: The Philosophy of Jacqueline Pascal, Gilberte Pascal Périer, and Marguerite Périer*. Notre Dame, IN: University of Notre Dame Press, 2019.

Constable, Giles. *Three Studies in Medieval Religious and Social Thought*. Cambridge: Cambridge University Press, 1995.

Cordier, Jean. *La famille sainte*. 3 vols. Paris: Denys Bechet, 1666.

Cutter, Elissa. "Monastic Reform in Seventeenth-Century France: The Cistercian and Tridentine Influences on Angélique Arnauld's Reform of the Convent of Port-Royal." *Cistercian Studies Quarterly* 52, no. 4 (2017): 425–51.

Dalmases, Cándido de. "Histoire de la rédaction des Exercices spirituels 1522 à 1548." In *Texte autographe des Exercices Spirituels et*

Documents contemporains (1526–1615), edited by Édouard Gueydan et al., 11–35. Paris: Desclée de Brouwer, 1986.

Dangles, Bernard. *Particuliere conduite asseurée a la perfection de chaque persone selon son estat*. Paris: Sebastien Cramoisy, 1638.

Darricau, Raymond. "Un débat sur la vocation au début du XXe siècle: l'affaire Lahitton (1909–1912)." In *La vocation religieuse et sacerdotale en France, XVII-XIX siècles : actes de la deuxième Rencontre d'histoire religieuse, organisée à Fontevraud, le 9 octobre 1978 par le Centre culturel de l'Ouest et le Centre de recherches d'histoire religieuse et d'histoire des idées (Université d'Angers)*, 65–77. Angers: Université d'Angers, U.E.R. des lettres et sciences humaines, Centre de recherches d'histoire religieuse et d'histoire des idées, 1979.

Davis, Pete. *Dedicated: The Case for Commitment in an Age of Infinite Browsing*. New York: Avid Reader Press, 2021.

D'Avray, David L. "The Gospel of the Marriage Feast of Cana and Marriage Preaching in France." In *The Study of the Bible in the Middle Ages*, edited by Katherine Walsh and Diana Wood, 3rd ed., 207–24. Oxford: B. Blackwell, 1985.

De Jong, Mayke. *In Samuel's Image: Child Oblation in the Early Medieval West*. Leiden: Brill, 1996.

Delumeau, Jean. *L'aveu et Le Pardon: Les Difficultés de La Confession, XIIIe–XVIIIe Siècle*. Paris: Fayard, 1990.

– *Le Péché et La Peur: La Culpabilisation En Occident, XIIIe–XVIIIe Siècles*. Paris: Fayard, 1983.

– *Rassurer et protéger: Le sentiment de sécurité dans l'Occident d'autrefois*. Paris: Fayard, 1989.

– *Sin and Fear: The Emergence of a Western Guilt Culture, 13th–18th Centuries*. Translated by Eric Nicholson. New York: St Martin's Press, 1990.

Diefendorf, Barbara B. "Give Us Back Our Children: Patriarchal Authority and Parental Consent to Religious Vocations in Early Counter-Reformation France." *Journal of Modern History* 68, no. 2 (1996): 265–307.

– *Planting the Cross: Catholic Reform and Renewal in Sixteenth- and Seventeenth-Century France*. Oxford: Oxford University Press, 2019.

Dinet, Dominique. "Les entrées en religion à la Visitation (XVIIe et XVIIIe siècles)." In *Visitation et Visitandines aux XVIIe et XVIIIe siècles. Actes du Colloque d'Annecy, 3–5 juin 1999*, edited by Bernard Dompnier and Dominique Julia, 177–93. Saint-Étienne: Publications de l'Université de Saint-Étienne, 2001.

– *Vocation et fidélité. Le recrutement des réguliers dans les diocèses d'Auxerre, Langres et Dijon (XVIIe–XVIIIe)*. Paris: Economica, 1988.
Dompnier, Bernard, ed. "Vocations d'Ancien Régime: Les gens d'Église en Auvergne aux XVIIe et XVIIIe siècles, special issue." *Revue d'Auvergne* 544–5 (1997).
Donlan, Thomas A. *The Reform of Zeal: François de Sales and Militant French Catholicism*. St Andrews: Centre for French History and Culture of the University of St Andrews, 2018.
Doohan, Leonard. *The Laity: A Bibliography*. Wilmington, DE: Michael Glazier, 1987.
– *The Lay-Centered Church*. Minneapolis, MN: Winston Press, 1984.
Drillat, Geneviève. "Les Visitandines francaises (1667–1767)." In *La Mort des pays de Cocagne*, edited by Jean Delumeau, 189–205. Paris: Publications de la Sorbonne, 1976.
Dupré, Louis. *Passage to Modernity: An Essay in the Hermeneutics of Nature and Culture*. New Haven, CT: Yale University Press, 1993.
Dusch, Brigitte. "Eléonore de Bergh, Dernière Princesse de Sedan." *Terres Ardennaises* 51 (1995): 14–18.
Eisenhart, Johann August Ritter von. "Heckenstaller, Urban." In *Allgemeine Deutsche Biographie*, 11: 206–7. Leipzig: Duncker & Humblot, 1880.
Elliott, George. *Discernment Do's and Don'ts: A Practical Guide to Vocational Discernment*. Charlotte, NC: TAN Books, 2018.
Emanuel de la Croix. *Le bon chois, ou instruction pour bien choisir un état de vie*. Lyon: Molin, 1667.
– *La buona elezione, o sia istruzione per ben eleggere uno stato di vita*. Translated by C.G.G. Milan: Giuseppe Pandolfo Malatesta, 1718.
– [as Emmanuel de la Croix]. *La Vocation, ou Instructions propres à diriger une âme dans le choix d'un état*. Translated by C.G.G. and Amédée Vignolo. Lyon: J.-B. Pélagaud et Cie, 1844.
Farr, James R. *Authority and Sexuality in Early Modern Burgundy (1550–1730)*. New York: Oxford University Press, 1995.
Fénelon, [François de Salignac de la Mothe]. "Avis de Monsieur de Fenelon Archevêque de Cambray, à une Dame de qualité sur l'éducation de Mademoiselle sa fille." In *De l'Education des filles*, nouvelle edition, 271–99. Paris: Emery, Emery, Saugrain, et P. Martin, 1719.
– *Éducation des filles*. Paris: Pierre Aubouin, Pierre Emery, & Charles Clousier, 1687.
"Final Document of the Synod of Bishops on Young People, Faith and Vocational Discernment," October 2018. http://www.synod.va/content/

synod2018/en/fede-discernimento-vocazione/final-document-of-the-synod-of-bishops-on-young-people--faith-an.html.

Forrestal, Alison. "A Spiritual Inheritance? Family Spirit, Virtue and Vocation in the Vies of the Lamoignon *Dévots*." *French History* 35 (2021): 24–48.

– *Vincent de Paul, the Lazarist Mission, and French Catholic Reform*. Oxford: Oxford University Press, 2017.

Fox, Zeni, and Regina Bechtle, eds. *Called and Chosen: Toward a Spirituality for Lay Leaders*. Lanham, MD: Rowan and Littlefield, 2005.

Fraine, Jean de. *The Bible on Vocation and Election*. De Pere, WI: St Norbert Abbey Press, 1966.

Francis. "Christus Vivit, Post-Synodal Exhortation to Young People and to the Entire People of God," 25 March 2019. http://www.synod.va/content/synod2018/en/fede-discernimento-vocazione/-christus-vivit---post-synodal-exhortation-to-young-people-and-t.html.

– "Morning Meditation in the Chapel of the Domus Sanctae Marthae: Sisters and Priests Free from Idolatry." Vatican City, 3 March 2014. https://w2.vatican.va/content/francesco/en/cotidie/2014/documents/papa-francesco-cotidie_20140303_sisters-and-priests.html.

François de Sales. *Oeuvres de Saint François de Sales évêque et prince de Genève et docteur de l'église*. Ed. complète. 27 vols. Annecy: J. Niérat, 1892–1964.

Freedman, Paul. *Images of the Medieval Peasant*. Stanford, CA: Stanford University Press, 1999.

Gay, Jean-Pascal. *Morales en conflit: Théologie et polémique au Grand Siècle (1640–1700)*. Paris: Cerf, 2011.

Gerken, John D. *Toward a Theology of the Layman*. New York: Herder and Herder, 1963.

Gibson, Ralph. "Hellfire and Damnation in Nineteenth-Century France." *Catholic Historical Review* 74, no. 3 (1988): 383–402.

Giesey, Ralph E. "Rules of Inheritance and Strategies of Mobility in Prerevolutionary France." *American Historical Review* 82, no. 2 (1977): 271–89.

Gilbert, David. *"Le grand secret de la vocation": Louis Tronson (1622–1700)*. Paris: Honoré Champion, 2018.

Giordano, Silvano, ed. *Le Carmel en Terre Sainte: Des origines à nos jours*. Paris: Médiaspaul, 1995.

Gobinet, Charles. *Instruccion de la juventud en la piedad christiana*. Translated by Juan Antonio Tubique. Barcelona: Joseph Texidò, 1731.

– *Instruction de la jeunesse en la pieté chrestienne*. Paris: François le Cointe, 1655.

– *Instruction de la jeunesse en la piété chrétienne*. Nouvelle edition. Paris: François le Cointe et Urbain Coutelier, 1688.

– *Instruction sur la Penitence, et sur la sainte Communion, seconde partie de l'Instruction de la jeunesse*. Lyon: Jaques Faeton, 1674. Originally published Paris: François le Cointe, 1668.

– *The Instruction of Youth in Christian Piety*. Translated by [Nicholas Leyburn]. London: Henry Hills, 1687.

– *The Instruction of Youth in Christian Piety: Taken Out of the Sacred Scriptures and Holy Fathers*. Boston: P. Donahoe, [1850?].

– [as Carlo Gobinet]. *Instruzione della gioventù nella pietà cristiana*. Translated by Giuseppe Antolini. 2 vols. Venice: Paolo Baglioni, 1708.

– [as Kārlūs Ghūbīnīt]. *Kitāb irshād al-aḥdāth mundhu al-ṣubūwah wa-al-shubūbīyah fī manhaj al-taqwá al-Masīḥīyah*. Jerusalem: Maṯba'at al-Ābā' al-Faransīskānīyīn, 1879.

–[as Karol Gobinet]. *Nauki o nabywaniu cnoty w młodości i obraniu stanu życia na pięć części podzielone*. Translated by Martynian Nafalski. Warsaw: J.K. Mci y Rzpltey, at the Kollegium Scholarum Piarum, 1768.

– [as Karel Gobinet]. *Onderwijs der jeugd in de Christelijke godvruchtigheid*. Antwerp: Henrik van Rhyn, 1693.

– [as Carolus Gobinet]. *Underweisung der Jugend, in der Christlichen Gottseeligkeit*. Translated by Urban Heckhenstaller. Freising: Johann Christian Carl Immel, 1714.

Gonsin, Charles. *Catechisme dogmatique et historique, à l'usage du Diocese d'Amiens*. Paris: L. Roulland fils, 1693.

Goré, Jeanne-Lydie. *L'itinéraire de Fénelon: humanisme et spiritualité*. Paris: Presses universitaires de France, 1957.

Grandet, Joseph. *Les saints prêtres français du XVIIe siècle*. Vol. 2. Angers, 1897.

Green, Thomas H. *Come Down, Zacchaeus: Spirituality and the Laity*. Notre Dame, IN: Ave Maria Press, 1988.

Gregory, Brad S. *The Unintended Reformation: How a Religious Revolution Secularized Society*. Cambridge, MA: Belknap Press of Harvard University Press, 2012.

Gres-Gayer, Jacques M. *Jansénisme en Sorbonne, 1643–1656*. Paris: Klincksieck, 1996.

Griselle, Eugène. *Bourdaloue: histoire critique de sa prédication*. 3 vols. Paris: Société française d'imprimerie et de librairie (vols. 1–2) and Gabriel Beauchesne (vol. 3), 1901–06.

Grisez, Germain. *Living a Christian Life*. Vol. 2. *The Way of the Lord Jesus*. Quincy, IL: Franciscan Press, 1993.

Hahnenberg, Edward P. *Awakening Vocation: A Theology of Christian Call*. Collegeville, MN: Liturgical Press, 2010.

Hankins, Kenneth Miles Wardle. "'The Contention of Power': The Role of the Jesuits in the Catholic Life of Bristol, 1700–1830." PhD diss., University of Bristol, 1998.

Hanley, Sarah. "Engendering the State: Family Formation and State Building in Early Modern France." *French Historical Studies* 16, no. 1 (1989): 4–27.

– "Family and State in Early Modern France: The Marital Law Compact." In *Connecting Spheres: European Women in a Globalizing World, 1500 to the Present*, edited by Marilyn J. Boxer and Jean H. Quataert, 53–63. New York: Oxford University Press, 1987.

Hardwick, Julie. *The Practice of Patriarchy: Gender and the Politics of Household Authority in Early Modern France*. University Park, PA: Pennsylvania State University Press, 1998.

Harman, Paul F. "Vocation and the Spiritual Exercises of St Ignatius of Loyola." In *Revisiting the Idea of Vocation: Theological Explorations*, edited by John C. Haughey, 97–118. Washington, DC: Catholic University of America Press, 2004.

Harrison, Henrietta. *The Missionary's Curse and Other Tales from a Chinese Catholic Village*. Berkeley: University of California Press, 2013.

Hébrard, Pierre. *Histoire de Messire Claude Joly, éveque et comte d'Agen (1610–1678)*. F. Brousse, 1905.

Helms, Chad. "Introduction." In *Fénelon: Selected Writings*, 1–113. Mahwah, NJ: Paulist Press, 2006.

Henryot, Fabienne. "Le Prédicateur et Ses Livres. Normes Oratoires et Sermonnaires Dans Les Couvents Mendiants Urbains à l'époque Moderne (Lorraine & Luxembourg)." In *La Parole Publique En Ville, Des Réformes à La Révolution*, edited by S. Simiz, 39–60. Nancy, France: Presses Universitaires du Septentrion (Villeneuve d'Ascq), 2011.

Hesburgh, Theodore M. *The Theology of Catholic Action*. Notre Dame, IN: Ave Maria Press, 1946.

Holl, Karl. "The History of the Word Vocation (Beruf)." Translated by Heber F. Peacock. *Review & Expositor* 55, no. 2 (1958): 126–54.

Ignatius of Loyola. *Exercitia Spiritualia*. Rome: Antonio Blado, 1548.

– *The Spiritual Exercises of St Ignatius: Based on Studies in the Language of the Autograph*. Translated by Louis J. Puhl. Chicago: Loyola Press, 1951.

– *Texte autographe des Exercices Spirituels et Documents contemporains (1526–1615)*. Edited by Édouard Gueydan et al. Paris: Desclée de Brouwer, 1986.

Jansen, Cornelius. *Augustinus*. 3 vols. Louvain: Jacobus Zegers, 1640.

John Paul II. "Christifideles Laici, Post-Synodal Apostolic Exhortation on the Vocation and Mission of the Lay Faithful in the Church and in the World," 30 December 1988. http://www.vatican.va/holy_father/john_paul_ii/apost_exhortations/documents/hf_jp-ii_exh_30121988_christifideles-laici_en.html.

– "Homily at the Eucharistic Concelebration in the Grounds of the Papal Seminary." Pune, India, 10 February 1986. https://w2.vatican.va/content/john-paul-ii/en/homilies/1986/documents/hf_jp-ii_hom_19860210_pont-ateneo-pune.html.

– "Message of His Holiness Pope John Paul II for the XXXII World Day of Prayer for Vocations." Vatican City, 18 October 1994. http://www.vatican.va/content/benedict-xvi/en/messages/vocations/documents/hf_ben-xvi_mes_20121006_l-vocations.html.

Joly, Claude. *Les devoirs du chrestien dressez en forme de catechisme*. 6th ed. Paris: Pierre le Petit, 1677.

– *Prones de messire Claude Joli, eveque et comte d'Agen, pour tous les dimanches de l'année*. Vol. 1. Paris: Edme Couterot, 1693.

Kaufman, Peter Iver. "John Colet's Opus de Sacramentis and Clerical Anticlericalism: The Limitations of 'Ordinary Wayes.'" *Journal of British Studies* 22, no. 1 (1982): 1–22.

Keller-Lapp, Heidi. "Devenir des Jésuitesses: les missionaires Ursulines du monde Atlantique." *Histoire et Missions Chrétiennes* 16 (2010): 19–51.

Kelly, Bernard J. *Lay Spirituality: Its Theory and Practice*. London: Sheed and Ward, 1980.

[La Chétardie, Joachim de]. *Catechismes ou abregés de la doctrine chrétienne*. 2nd ed. Bourges: François Toubeau, 1690.

La Colombière, Claude. *Reflexions chrêtiennes*. Lyon: Anisson, Posuel, & Rigaud, 1684.

La Font, Pierre de. *Prosnes pour tous les dimanches de l'année*. Vol. 1. Paris: J.B. Cusson et P. Witte, 1701.

– *Prosnes pour tous les dimanches de l'année*. Vol. 3. Paris: J. B. Cusson et P. Witte, 1701.

Lakeland, Paul. *The Liberation of the Laity: In Search of an Accountable Church*. New York: Continuum, 2003.

Lane, Christopher J. "Gentle Holiness in the Vocational Culture of

Seventeenth-Century French Visitandine Nuns." In *Lived Religion and Everyday Life in Early Modern Hagiographic Material*, edited by Jenni Kuuliala, Rose-Marie Peake, and Päivi Räisänen-Schröder, 51–75. Cham, Switzerland: Palgrave Macmillan, 2019.

Lanza, Janine Marie. *From Wives to Widows in Early Modern Paris: Gender, Economy, and Law*. Aldershot, UK: Ashgate, 2007.

Lawrence, C.H. *Medieval Monasticism: Forms of Religious Life in Western Europe in the Middle Ages*. 4th ed. London: Routledge, 2015.

Le Blanc, Thomas. *Le Bon Escolier, ou Instruction pour la jeunesse qui estudie*. Paris: Jean Riviere, 1664.

Le Jau, Jean. *Chemin royal pour conduire les ames à faire eslection d'un genre de vie qui soit conforme à la volonté de Dieu*. Paris: Denys Moreau, 1628.

Les Constitutions du monastere de Port Royal du S. Sacrement. Mons: Gaspard Migeot, 1665.

Le Vray thresor du chrestien. Ou Instruction familiere de catechisme, dressé en faveur de la jeunesse, qui desire de s'avancer en la cognoissance de Dieu. Par le commandement de Monseigneur l'Evesque & Comte de Noyon, Pair de France. S. Quentin: Claude le Queux, 1648.

Leclercq, Jean. "Lettres de Vocation à La Vie Monastique." In *Analecta Monastica: Textes et Études Sur La Vie Des Moines Au Moyen Âge, Troisième Série*, 169–97. Studia Anselmiana, Fasc. 37. Rome: Herder, 1955.

Lehmann, Hartmut, and Guenther Roth, eds. *Weber's Protestant Ethic: Origins, Evidence, Contexts*. Washington, DC: German Historical Institute, 1993.

Lessius, Leonardus. *Disputatio de Statu Vitae Deligendo et Religionis Ingressu*. Antwerp: Plantin, 1613.

Lindeborn, Jan. *Instructions chrestiennes sur le sacrement de mariage et sur l'education des enfans*. Paris: Helie Josset, 1679.

Loriot, Julien. *Sermons sur les plus importantes matieres de la morale chrétienne*. 3rd ed. Vol. 4. Paris: Charles Robustel, 1700.

Luther, Martin. "De captivitate Babylonica ecclesiae, praeludium. 1520." In *D. Martin Luthers Werke: kritische Gesamtausgabe*, 6: 497–573. Weimar: Hermann Böhlau, 1888.

– "De votis monasticis iudicium. 1521." In *D. Martin Luthers Werke: kritische Gesamtausgabe*, 8: 573–669. Weimar: Hermann Böhlau, 1889.

– "On the Estate of Marriage." In *Luther's Works*, edited by Walther I. Brandt and Helmut T. Lehmann, translated by Walther I. Brandt, 45: 11–49. Philadelphia: Muhlenberg Press, 1962.

Malou, Jean-Baptiste. *On the Choice of a State of Life*. Translated by Aloysius Del Vittorio. London: Burns & Oates, 1874.

– *Regeln für die Wahl eines Lebensstandes*. Translated by J.B. Jungmann. Mainz: Kirchheim, 1863.

– *Règles pour le choix d'un état de vie proposées à la jeunesse chrétienne*. Brussels: H. Goemaere, 1860.

Marin, Juan M. "A Jesuit Mystic's Feminine Melancholia: Jean-Joseph Surin SJ (1600–1665)." *Journal of Men, Masculinities and Spirituality* 1, no. 1 (2007): 65–76.

Martin, Philippe. *Une religion des livres (1640–1850)*. Paris: Cerf, 2003.

Mascaron, Jules. "Oraison funebre de trés-haut et trés-puissant prince Henry de la Tour-d'Auvergne, vicomte de Turenne." In *Recueil des oraisons funebres*, Nouvelle édition, 317–424. Paris: Jean Dessaint, 1745.

McGoldrick, Terence. "'Everything in Marriage Is Holy.' Francis de Sales, a Christian Humanist Theology of Marriage." *Salesianum* 75 (2013): 761–80.

Melanchthon, Philipp. "Apology of the Augsburg Confession." In *Concordia Triglotta: Libri Symbolici Ecclesiae Lutheranae, Germanice-Latine-Anglice*, edited by F. Bente, translated by F. Bente and W.H.T. Dau, 97–451. St Louis, MO: Concordia Publishing House, 1921.

Mellinghoff-Bourgerie, Viviane. "Four Centuries of Editions of the *Introduction to the Devout Life*: Bibliographical Lessons." In *Encountering Anew the Familiar: Francis de Sales's* Introduction to the Devout Life *at 400 Years*, edited by Joseph F. Chorpenning, 1–22. Rome: International Commission for Salesian Studies, 2012.

Melloni, Javier. *The Exercises of St Ignatius Loyola in the Western Tradition*. Leominster, UK: Gracewing, 2000.

Miron de l'Espinay, A. *Robert Miron et l'administration municipale de Paris de 1614 à 1616. Le tiers aux États généraux de 1614. L'ambassade française en Suisse de 1617 à 1672*. Paris: Plon-Nourrit, 1922.

Nepveu, François. *Pensées, ou réflexions chrétiennes pour tous les jours de l'année*. 3rd ed. Vol. 3. Lyon: Antoine Boudet, 1700. Originally published Paris: E. Michallet, 1695.

O'Brien, William P. "Claude La Colombière (1641–82), Marguerite-Marie Alacoque (1647–90), and Devotion to the Sacred Heart." In *A Companion to Jesuit Mysticism*, edited by Robert A. Maryks, 166–92. Leiden: Brill, 2017.

– "Une 'manière' de prêcher: Rhétorique et sainteté chez Claude la Colombière." *Archivum Historicum Societatis Iesu* 79, no. 157 (2010): 127–71.

O'Connor, William R. *The Layman's Call*. New York: P.J. Kennedy & Sons, 1942.

O'Gara, James, ed. *The Layman in the Church*. New York: Herder and Herder, 1962.

Olin, John C. *The Catholic Reformation: Savonarola to Ignatius Loyola*. New York: Harper & Row, 1969.

O'Malley, John W. *The First Jesuits*. Cambridge, MA: Harvard University Press, 1993.

Ozment, Steven E. *The Age of Reform (1250-1550): An Intellectual and Religious History of Late Medieval and Reformation Europe*. New Haven, CT: Yale University Press, 1980.

– *The Reformation in the Cities: The Appeal of Protestantism to Sixteenth-Century Germany and Switzerland*. New Haven, CT: Yale University Press, 1975.

– *When Fathers Ruled: Family Life in Reformation Europe*. Cambridge, MA: Harvard University Press, 1983.

Parish, Richard. *Catholic Particularity in Seventeenth-Century French Writing: "Christianity Is Strange."* Oxford: Oxford University Press, 2011.

Pascal, Jacqueline. *A Rule for Children and Other Writings*. Edited and translated by John J. Conley. Chicago: University of Chicago Press, 2003.

Parsons, Jotham. "Vocation in Seventeenth-Century France: The Catholic Ethic and the Spirit of Étatisme." *French History* 28, no. 3 (2014): 322–42.

Peregrinus de Opole. *Sermones de Tempore et de Sanctis*. Edited by Ryszard Tatarzyński. Warsaw: Institutum Thomisticum PP. Dominicanorum Varsaviensium, 1997.

Phillips, Gerard. *Le Rôle du Laïcat dans l'église*. Tournai: Desclée de Brouwer, 1954.

– *The Role of the Laity in the Church*. Translated by John H. Gilbert and James Moudry. Chicago: Fides, 1957.

Pillorget, René. "Vocation Religieuse et état en France aux XVIe et XVIIe siècles." In *La vocation religieuse et sacerdotale en France, XVII–XIX siècles : actes de la deuxième Rencontre d'histoire religieuse, organisée à Fontevraud, le 9 octobre 1978 par le Centre culturel de l'Ouest et le Centre de recherches d'histoire religieuse et d'histoire des idées (Université d'Angers)*, 9–18. Angers: Université d'Angers, U.E.R. des lettres et sciences humaines, Centre de recherches d'histoire religieuse et d'histoire des idées, 1979.

Placher, William C., ed. *Callings: Twenty Centuries of Christian Wisdom on Vocation*. Grand Rapids, MI: Eerdmans, 2005.

Platus, Hieronymus [Girolamo Piatti]. *De bono status religiosi libri tres: ab ipso auctore nunc denuo aucti atque recogniti, & et in Germania primum excusi*. Ingolstadt: David Sartorius, 1590.

Pocetto, Alexander. "Jean-Pierre Camus (1584–1652) as Disseminator of the Salesian Spirit." International Commission for Salesian Studies, September 2001. http://www.franz-von-sales.de/icss_de/artikel/english/pocetto08.html.

Pommereuse, Marie de. *Les Chroniques de l'ordre Des Ursulines*. Troisiéme Partie. Paris: Jean Henault, 1673.

[Pouget, François-Aimé]. *Instructions générales en forme de catechisme*. 4 vols. Paris: Augustin Leguerrier, 1702.

Price, Richard. "Did the Early Monastic Tradition Have a Concept of Vocation?" In *The Disciples' Call: Theologies of Vocation from Scripture to the Present Day*, edited by Christopher Jamison, 29–42. London: Bloomsbury, 2013.

Pringy, [Jeanne-Michelle] de. *La vie du Pere Bourdaloue de la Compagnie de Jesus*. Paris: Pierre Ribou, 1705.

Quantin, Jean-Louis. "Catholic Moral Theology, 1550–1800." In *The Oxford Handbook of Early Modern Theology, 1600–1800*, edited by Ulrich L. Lehner, Richard A. Muller, and A.G. Roeber, 119–34. Oxford: Oxford University Press, 2016.

– *Le rigorisme chrétien*. Paris: Cerf, 2001.

Rahner, Karl. "Notes on the Lay Apostolate." In *Theological Investigations*, Vol. 2. Baltimore: Helicon Press, 1963.

– "Uber Das Laienapostolat." In *Schriften Zur Theologie*, vol. 2. Einsiedeln: Benziger, 1955.

Rapley, Elizabeth. "Fénelon Revisited: A Review of Girls' Education in Seventeenth Century France." *Histoire Sociale/Social History* 20, no. 40 (1987): 299–318.

– "Women and the Religious Vocation in Seventeenth-Century France." *French Historical Studies* 18, no. 3 (1994): 613–31.

[Richard, Jean]. *Discours moraux, sur les evangiles de tous les Dimanches de l'année*. Vol. 1. Paris: Jean Couterot & Loüis Guerin, 1684.

Rieff, Philip. *The Triumph of the Therapeutic: Uses of Faith after Freud*. New York: Harper & Row, 1966.

Roger, Alexandra. "Contester l'autorité parentale: les vocations religieuses forcées au XVIIIe siècle en France." *Annales de démographie historique* 1, no. 125 (2013): 43–67.

Roper, Lyndal. *The Holy Household: Women and Morals in Reformation Augsburg*. Oxford: Clarendon Press, 1989.

Saint-Cyran, Jean du Verger de Hauranne, abbé de. *Lettres chrestiennes et spirituelles de Messire Jean Du Verger de Hauranne, abbé de S. Cyran*. 2 vols. Paris: Jean le Mire, 1645–7.

Schillebeeckx, Edward. *The Layman in the Church and Other Essays*. Staten Island, NY: Alba House, 1963.

Schleck, Charles A. *The Theology of Vocations*. Milwaukee, WI: Bruce Publishing Company, 1963.

Schutte, Anne Jacobson. *By Force and Fear: Taking and Breaking Monastic Vows in Early Modern Europe*. Ithaca, NY: Cornell University Press, 2011.

Selderhuis, Herman J. *Marriage and Divorce in the Thought of Martin Bucer*. Translated by John Vriend and Lyle D. Bierma. Kirksville, MO: Thomas Jefferson University Press at Truman State University, 1999.

Shagan, Ethan H. *The Rule of Moderation: Violence, Religion and the Politics of Restraint in Early Modern England*. Cambridge: Cambridge University Press, 2011.

Sluhovsky, Moshe. *Becoming a New Self: Practices of Belief in Early Modern Catholicism*. Chicago: University of Chicago Press, 2017.

Smith, Christian, and Brandon Vaidyanathan. "Multiple Modernities and Religion." In *The Oxford Handbook of Religious Diversity*, edited by Chad Meister, 250–65. Oxford: Oxford University Press, 2010.

Stedman, Chris. "Do Only Religious People Have a 'Calling'?" *Huffington Post*, 24 January 2011. http://www.huffingtonpost.com/chris-stedman/can-atheists-have-a-calli_b_812433.html.

Stopp, Elisabeth. "St. Francis de Sales at Clermont College: A Jesuit Education in Sixteenth-Century Paris." In *A Man to Heal Differences: Essays and Talks on St Francis de Sales*, 23–50. Philadelphia: St Joseph's University Press, 1997.

Suenens, Leon-Joseph. *Co-Responsibility in the Church*. New York: Herder and Herder, 1968.

Suire, Éric. *La sainteté française de la Réforme catholique (XVIe-XVIIIe Siècles): d'après les textes hagiographiques et les procès de canonisation*. Pessac: Presses Universitaires de Bordeaux, 2001.

Surin, Jean-Joseph. *Catechisme spirituel*. 2nd ed. Vol. 1. Paris: Claude Cramoisy, 1667.

Swatos, William H., and Lutz Kaelber, eds. *The Protestant Ethic Turns 100: Essays on the Centenary of the Weber Thesis*. Boulder, CO: Paradigm Publishers, 2005.

Sweeney, Conor. *Abiding the Long Defeat: How to Evangelize Like a Hobbit in a Disenchanted Age*. Brooklyn, NY: Angelico Press, 2018.

Tanner, Norman P., ed. *Decrees of the Ecumenical Councils*. Vol. 2. Washington, DC: Sheed & Ward and Georgetown University Press, 1990.

Taylor, Charles. "A Catholic Modernity?" In *A Catholic Modernity?*, edited by James M. Heft, 13–37. New York: Oxford University Press, 1999.

– *A Secular Age*. Cambridge, MA: Belknap Press of Harvard University Press, 2007.

– *Sources of the Self: The Making of the Modern Identity*. Cambridge, MA: Harvard University Press, 1989.

Taylor, Larissa. *Soldiers of Christ: Preaching in Late Medieval and Reformation France*. New York: Oxford University Press, 1992.

Tentler, Thomas N. *Sin and Confession on the Eve of the Reformation*. Princeton, NJ: Princeton University Press, 1977.

Thayer, Anne T. *Penitence, Preaching, and the Coming of the Reformation*. Aldershot, UK: Ashgate, 2002.

Thorman, Donald J. *The Emerging Layman: The Role of the Catholic Layman in America*. Garden City, NY: Doubleday & Company, 1962.

Tulchin, Alan. "Low Dowries, Absent Parents: Marrying for Love in an Early Modern French Town." *Sixteenth Century Journal* 44, no. 3 (2013): 713–38.

Turrini, Miriam. "La vita scelta? Appunti per una storia della vocazione in età moderna." In *Dai cantieri della storia: Liber amicorum per Paolo Prodi*, edited by Gian Paolo Brizzi and Giuseppe Olmi, 145–59. Bologna: CLUEB, 2007.

Van Engen, John H. "Professing Religion: From Liturgy to Law." *Viator* 29 (1998): 323–44.

– *Sisters and Brothers of the Common Life: The Devotio Moderna and the World of the Later Middle Ages*. Philadelphia: University of Pennsylvania Press, 2008.

Vermeersch, A. *Religious and Ecclesiastical Vocation*. Translated by Joseph G. Kempf. 2nd ed. St Louis, MO: B. Herder, 1930.

Viguerie, Jean de. "La vocation sacerdotale et religieuse aux XVIIe et XVIIIe siècles: la théorie et la réalité." In *La vocation religieuse et sacerdotale en France, XVII–XIX siècles*, 27–37. Angers: Université d'Angers, U.E.R. des lettres et sciences humaines, Centre de recherches d'histoire religieuse et d'histoire des idées, 1979.

Villiers de Saint-Etienne, Cosme de. *Bibliotheca Carmelitana*. Vol. 1. Orleans: M. Couret de Villeneuve & Joannes Rouzeau-Montaut, 1752.

"Vocations and Discernment FAQ." Office of Vocations, Diocese of Harrisburg, PA. Accessed 8 April 2020. https://www.hbgdiocese.org/clergy/vocations/vocation-discernment/vocations-faq.

Walch, Agnès. *La spiritualité conjugale dans le catholicisme français (XVIe–XXe siècle)*. Paris: Cerf, 2002.

Walker, D.P. *The Decline of Hell: Seventeenth-Century Discussions of Eternal Torment*. Chicago: University of Chicago Press, 1964.

Weber, Max. "Die Protestantische Ethick Und Der 'Geist' Des Kapitalismus." *Archiv Für Sozialwissenschaft Und Sozialpolitik* 20, 21 (1905): 1–54, 1–110.

– *The Protestant Ethic and the "Spirit" of Capitalism and Other Writings*. Translated by Peter Baehr and Gordon C. Wells. New York: Penguin, 2002.

Winfrey, Oprah. "What Oprah Knows for Sure about Finding Your Calling." Oprah.com. Accessed 8 April 2020. http://www.oprah.com/spirit/oprah-on-finding-your-calling-what-i-know-for-sure.

Wingren, Gustaf. *Luther on Vocation*. Translated by Carl C. Rasmussen. Philadelphia: Muhlenberg Press, 1957.

Witte, John, Jr. *From Sacrament to Contract: Marriage, Religion, and Law in the Western Tradition*. 2nd ed. Louisville, KY: Westminster John Knox Press, 2012.

Worcester, Thomas. *Seventeenth-Century Cultural Discourse: France and the Preaching of Bishop Camus*. New York: Mouton de Gruyter, 1997.

– "St Francis de Sales and Jesuit Rhetorical Education." In *Traditions of Eloquence: The Jesuits and Modern Rhetorical Studies*, edited by Cinthia Gannett and John C. Brereton, 102–15. New York: Fordham University Press, 2016.

Wright, Anthony D. *The Divisions of French Catholicism, 1629–1645: "The Parting of the Ways."* Farnham, UK: Ashgate, 2010.

Index